MORNING BY MORNING

The Autobiography

of

AYO BANJO

MORNING BY MORNING

The Autobiography
of

AYO BANJO

Safari Books Ltd.
Ibadan

Published by
Safari Books Ltd
Ile Ori Detu
1, Shell Close
Onireke
Ibadan.
Email: info@safaribooks.com.ng
Website: http://safaribooks.com.ng

© 2019, Ayo Banjo

First published 2019

All rights reserved. This book is copyright and so no part of it may be reproduced, stored in a retrieval system, or transmitted, in any form or by any means, electrical, mechanical, electrostatic, magnetic tape, photocopying, recording or otherwise, without the prior written permission of the author.

ISBN: Paperback - 978-978-55986-6-7
          Cased - 978-978-55986-7-4

Dedication

In Memoriam:
Comfort Jokotola Banjo, 1910-1947
Alice Oritseweyinmi Banjo, 1936-2014
Two women who never met.

Morning by morning new mercies I see;
All I have needed Thy hand hath provided
Great is Thy faithfulness, Lord unto me!

Contents

Dedication.. *v*
Foreword.. *ix*
Acknowledgements.. *xv*
Introduction.. *xvii*

Chapter One:	In The Beginning	1
Chapter Two:	The Lagos Years..	13
Chapter Three:	An Ibadan Interlude.................................	47
Chapter Four:	Sojourn in Great Britain...........................	55
Chapter Five:	A French Interlude...................................	79
Chapter Six:	In the Delta..	87
Chapter Seven:	From Leeds to UCLA................................	99
Chapter Eight:	Thoughts on the Nigerian University System..	141
Chapter Nine:	Back in Ibadan...	173
	Epilogue	199
	Appendices...	207
	Index..	239

Foreword

Morning by Morning reflects, in its subject and its medium, the virtues for which Ayo Banjo is so widely respected and admired. Three comments recur in the formal and informal tributes of his friends, associates and colleagues. The remarkable simplicity of his language and lifestyle, the quiet efficiency of his leadership reflected in the conduct of official business, and the ease and familiarity that his comportment encourages. A reader who is struck by the simplicity of style and clarity of worldview in this text might be reminded of the discipline that the King James Version has taught writers down the ages. But there are other, direct influences evident in *Morning by Morning*, especially the elite education of the future Emeritus Professor of English, and the professional distinction and traditional Christian culture of his upbringing. There is, in addition, the effect of the African autobiography, perhaps the most faithful representation of the evolution of the educated elite in modern African writing. The form is decisive in influencing the way that modern society perceives its exceptional men and distinguished leaders like Banjo. Before our time, societies where the autobiography had not fully developed glorified their heroes and religious leaders. The charisma that inspired the comments on Banjo makes it easy to envisage that he could have been a subject of veneration in an earlier age. The reason why that cannot be so these days is tied up with the autobiographical form in which his story is told.

The autobiography has a special place in the habits of the Nigerian reading public, especially the reasons for their different uses of literacy. Apart from the other familiar uses of reading – aesthetic pleasure enabled by leisure and literature, educational knowledge available in textbooks, and information on public affairs that the print media provides, the autobiography satisfies the wish to understand the sources of a great man's mystique or the springs of a public figure's charisma and success. What readers seek in an autobiography is realism – the clarification, explanation, confession that only a participant or eyewitness can provide. When these are not available, the alternative is myth making or hero worship. The deification of Sango, the fourth Alaafin of Oyo, took place in the age of heroes. In our own age of literacy, the culture that made such traditional gods and heroes possible is in decline, leaving only echoes in praise poems and those museum relics that are not just memorials, but icons of outstanding mortals re-created as immortals. In the modern age, the deification of a great statesman, Awolowo, did not take place. It could not have taken place in this age of realism because too much that is human about him is documented, and too little is magical. Fagunwa's image is similarly being shaped by this realist tendency of modern culture. We read in *Morning by Morning* that he was Banjo's headmaster. Is he then not what we would have imagined – an incarnation of the forest spirit of storytelling, who sometimes gets scribes to transcribe his adventures or leads them on a tour of his wonder world of tales? Banjo similarly spoils the fun for hero worshippers by crowding his chapters with other legendary persons with whom he had interacted throughout his eventful life and who turn out to be his schoolmates and teachers, associates and colleagues, friends and relations. Now that we know that these famous persons are human, no hagiographer can turn them into gods. For that, blame literacy and modern education; blame the mission institutions that trained Banjo's generation and the generation before.

The implied lesson is a simple one even from the style alone. What needs to be said can be said by using the resources within reach, not by striving for excess. In the modern age, where even language, like lifestyle, is not immune from inflation in politics and the economy, the fantastic tale with its special kind of form and style for the glorification of individuals has been edged out by the realism of the prosaic and commonplace. Of course, writers with exceptional talent and genius can claim the right to be different; but even they cannot be stripped of their humanity. But that does not mean that our capacity for wonder is dead. *Morning by Morning* teaches us to savour the modern transformations of magical experience in the child's ageless capacity for delight at his idyllic environment, and in the sense of fulfillment when a leader overcomes professional challenges and successfully upholds tested academic traditions, as Banjo has done, not only when he was in the saddle, but in his continuing performance after retirement.

To the reader, *Morning by Morning* soon takes on a cultural significance beyond its account of the author's life and times. It is representative of the autobiography as a key document of modern Nigeria's literary culture. The Nigerian autobiography is authorized by the educated middle class in the sense that its author, its subject and its readers belong to the same educated middle class. That class was the modernizing agent that shaped the emergent literary culture of Nigeria and became an organ of national development. So, the autobiographer's personal account of his life and times is valuable material for the professional historian. Like history, its close relation, the autobiography's formal and psychological resources are the obvious model for the modern realist novelist. One of the attractions of this autobiography and others, is that the recollection and careful relation of things, places, people and events – even those that would be ignored in conventional history, accumulate into a significant social context, and enable the reader to enter into a world that now exists only in memory, memoirs and autobiographies. Memory is particularly vital to the autobiographer since his or her account is open to challenge from other sources. It is usual to consider the difference between the modern novel and the autobiography to be the novelist's freedom to organize his fictional material on aesthetic terms. But they do have a common source in the creative urge, as Banjo says in his introduction. For while the autobiographer cannot alter the facts of his life and their order, he can discern their inner form by his insight into how they came about and feel a sense of purpose in their unfolding, as Banjo does in *Morning by Morning*. Always faithful to the principles of his faith, Banjo sees the plan of providence in his progress from privileged beginnings to professional fulfillment, and his narrative takes shape from this world view.

The reader is unlikely to miss the manner in which character reveals itself in this narrative. Throughout his travels, Banjo carries along with him an appreciation of the essential inner beauty of virtually all the places that he visits in Africa, Europe and the West Indies, and the basic goodness of the people that he meets. Such is his openness and warmth to people of all races and classes that the reader might wonder whether, with one exception, it is only a guest's conventional courtesy to a host, the usual traveller's romantic view of new places and people, or perhaps he was just being gracious – an incidental outflow or sharing of his own sense of fulfillment. An autobiography encourages a reader to make connections between seed and fruit, source and effect. So, given Banjo's warm memories of his childhood, including the excellence of his primary and secondary school education, the reader is left to infer that the goodness of the narrator in *Morning by Morning* is inbred, and that this beholder's eye bathes new places and people in goodness and integrity, and leaves things that way until experience directs differently; that his candour is as present at these encounters as his courtesy. It is in character for Banjo not to project a related dimension of his character in his autobiography – the equanimity that enables him to rein in strong action until he needs to stop matters from getting out of hand.

It is fit that Banjo's latest assignment should be the chairmanship of the National Universities Commission. It is not only fit, it is providential in many senses: it concludes the plot of this autobiography; it is the logical step after his earlier services as Pro-Chancellor at different institutions; and, given the present state of tertiary education, it launches him into a more profound phase of reflection and ideas on the way to national debate, policy making and resolution.

By the late twentieth century, Nigerian tertiary education was already a troubled system – a reflex reaction to the country's social and cultural pressures. It is still troubled two decades into the twenty-first century when all issues should have been resolved. It is easy to misjudge the long term outcomes of this development. Institutions and systems that are conventionally considered to be largely isolated (and insulated) from society, as if they were real ivory towers, may be so deeply implicated in social matters as to determine the nation's development, especially if we are prepared to consider secondary and tertiary education as one connected system. The university teacher and seasoned manager of institutions whose story is told in these pages, Professor Emeritus Ayo Banjo, may have ideas that policy makers will do well to consider.

Professor Emeritus Dan Izevbaye, FNAL
February, 2019

Acknowledgements

The author of an autobiography must have a whole lot of people to acknowledge. First to be recognized, surely, is the Almighty, who provided the plot for the narration. Then an innumerable number of people have pitched in and have been used to give life to the plot, without necessarily being aware of their roles. While being thankful to all of them, it behoves me to mention some of those who are or were certainly conscious of their roles. These are, in the first place, my parents, followed by my wife, siblings and children. Then I must recognise my teachers at various levels, my students and my friends. They have all participated in the story told here because they made it possible.

As for the process of publishing the story, again I have to thank, in particular, my siblings and my children, all of whom were witnesses to the narration as it unfolded. Their positive response, the eager expectation to read the next bit, encouraged me, and I decided that the publication of the book would not be a bad way of celebrating my eighty-fifth year. I am grateful to all of them.

I had no difficulty deciding who the publisher should be. Joop Berkhout, a friend of fifty-two years and an Ife chief, has run two publishing businesses in the city of Ibadan and has invited me to the board of both of them. I am grateful to him for offering to publish this volume on extremely generous terms.

Introduction

Almost certainly, the first Nigerian to write his autobiography in English was Olaudah Equiano (1745 - 1797), also known as Gustavus Vassa. Olaudah had hailed from the Igbo stock in eastern Nigeria and, in his boyhood, had gone through the traumatic experience, which had been the lot of some other Nigerian boys of the eighteenth century, of being captured by slavers but later luckily manumitted. In Olaudah's case, he ended up in the care of Quakers in England where he prospered, as much as could be expected of a person in his circumstances and, naturally, joined the abolitionist movement.

We treasure his autobiography titled *The Interesting Narrative of the Life of Olaudah Equiano* (1789) today as representing the earliest publication in the English language by a man of Nigerian origins, and it is perhaps fitting that all Nigerians subsequently writing their autobiographies should pay homage to him. His autobiography was very well received by all classes in England and went into several editions.

We may well ask why he felt the need to write an autobiography. The short answer would simply be that he experienced an irresistible creative impulse. But in addition, he must have felt the need to tell his own story, to identify with his origins in spite of his great success in English circles.

Many public figures have their biographies written about them, but it is doubtful if even the best biographies can be as authentic as an honestly written autobiography. In an autobiography, the author tells his own story in his own way, and normally, there are two major aspects of an autobiography. The first is that it tells us of the events which have shaped the life of the author and, secondly, the work throws some light on the author's country's social history, showing us how the country itself has developed, or at least manifested changes, over a course of time.

This work is no different from other autobiographies. In casting a nostalgic glance back to the events of my life which have resulted in who I am, I have, at the same time, endeavoured to satisfy the curiosity of family members, especially the children and the grandchildren, who are fascinated by the differences between the past and the present. While not setting out to write a social history of Nigeria, I have nevertheless inevitably presented a picture of some of the dynamics of change in the country over a number of decades.

It would appear in some circles that autobiographies and memoirs are considered to be synonymous. Obviously, the two terms do have some semantic features in common, but at least one distinguishing feature is that whereas an autobiography endeavours to encompass the whole of the writer's life, a memoir can legitimately cover just a period of his life. My earlier publication, *In the Saddle* (1997) may perhaps be regarded as typically a memoir, dealing, as it does, with my years as the Vice-Chancellor of the University of Ibadan. Part of the function of the present work, on the other hand, is to attempt to contextualise the earlier work. Quite simply, *In the Saddle* attempts to answer the question: 'What is Ayo Banjo? 'whereas the present work attempts to answer the question: 'Who is Ayo Banjo?' A man may play several important roles in his life, each worthy of a memoir, but he has just one lifetime deserving one autobiography.

I have taken care not to unnecessarily repeat the material in the earlier publication, but of course, since the material there is part of my overall biography, without which the present work may not be complete or meaningful, references are made in this work to some of the events recounted in the earlier publication. Generally speaking, however, I have avoided an elaborate account of my years as Vice-Chancellor.

The ensuing story has been conditioned by many factors illustrating my good fortune. First of all was having a father who was a scholar in his own right. Then there were the circumstances in which I was brought up which conferred many advantages. There was the good fortune of attending Igbobi College when that school was among the very best in the country. Other institutions added value – Glasgow, Leeds and the University of California at Los Angeles.

These institutions in turn prepared me for a rewarding career at the University of Ibadan where, for twenty-five years of my life, I spent my entire professional career. At Ibadan, I encountered the cream of Nigerian scholars, not only in my own discipline but also elsewhere in the Humanities and Science. This fulfilling career ended with my being entrusted with the affairs of the university for a record period of eight years.

Indeed, I cannot be grateful enough to the University of Ibadan – Nigeria's 'first and best. 'In addition to offering me the opportunities of finding fulfilment, it has bestowed on me the highest academic honour in its gifts – the honorary degree of Doctor of Letters. Earlier, it had also honoured me with the status of Professor Emeritus. The university is one of Nigeria's greatest assets, and the government would do well to cherish it and make it, together with the other first generation universities, a model for the rest of the university system.

My thanks go to all those who have helped me along my way, and to my publisher, Chief Joop Berkhout, the executive chairman of Safari Books and a friend of more than fifty years. *In the saddle* was actually published in 1997 by his former company, Spectrum Books. He has perhaps tried to make a publisher out of me by making me a director both at Spectrum and at Safari.

1

IN THE BEGINNING

I was born on Wednesday, 2 May 1934 to Samuel Ayodele Banjo and Comfort Jokotola Banjo (nee Osinuga). My father's family had hailed originally from the Arobieke family of Oke-Jaga, Ijebu-Igbo, but my father had been raised by his parents, John and Dorcas Banjo, in Ibadan. There my father went to school at St David's Primary School, Kudeti. From there, at the age of 14, he entered the famous St Andrew's College, Oyo, in 1916. On finishing at St Andrew's in 1921, he went out to teach at Ijebu-Jesha and Ilesha, and then returned to St Andrew's College in 1927 as a tutor, and later, senior tutor. He was to remain there for the next eighteen years.

During this period, in 1933, he graduated B.A. Honours in Philosophy of the University of London as an external candidate, one of the first two or three Nigerians ever to perform this feat.

Meanwhile, my grandparents had relocated to Ijebu-Igbo, where they played a prominent part in the affairs of St John's Church, Oke-Sopen, while my grandfather also served as the *Oloritun* (that is, head) of Oke-Sopen, and a member of the Customary Court.

My mother, Comfort Jokotola Banjo (nee Osinuga) could also be considered a trailblazer in her own way. Her father, Jonathan Osinuga, had hailed originally from Sagamu, from the household of the Balogun of Makun. Though he lived and prospered in Ibadan, he himself held the title of Balogun of Makun, which passed on later to one of my uncles. My maternal grandfather lived and flourished in Ibadan, having taken an Ibadan wife, who also turned out later to be a very prosperous business woman in her own right. Tragically, he died in the city of Ibadan by being thrown off his horse, causing much panic and consternation.

Coming from a well-off family in Ibadan, my mother went to Kudeti Girls' School, Ibadan, from where she went on to be one of the foundation students of United Missionary College (UMC), Ibadan. Her fellow-pioneers included girls who were later to become the mothers of Professor Bolanle Awe, Professor Jade Akande and Joko Ojo. UMC was the product of unprecedented collaboration between the Church Missionary Society (CMS), the forerunner of today's Anglican Communion, and the Methodist Church Nigeria. As fate would have it, I was also, many years later, to be a beneficiary of a second collaboration between these same two Churches at Igbobi College, Yaba, though of course, not as a foundation student. It is, indeed, an interesting fact, in the circumstances, that my paternal grandfather was an Anglican, and my maternal grandfather a Methodist.

On passing out of UMC, my mother lost no time in getting married to my father. The marriage took place in December 1930 at St David's Church (now Cathedral), Kudeti, Ibadan. She moved to Oyo to join my father and settled down to being a housewife. As time went on, she lavished her training as a teacher and prospective mother on the upbringing of her children, the first of whom, Bayo (later to become a famous medical practitioner in Ibadan, and indeed in Nigeria), came on 12 November, 1931. He was appropriately christened Olumide Adebayo.

I arrived two and a half years later, on Wednesday, 2 May 1934, that is, the year after my father's graduation; hence my name, Ladipo Ayodeji. But actually, that name is ambiguous, as it is also an appropriate name for a second child in a family. It is one of those ambiguities that I silently enjoy. The other comes from the inscription 'Villayo' on my residence in New Bodija, Ibadan. I think it would be correct to say that everyone assumes that I had named the house after myself. But they could not be more wrong. The building was actually named after my father, who, like (and before) me, was Ayo. But the ambiguity has never been lost on me. My elder brother had named his own residence on Ring Road, Ibadan, 'Jokotola Lodge' after our mother; so I felt called upon to balance the equation!

I started school in 1938 in the kindergarten section of St Andrew's Primary School, the demonstration school of St Andrew's College. My headmaster turned out to be none other than D.O. Fagunwa. Like us, Fagunwa lived in the staff quarters of the college; and in fact, his residence was not far from ours. I recall many pleasant moon-lit evenings listening, in the company of some other staff children, to fantastic Yoruba stories told in his inimitable Yoruba accent by our headmaster as we gathered round him at his quarters. One of those stories was about a brave hunter in a forbidding forest. We listened open-eyed and open-mouthed as we were transported to this mysterious forest. Imagine my great surprise and pleasure, therefore, on finding, some years later, that Fagunwa had published the story as *Ogboju Ode Ninu Igbo Irunmole*. I read it avidly, thinking that what was missing was the author's enchanting voice. The publication instantly made Fagunwa the most significant Yoruba author. Other publications followed confirming the author's position.

After kindergarten, I moved on to the primary school proper. The school was built next to the college, but to get there in the mornings, we staff children had first of all to exit the college, walk along the fence for some yards and then enter through the school's own gate, along with the pupils from town. I wondered many times why a short cut through the college was not provided for staff children. Perhaps it was felt that that would have been too much of an indulgence.

Although I hardly realised it then, we were, in fact, being given a highly privileged education. Most of the teachers, including the headmaster himself, Mr G. Lasebikan, whose son in later years became an academic and, later still, the Archbishop of the Anglican Province of Ondo, were products of the college. In addition, being a demonstration school, our school was used for teaching practice for students from the college, who performed under the eagle eyes of their tutors.

No doubt, my mates and I were beneficiaries of the most up-to-date developments in curriculum and teaching methods. For example, we were made to read and write in Yoruba before being taught to do the same in English – a language-learning methodology which successive Nigerian governments seem to be struggling in vain to establish throughout the country. I recall how we were made to memorize some beautiful Yoruba poems, which we then recited before the class. Some of these poems have remained stuck in my memory.

There were quite a few extra-curricular activities. For example, scouting, which was strongly pursued at the college itself, was extended to the school. In my first year, I was inducted into the movement as a wolf cub, being too young to be even an adolescent boy scout. And how I loved being a wolf cub! The green shirt, the yellow scarf, the beret: I just felt excited by what I considered to be my new status. And there were very practical things as well, such as learning to tie different kinds of knots. In all this, my brother and I were encouraged by my father, who was the leader of the scouts in the college. His passion for the movement was so strong that, later in life, he became the scout commissioner for Western Region of Nigeria.

But my excitement always peaked at the meetings, to which I eagerly looked forward:

> DYB, DYB, DYB! (Do Your Best, pronounced 'deeb, deeb, deeb'), hollered our scoutmaster.
>
> We'll DOB, DOB, DOB! (We'll Do Our Best, pronounced 'dob, dob, dob') we yelled back with every ounce of energy in our tiny bodies.

That was most exhilarating. Then there was camping. I remember Jobele, Akinmorin, Awe... These were at different times the venues of our camping. We set up camp in clearings away from any form of civilisation; and then, of course, fended for ourselves, shouldering responsibilities beyond our age, but never forgetting to 'do our best'.

There was a measure of trepidation on the first night, of course, for some of us had not forgotten Fagunwa's stories, and wondered whether we were not exposing ourselves to unnecessary danger. But then, the camp fire was lit, and we sang and danced round it. Exhausted after the day's labours and excitement, we finally fell into deep sleep in our tents, forgetting all about *Igbo Olodumare*.

After a few days of such surreal existence, we later returned to normal life, feeling a little superior to non-cubs in our school.

Then there was a date securely inscribed on our brains: 24 May, which in colonial Nigeria was Empire Day. That was the date when, every year, all the primary schools in Oyo and environs gathered at a place called Durbar to be addressed by the British District Officer. Each school marched, to the beat of its school band, past the District Officer, who took the salute. Of course, this provided great scope for rivalry among the schools, but I thought all the other schools conceded that St Andrew's was the best, led, as it was, by its well-trained boy scouts and wolf cubs!

The ancient town of Oyo, in those days, was a quiet, almost sleepy town all too conscious of its place in Yoruba history.

It was, to be sure, already a large town. But if it appeared somewhat somnolent in the day-time, one had to visit Akesan market at night to witness the vivacity of the town. There was no electricity in the town, and Akesan market was lit by scores, I even thought hundreds, of oil lamps. I thought it looked like fairyland as shadowy figures milled around and moved from stall to stall amidst a general din. It was believed that young people found suitable corners for assignations, and that many marriages in fact had their origins at Akesan market.

The Alaafin was venerated and widely regarded as a demi-god. He resided in his beautiful vast palace, not too far from the Romanesque Atiba Hall, with his numerous wives, and seldom made a public appearance – not even at Durbar on Empire Day. However, my school made the occasional pilgrimage to the palace. On such occasions, the monarch sat resplendent in one of the courtyards of his palace, surrounded by some of his high chiefs, and ministered to by his servants. These servants had peculiar hairdos and appeared very well nourished. It was rumoured in our school that they were all eunuchs – presumably for the safety of the king's harem!

We never ever saw the monarch's face during any of our visits, as this was completely obscured by beads extending from his crown. Nor did we ever hear his voice. Rather, one of the chiefs sitting next to him delivered the Alaafin's thoughts to us as his spokesman. It was all so awe-inspiring.

Then there was the oasis which the college represented in this rural setting. Here, since the closing years of the nineteenth century, had gathered the cream of young Nigerians under the pupillage of tutors carefully selected not only from all over the country, but from Great Britain as well. It was such a remarkable study in contrasts: the town under the Alaafin, depository and guardian of ancient Yoruba ways; the college under a British principal, looking forward into the far future. And there in the middle was I, like the other staff children, forming a bridge between the two. It has to be said, however, that for us, there was no sense of conflict, just that we felt more at home in the college surroundings than in town. Indeed, our contact with town was minimal. For me, it consisted, essentially, in being a chorister at St Michael's Church (now Cathedral), Agunpopo, also known as Esiele, which admittedly was even located not too far from the college. That was the beginning of my love for singing, and for music in general, particularly art music. From being a treble voice in Oyo, I moved on, in later years, briefly to alto, and then settled much longer on tenor until finally stabilizing as a bass.

***

My earliest memories naturally go back to Oyo, where I spent the first ten years of my life in the premises of St Andrew's College, at that time the finest institution of its kind in Nigeria. I had thought then that I was living in a fairly large house, until I visited two decades later and found, to my amazement, that it was nothing but a modest structure. But it was big enough to contain a sitting room, two or three bedrooms and the *sanctum sanctorum* of the building – my father's study.

My earliest memories of sounds were a cacophony of sounds emanating persistently every early evening from across the fence in front of our house. It turned out to be the sounds produced by students practising in a block housing harmoniums. The college took very seriously the business of making an organist out of every student, so that they would be able to serve as Church organists in addition to their teaching duties.

One practical result of this aspect of an Andrian's training was, in fact, once brought home to me. During a service at St Michael's, we choristers filed into our stall without any sign of the organist. The service was to be conducted by my father, who by now had been ordained priest, and he was also to preach the sermon. From my vantage position in the choir stall, I observed him moving repeatedly from the chancery to the

Church organ as he served, I thought brilliantly, as priest and organist for that service. I suspect many other Andrians have played similar roles or, at any event, been asked peremptorily to exchange their seats in the congregation for the organist's stool, to save embarrassments.

Life as a boy at St Andrew's was pleasant enough. The students looked big to my child's eyes. Some of them called occasionally at our house, but some groups of them also came regularly for what looked like open-air tutorials. One or two of the students, like Ade Akomolafe, later Chief, took a great liking to my brother and myself and occasionally took us to their dormitories. Akomolafe was later to be my teacher at Christ Church Cathedral School, Lagos, and Igbobi College, Yaba. He retained a profound affection for our family.

We were able to witness some of the students' activities. We regularly went to watch football matches and, once a year or so, were at soirees where the students presented cultural music and dances from various parts of the country. My father played lawn tennis regularly with some of his colleagues, and we staff children enthusiastically served as ball boys. I simply loved the smell of new tennis balls as they were taken out of the containers.

On Sundays, we were also allowed to attend Chapel services with our parents; and that was where my love for Church music was further reinforced. Incidentally, I also fell in love at first hearing with the college anthem, the score of which has now been taken over by Ajayi Crowther University, which has risen on the ashes of St Andrew's College.

But one annual event which I cannot forget was the ritual of breaking new students into the life of the college, dominated, as it was, by the importance of seniority. To my thinking at the time, some of the chores that the new students were made to perform by their stern-looking seniors bordered on sheer wickedness. But then, these seniors, too, in their own time, had been at the receiving end of the martial treatment. Strangely enough, the following day, life went on as normal, and slave-drivers had turned amiable seniors.

We staff children bonded very well. We exchanged visits, and went together to explore the campus, paying particular attention to the mango trees which formed the avenue leading to the principal's residence. When the fruits were in season, we gorged ourselves with them, occasionally to the point of diarrhoea. At other times, we would go round the compound looking at some of the trees, which must have been standing there for half a century. Each tree was labelled with the botanical Latin name which sounded curious to us but surely to the delight of the students.

Some of my friends had a passion for eating crickets. We would go round looking for holes from which we ferreted out the poor creatures. At first, it appeared strange and even repulsive to some of us; but gradually, we found the aroma from frying the insects quite pleasant, and when at last we agreed to have a taste, we thought it was marvellous. Thereafter, all of us devoted much of our time to hunting for the insects, which was not difficult because they always gave themselves away with their shrill sounds. We would dig them out of their holes, fry them and have a snack. It is interesting that the rest of the world is now just finding out what we discovered more than seventy years ago, and insect farming is becoming fashionable and considered an additional source of protein.

Talking of protein, our daily beef supplies were delivered to us at home by a butcher named Ango. Ango lived in a Fulani camp situated between the college and the town. If we children had to pass through that camp at dusk, we were very scared. The sight of scores of cattle huddled up motionless and appearing to us to be about to attack us made us, in such circumstances, always sprint across the camp. But when we passed through in day time, we found the head of the camp very friendly. And so was Ango, from whom we picked up a few words of greetings in Hausa, just as he practised his Yoruba on us.

Meanwhile, primary school continued to be delightful. Now looking back, I believe we had the best teachers that could be found anywhere in Nigeria. We were also kept happy with singing and drumming. My brother and I spent many Sunday afternoons having lunch with the principal of the college and his wife, Venerable Archdeacon and Mrs. George Burton, at their residence. The couple were quite close to my parents. The college had no statutory vice-principal, and so the duties of that office were performed by the Senior Tutor, a position held by my father for about a dozen years before we moved to Lagos. But the real reason, I suppose, why we were such frequent guests at the principal's residence was, as I got to know at some point, that Mrs. Burton was, in fact, my God-mother.

Meanwhile also, the family continued to grow. A year after I was born, my father left for Fourah Bay College, Sierra Leone, for a postgraduate diploma course in education of the University of Durham, England. He returned the following year, and on 1 April 1937, we welcomed the addition of a baby sister. Predictably, she was named Aduke Tokunbo. My mother was, naturally, very excited, but my brother and I did not mind that our new sister was getting more than her fair share of attention. We received visitors from time to time in our house, my mother being perceived as a very hospitable and generous woman; but the visitor that has stuck in my memory was Bishop I.B. Akinyele, who had known my parents from their early years. He came in from time to time and spent a few days. We children simply loved this grandfather figure. He came down to our level and cracked jokes with us. There was an aura of genuine goodness about him. It has since occurred to me that that was my first encounter with a saintly person.

Three years after Tokunbo's arrival, my father took a profound decision, the origins of which went all the way back to the circumstances of his own birth. After their marriage, my grandparents had experienced delay in starting a family. My grandmother was understandably agitated; and so, like the Biblical Hannah, she had made a pledge with God that if He would give her a male child, she would dedicate the child's life to Him. That child happily arrived on 13 November 1901. What better name for him in the circumstances than Ayodele! My grandparents had only one child thereafter, a girl fittingly named Oluwaloni (Loni, for short). Apparently, my grandmother had made a pledge, not only about a son, but about a daughter as well. And because there were just two of them, the extended family in later years was closely knit, with my first cousins regarded in every way as my siblings.

My grandmother must have constantly reminded my father of the pledge surrounding his birth, but he was really a born teacher and was enjoying his career at Oyo. Then, in 1940, he took the decision long-awaited by my grandmother. He decided to become a clerk in holy orders. As he had to be ordained at Christ Church Cathedral, Lagos, the whole family made a trip to Lagos. I was barely six years old then, but do recall the splendour of the occasion: the majestic booming of the pipe organ, the profoundly, to me, mystifying candle-lit ritual, the enchanting singing of the choir. I could not but take it that something very important was happening in our lives.

We returned to Oyo, where my father now performed as a teacher and a cleric. But before the year ran out, we welcomed another addition to the family. Arriving in the year of my father's ordination, a male child was born on 19 November. The appropriate name came quite easily: Abimbola Olugboyega.

Three years after my father's ordination, my elder brother, Bayo, had to return to Lagos, this time as a student at the CMS Grammar School, the precursor of the present-day Anglican Grammar School, and the oldest grammar school in the country. The principal then, the Reverend (later Bishop) S.I. Kale, was a very good friend of my father's, so it was agreed that, at least for the first year, my brother, considering his age, should live with the principal, where he enjoyed the company of a handful of other grammar school boys in a mini boarding-house. Boarding accommodation in the school was, in any case, in short supply.

I was then only in Primary 2, and was fascinated with the books that my brother brought home during vacations, especially the dictionary. Also, I thought it showed how my brother was going up in the world that he was allowed to use a fountain pen, while I was still confined to my pen and inkpot. Even more importantly, he had exchanged the khaki uniform of Oyo for the gleaming white uniform of Lagos.

Life went on as normal with the family in Oyo; and then I started hearing some rumblings. I thought it was being rumoured that the entire family would soon be relocating to Lagos. Was there a similar college in Lagos?

Then gradually, the picture became more focused. My father was about to exchange a part-time career as cleric for a full-time one. Increasingly, the word 'Aroloya' cropped up in conversations around me. It sounded magical to my ears. Eventually, I got to know what it was all about. My father was going to Lagos to become the vicar of St. John's Church, Aroloya. I was told that this was the second oldest Anglican Church in Lagos, indeed in Nigeria, the oldest being St. Paul's, Breadfruit. My father was going to take over from Canon (later, Bishop) Adelakun Williamson Howells, who was going over to Christ Church Cathedral, Lagos, as the new Provost.

On the due date in December, 1944, we packed our belongings into a lorry which had been hired, and made for Lagos. My parents sat with the driver in front while we children sat on wooden benches in the back of the lorry with all the baggage. As far as I was concerned, we were venturing into the unknown. Curiosity, tinged with excitement, preoccupied my young mind.

2

THE LAGOS YEARS

Aroloya

We arrived in Lagos at dusk, which made things even more unreal. This was in the mid-forties, but even then, the noise, the energy of Lagos, took me by surprise. And there were more surprises that evening before we went to bed. There was electricity all over the house! I looked out of the window on Palm Church Street, and there were street lights! There was hooting of cars; there were street-cries. Even Akesan market was not like this. After observing the street scene for a while we turned round to begin the unpacking. In contrast to our quarters at Oyo, our new home was a large mansion of late Victorian architecture.

We were shown our various rooms, and I shared one with my brother, Bayo, who had that evening rejoined the family. We had a family prayer of thanksgiving and dispersed. In spite of the unfamiliarity of the surroundings, I recollect that I slept soundly that first night, the long journey having taken its toll.

Next morning, I woke up and felt disoriented. For a split second I wondered where I was. Then I remembered. There was no sound of the familiar cockcrow as life gradually returned to Palm Church Street. After breakfast, we carried the unpacking a stage further, and then it was time for us children to explore our new surroundings. We found that the vicarage, a corner piece between Aroloya and Palm Church Streets, was part of a group of buildings securely walled round – a far cry from the expansive campus of St. Andrew's College. Here, the structures were closely packed together. Apart from the vicarage, the other buildings were the Church, which I thought was much bigger than St. Michael's, Oyo, and the primary school buildings. These had a common gate, different from the one leading to the vicarage, but there were no physical demarcations once one entered through either gate.

Downstairs, we found there were two large bedrooms, and a hall which looked like a classroom. As the whole family lived upstairs, I wondered what the accommodation downstairs was intended for. Before long, I found out. It was apparently a tradition at vicarages in Lagos to take in lodgers – mainly boys of school age – to live under the influence of the vicar. One of the earliest boys to be admitted by my father was Rotimi Alade Blaize, whose father must have been the first successful indigenous bottler of orange drinks in Lagos. The other boys were also of my brother's age except for Funso Vaughn, who was the same age with me, and with whom I immediately bonded. Born and bred in Lagos, Funso, son of a lawyer, knew every street and alley of Lagos, which I thought was remarkable for a boy his age. No wonder, I thought, his father sent him to the vicarage.

There were also two or three female boarders – girls attending girls schools in Lagos. They were usually relations, and lived upstairs with the family, to which they were more closely integrated. Among them once was Atinuke Oloko, later to become the Hon. Justice Atinuke Ige.

Next, we took a peek at the Church, inside and outside. I thought it was a really big edifice, at least three times the size of St. Michael's. It was clear that it was an old Church, but well maintained. We went round and saw the supporting columns at the back. This was the part of the Church which, in later years, I carefully avoided, for my new friends assured me that it was the habitation of spirits. One or two of them claimed to have been eye-witnesses, and as echoes of Fagunwa's stories were still ringing in my ears, I gave the place a wide berth after dusk in future years. I wondered where the spirits disappeared to in the daytime, but was not prepared to argue with an eye-witness.

Then we virtually tip-toed into the Church. The atmosphere was so awe-inspiring. It was clear that the Church had been very well maintained. Everything was spick and span. And then there was the pipe-organ, the type, I imagined, that had been played at the Cathedral at my father's ordination. It was a big organ, but I was later to see an even bigger one at the Cathedral. I knew I was destined for the choir stall every Sunday from then on, and wondered whether this choir would produce as beautiful music as the Cathedral had done.

Next we looked round the school buildings. The school was on holiday, and so we were able to wander around, and were impressed by the evident high standard of maintenance. I was happy I would take my place in Primary 4 when the school resumed. I found later that my father was statutorily the manager of the school. We then went into the playground, which was nothing to write home about. Not only was it small in size, it had no grass. White sand covered the whole area like a beach. That was enough for one day. The following day, or at the first available opportunity, we would go out of the vicarage complex and explore our area of Lagos.

Here, Funso came in very handy. He actually knew that our neighbour across the road was Dr Omololu, who also ran a clinic there. Later on, a familiar sight practically every early evening was Dr Omololu and Chief Adebayo Doherty, whose arrival was utterly predictable in his Chevrolet, sitting in the verandah of the clinic sipping tea.

***

Funso and I then wandered up Palm Church Street. After a few yards, we came to an imposing structure, and Funso informed me that the Akereles lived there. In the coming weeks, I discovered that there was an Akerele boy who was about my age, and we struck up a friendship. Funso and I walked further up and came to a magnificent corner piece, and Funso said it was Dr Phillips' house. Dr Phillips was a dentist or opthalmologist, he was not sure which.

That took us into Alli Street, and Funso suggested we should go on and see the famous Tinubu Square. There was a cluster of two or three-storey buildings around the square, a kind of vista which was new to me. Funso pointed at Broad Street to me, with the Santana Courts just visible from where we were standing. We thought that was enough for one day and, in any case, it was about time for lunch. So we returned home, and I was already feeling like a Lagos boy.

Funso had won my admiration for his knowledge of Lagos and of its famous personalities; but as time went on, it became clear to me that there were, in fact, many boys like Funso in Lagos. They made it their business to familiarize themselves with the various areas of the city, and with the residences of the makers and shakers of the city. They also knew by heart the car registration number of each one of them! I myself soon acquired that knowledge, after further explorations had led me to various parts of the city.

One day, Funso suggested we should go to Balbina Street and we might just be lucky to catch a glimpse of the legendary Herbert Macaulay. So off we went, and I shall never forget the image of Macaulay, famous moustache and all, at the upstairs window of his Kirsten Hall, looking below at how lesser mortals were getting on with their lives.

Further explorations inevitably led us to the Bar Beach. The most famous building at Bar Beach at the time – in fact, a solitary one – was Dr Akinola Maja's impressive beach house. At that time, it was perhaps some half-mile from the roaring waves. In later years, however, almost before our very eyes, the waves approached steadily and swallowed up the house, which I imagine is at present somewhere in the middle of the Atlantic. Keeping the waves back has since been almost a quixotic battle for Lagos State and the federal government, and it remains to be seen whether the battle has finally been won.

Funso suggested we should have a dip, but I was clearly too scared to do such a thing. On a subsequent visit, however, he did take a dip while I watched him. When he came out, what I saw confirmed my resolution never to contemplate a swim in the Atlantic, because Funso's eyes were bloodshot. When we returned home, he had to avoid coming face to face with my parents until he had got rid of the tell-tale signs!

Soon it was time to resume schooling, as a Primary 4 pupil at St John's School, Aroloya. The first discovery I made, to my amazement, was that I was in the top class. I later found that all the Anglican primary schools at that time stopped at Primary 4. All the products from such schools – St Paul's, Breadfruit, St John's, Aroloya, St Peter's, Faji, Holy Trinity, Ebute-Ero – then vied for places at the Christ Church Cathedral School on Broad Street. This school had only Primaries 5 and 6, but four arms of each.

I soon learnt what a privilege it was to be at St John's, for if St John's Church was the second oldest Anglican (then called CMS) Church in Lagos, after St. Paul's Breadfruit, it followed, in accordance with practice, that my new school was the second oldest Anglican primary school in Lagos. Expectedly, it had produced many of the leading personalities in Lagos, and Nigeria. Such products went on to be bishops, doctors, engineers and lawyers. I was informed that my hero at the time, Bishop I.B. Akinyele, had also attended the school. There were teachers there who had been trained at St Andrew's College, Oyo; and indeed, my own class teacher had been my father's student at Oyo.

Obviously, I had only one year to spend at the school, but it was a very pleasant year. I had had the good fortune of transferring from one very good school to another. The cleanliness was very impressive, and the teachers all came formally dressed to school. My own teacher always turned out in a complete suit. He would then hang his jacket round the back of his chair, and sometimes roll up his sleeves. I must say they made the teaching profession very attractive.

I was soon drafted into the school band as a drummer. Each morning, I could not wait to get to school – which was only two minutes away! – to take my place in the band and bang away on the drums. It was such a good start to every morning.

I later transferred the skills I had acquired here to the Boys Brigade of the Church, which my father started soon after his arrival at Aroloya. My brother, Bayo, and I featured prominently in the movement, and particularly enjoyed the occasional marches into town. Unlike me, my brother retained his interest in the movement and became, much later in life, the patron of the movement in Ibadan.

This was in addition to our both being choristers in the Church. My brother started off as an alto, and I as a treble. There were many famous families represented in the congregation, but among the most prominent members were the middle-aged Taiwo twins. The two families spread over the same pew every Sunday, but one of the twins was a fantastic tenor who sang in the choir.

I became an eager chorister, looking forward both to the choir practices during the week, and to the performances at Matins and Evensong every Sunday. We were blessed with a charismatic organist, Mr Sandey, and a taciturn assistant organist, Mr Majekodunmi. Mr Sandey was fun to work with, interspersing rigorous practice with hilarious jokes. 'Use your head voice!' he would urge us trebles.

We knew when Mr Majekodunmi was truly inspired at the organ. At such moments, he would, we imagined, pull out all the stops and drown the entire congregation in exhilarating sounds. We choristers would look at one another and smile, in appreciation of his performance. It was believed among us that at such inspired moments, his thick moustache would stand on end! It had to be true.

The Anglican Churches in Lagos at this time were famous for their choirs – and, for that matter, for their organists. I thought our performance could not have been far behind the Cathedral's, even though they had the formidable T.K.E Phillips as their organist. We sang beautiful anthems and, on one occasion, proudly presented a cantata, 'Lord of Gold', to the admiration of all of Lagos. I still find myself up till today humming snippets from the score.

Meanwhile, the explorations continued. Having witnessed the rage of the Atlantic, it was surely time to contemplate the calmness of the lagoon. So we headed for the Marina, and I was struck by the contrast between the two bodies of water. Funso warned me, however, that there was a constant battle between the sea and the lagoon. He was obviously referring to the meeting point between the two. There was a liner at anchor on the Marina, and far away, we could just make out ships berthed at the Apapa wharf.

We walked up the Marina and got to Christ Church Cathedral. I had not realized it was as beautiful as this from the outside. My recollection, going back to five years previously, had been of the inside. But this Gothic piece of architecture was very impressive. We did not attempt to go inside, but stood contemplating it from across the road, while at the same time enjoying the welcome breeze.

Now, I had seen the sea, and I had seen the lagoon. I had seen some canoes on the lagoon. Surely, the next thing for me to experience was a sail on the lagoon. That opportunity in fact came before too long. The incumbent Bishop of Lagos, the Rt. Rev. Leslie Gordon Vining, ran a mini boys' club at his Bishopscourt on the Marina. I joined up and interacted regularly with a group of boys roughly my own age. On one occasion, the bishop decided that we should go on an excursion to Kuramo, which at that time was a small island by itself off Victoria Island. About six of us packed ourselves into a boat, with the bishop himself resplendent in the middle, wearing a white helmet. I already considered myself an experienced camper by this time and, at any rate, there was no thick forest to conquer here, just a mangrove one.

***

By the end of 1945, I was already feeling very well adjusted to my new surroundings. Work was proceeding smoothly at school, and I do not recall that there was any tension, considering that we were due to compete for entrance to Christ Church Cathedral School. Almost effortlessly, quite a few of us were admitted, and my school was now going to be, not two minutes away but, as I imagined, many miles away, taking me through the centre of Lagos every day.

In fact, my situation turned out to be much better than that. The distance was not as much as I had feared, taking me only half an hour of not too hurried walk. What gave me even greater pleasure and satisfaction was the fact that the school was next door to the CMS Grammar School, where my brother, Bayo, was going into his fourth year. In fact, the two schools were separated only by a wall. I was in luck. Until I had developed enough confidence to go on my own, I simply tagged on to my brother every morning, taking careful note of the landmarks as I had to return on my own. As it happened, anyway, I already knew how to get to Tinubu Square, thanks to Funso, who had also already pointed to Broad Street during one of our earlier explorations to the Square. All I had to do was just go down Broad Street until I came, first to the grammar school, and then, my new school, both of them on my left.

Christ Church Cathedral School was a huge building (or so it seemed to me then) almost directly facing the CMS Girls' School, which more directly faced the boys' counterpart. Further down the road was the Methodist Boys' High School. So, every morning, there was usually a large crowd of boys and girls going down Broad Street, something which I found in itself rather exhilarating. What struck me as being odd about my new school, though, was that it was a storey building with nothing at all happening on the ground floor. All the classes were on the first floor, which was accessed through an outside stair-case. So, we all streamed up every morning, and streamed down every afternoon, observed, no doubt, by passers-by on Broad Street.

My first impression on taking my first ascent to the classrooms was that of a make-shift arrangement. There were no concrete demarcations between the classes and, as I found later, teachers' voices filtered from each 'classroom' to adjacent ones through flimsy screens. There were three 'classrooms' on my part of the floor, and I only had to turn round on my feet to see the teachers in front of the other classes, apart from hearing their voices. This was very unlike any previous experience I had had. But in spite of that, the school had a very high reputation, since it had very good teachers and very good pupils. I thought we all deserved high commendation for concentration!

I now do believe that it was a make-shift arrangement, pending the time when all the contributing schools would be able to go up to Primary 6. This in fact later happened, and Christ Church Cathedral School was phased out, having served its purpose magnificently.

On my first day, I was shown to my class. On seeing me, my new class teacher smiled and said, 'You must be Banjo', and I responded in the affirmative. I later discovered that he was an Andrian, possibly a contemporary of my father's. There were three pupils to each desk, and I recall that my two companions, one on my left and the other on my right, were Kehinde Barber, the daughter of the headmaster, no less, and Nike Adejumo, who was later to be the wife of Professor Emeritus Ayo Bamgbose, a man with whom I later in life developed a close relationship at the University of Ibadan.

By the end of my first week, I had made the discovery that practically all the male teachers in the school were Andrians. In fact, there was only one female teacher, Mrs Lewis. My biggest find, however, was Mr Ade Akomolafe, who rekindled my Oyo days. From that day that I was reunited with him, contact between us has remained unbroken, as will be clear in the course of this narrative. One or two other teachers I could vaguely remember from my Oyo years. I was, after all, not in totally strange surroundings.

The tradition was that after one year at the school, most pupils gained admission to secondary schools of their choice. The few who failed to do so then went on to Primary 6 to try again. The school was thus really a prep school, and everyone prayed not to have to spend more than one year.

Then the season of entrance examinations arrived. Before this, all of us in Primary 5 had decided which schools to apply to. Some had applied to more than one school, and provided there was no clash of entrance examination dates, were able to take all the examinations. As for me, the choice would appear already to have been made. I would move next-door to join my brother at the Grammar School. Another incentive for me had been the seraphic sight of the Grammar School boys in their gleaming white uniforms during their breaks, running about and enjoying themselves on their relatively cramped playground. We could see them by looking down over the wall from a section of our building. I even tried occasionally to see if I could catch a glimpse of my brother; but of course he was now in Form 4 and was making better use of his time.

I do not recollect that I particularly bonded with any pupil in the school. All the same, it was a time when, unbeknownst to me, the foundation for a life-long friendship was laid. I had run into one of the boys in a different arm of Primary 5 from mine and got to know that his name was Wusu – Ladipo Wusu. That name immediately reminded me of a certain Mr Wusu, a very gifted artist who was the Art Tutor at St Andrew's College, Oyo. Ladipo and I did not even get close enough for me to find out whether they were related. Two years later, however, I found myself in the same class and the same boarding house with Ladipo, and we got close, being old boys of the same primary school. And that was not all, for after secondary school, we found ourselves fortuitously in the same university in Britain. The friendship has been strengthened and sustained ever since.

The year 1946 all too soon came to a close, and most pupils in my class had secured admissions to secondary schools of their choice. I had been offered admission to the Grammar School. All through the Christmas holiday, I kept picturing myself among the boys larking about on that school's playground. I was anxious, but also confident because I had a brother who would be going into Form 5 in the same school. Surely, he would offer me any protection that I might need, and act generally as a guide. It was an added advantage, I felt, that the principal of the school, the Revd S.I. Kale, was a friend of the family. I could not wait to get into my new white uniform, which would signify my enhanced status among the boys and girls walking down Broad Street every morning.

At the Grammar School, I found myself in a more rarefied atmosphere than I had known at Oyo, Aroloya or Cathedral School. There was a pervading atmosphere of sophistication.

The senior boys carried themselves with unmistakable self-assurance, and the junior boys, too, looked happy and relaxed. The new boys like me, however, for a while wore a look of wonderment on their faces but tried not to show any signs of intimidation, as they gradually got absorbed into the spirit and culture of the school.

Discipline was strict at the Grammar School, and among new intakes like myself, the Principal, the Rev. S.I Kale, attracted admiration and fear in equal measure. He did not just sit all day in his office but periodically went round the corridors of the classrooms to ensure that there was order and seriousness. He was not known to spare the rod, but there was, at the same time, something charmingly avuncular about him.

The teachers were very good, possibly some of the best to be found anywhere in Nigeria at that time, and one of the classes I particularly enjoyed attending was Music. Before this time, I had been trying to teach myself the piano, using the famous Smallwood piano manual, but now the lessons on the theory facilitated my efforts. Unfortunately, I was to have this benefit for only one year. I was doing quite well in the other subjects, and my mother had further inspired me by promising me a big present if I could top the class in the June examinations.

***

Then tragedy struck. The year 1947 had opened for me with exciting possibilities, but on 17 July, the family was dealt a devastating blow by the loss of my mother at the age of thirty-seven. A huge pall of gloom descended on the vicarage, and we children were in utter confusion. For several days, there was an unending flow of callers who had come to comfort us. Many of them were parishioners of St. John's, but many also had come from other parts of Lagos, and even from outside Lagos.

My mother had been admitted into Dr Akanni Doherty's Daddy's Nursing Home on Idumagbo Avenue, a little distance from Aroloya. She had gone to deliver a baby, and we did not expect anything unusual. There was a family relationship between Dr Doherty and my mother, and so we were assured of special care. As her due date drew nearer, my brother Bayo and I went over every late afternoon to visit her, and our father was always around.

Then one afternoon, we paid what had become our usual visit, and I was in particularly high spirits that day because I was going to inform mother that I had, indeed, passed the June examinations at the top of my class. But when we got to the Nursing Home, we were prevented from going into the room. The lugubrious expression on the faces of the staff did not mean much to us, for on the previous day, mother had appeared to be at last on the mend, to the extent that, for the first time, she had got out of bed and was seated in a chair, with father sitting by her on the arm of the chair. We were asked to return home, and soon the news came to shock us. There was wailing in the household, and it became clear to me that we would never see mother again. And I never even did get to tell her that I had passed my examinations at the top of my class. What cruel fate!

Then the Yoruba support mechanism immediately came into play. My aunt, my father's only sibling, came in to cushion the shock for us children. During the next few months, we went over to Ebute-Metta to spend Sunday afternoons with her and our cousins – Bisi, Funke and Sola. She genuinely treated us like her own children.

Also, from the day of bereavement and for several weeks – or perhaps even months – thereafter, my father's first cousin, Uncle David, left his own home on Idumagbo Avenue to spend every night with us at the vicarage. On mother's side, our three uncles were similarly marvellous – Uncle Bode, a civil servant in Lagos, Uncle Afolabi, an engineer and Uncle Layi, a magistrate. They all overwhelmed us with love, and reflected on us the deep affection that had subsisted between them and their only sister.

The funeral service was held, naturally, at St. John's, and it occurred to me that that was the first time of my worshipping among the congregation, rather than from the choir stalls. Even Mr Sandey, and his assistant, Mr Majekodunmi, looked grief-stricken, and somehow they managed to coax out of the organ a truly melancholic tone. As for father, he was the very picture of grief. At forty-five, he had lost his soul-mate and become a widower.

The stream of visitors slowly petered out, and the family now had to face the new reality. We carried on as best we could, but it became clearer everyday that father was ill at ease and was desirous of a change of environment. I am not sure of the options that he considered, but the notion soon crystallised that he had been invited to Ibadan to start an Anglican teacher-training college – St Luke's College – thus making it possible for him to return to his first love. I understand that an invitation to return to St Andrew's College, Oyo, his alma mater, as principal, was also on offer, but he felt, having spent eighteen years there before, the challenge of starting a brand new college was more appealing.

Soon, active plans began to be made for the family to relocate to Ibadan by the end of 1947. This had important implications for my brother Bayo and myself, in particular, for both of us were at the Grammar School in Lagos, I in my first year, and he in his penultimate. My brother obviously would have to stay on in Lagos to complete his course there; but the question was what to do about me.

Igbobi

In December, 1947 the family moved to Ibadan and took up residence at Yemetu, in what used to be the palace of one of the high chiefs of Ibadan, and there, St. Luke's College had its origins. The surroundings seemed strange to us at first – a far cry from Aroloya – but we gradually got used to them. The immediate preoccupation, for my father, apart from providing the minimum facilities for the take-off of the new college, was the disposition of his own children. Femi, the youngest member of the family had stayed back in Lagos to be cared for by our aunt, and the ultimate decision was that Tokunbo, my only sister, should also stay in Lagos with our aunt where, indeed, she would be among three female first cousins and enjoy the love and care of our aunt. As for Gboyega, seven years old, and Kunle, four years old, an appropriate primary school could be found for them in the neighbourhood without much difficulty. My brother, Bayo, obviously had to stay on at the Lagos Grammar School to complete his course. With regard to myself, two possible options would appear to be open. The first was to remain at the Grammar School and at least provide companionship for my brother for one more year. The problem, however, was that it would not be easy to secure accommodation in the boarding house. There was little doubt, it has to be said, that the principal would probably have gladly obliged, but my father had already fallen under another strong influence which threw open the second option.

During our years at Aroloya, I had observed that two gentlemen paid fairly frequent visits to my father, usually on Saturdays. I soon discovered that they were both Andrians, former students of my father. The more frequent of the two was Mr Ighodaro, who appeared to have taken a liking to my father. He was later to become the Hon. Justice Ighodaro, and Iyase of Benin Kingdom. The other gentleman was Mr Kalejaiye. In the course of time, I discovered that they were both masters at a relatively new boarding school in Lagos producing consistently excellent results in the School Certificate examination and holding its own in sports. It was, possibly, they who suggested the idea of getting me transferred to Igbobi College when the family moved to Ibadan.

Even at that late hour, my father made contact with the then acting principal of Igbobi College, Mr Norman P. Morris, who turned out to be most obliging. Yes, he would accept me, but there would be difficulty with accommodation in the boarding house. Father gladly accepted the offer, and Mr Kalejaiye most graciously offered to have me stay with him for the first year. Mr Kalejaiye, the school's geography master, was the House Master of Freeman House, but I was assigned to Oluwole House, into which I would move physically the following year.

As it turned out, I was a day boy only in name. Apart from board and lodging in Mr Kalejaiye's quarters, I followed the routine of the boarders, and many boys at the school must have assumed that I was indeed a boarder.

This was a totally new experience for me: having to leave home for the first time. But it was lucky for me that at the beginning, I was able to combine the homeliness of staying with a family with the more independent life of a boarder. I felt very grateful to Mr Kalejaiye and his family.

***

I fell in love with Igbobi at first sight. First, the layout of the school compound, with the carefully trimmed hedges and well-manicured lawns (on which, I quickly discovered, any boy stepped at his own peril), and I was fascinated by the yellow-and-blue school cap. I thought it was the most beautiful school cap in the whole of Lagos, and it made the boys look distinctive whenever they stepped out into town on open days. On such days, the boys wore their white uniforms, but the daily working uniform was khaki which, for me, was a throw-back to my days at Oyo, Aroloya and Christ Church Cathedral School. This time, however, the khaki seemed more dignified than in the past!

Igbobi College was founded in 1932 through a collaboration between the CMS (now Anglican) Church and the Methodist Mission (now Methodist Church Nigeria) following an earlier successful experiment with United Missionary College (U.M.C.) four years earlier in Ibadan. Possibly unlike any other school before or after it, the school opened with a full complement of boys from Form 1 to Form 6. It thus exemplified the Yoruba mythical *Ajantala*, the boy who grew into full manhood on the very day that he was born.

What the collaborating Churches did was to turn to the two elite schools already owned by them and (according to Igbobi folklore) 'cream off' the best boys in the various classes and constitute them into the pioneer boys of Igbobi. The boys came from the CMS Grammar School and the Methodist Boys' High School. That the 'creaming' was successful was shown in the calibre of these original Igbobians. They included Teslim Elias, who later became a legendary jurist, Professor of Law, Attorney-General of the Federation, Chief Justice of Nigeria and President of the World Court at the Hague. In the same class with him was Horatio Oritsejolomi Thomas, who became a famous professor of surgery and Vice-Chancellor of the University of Ibadan. Others included G.B.A. Coker, later to become a judge of the Supreme Court, and his brother, F.C.A Coker, who later became the first Nigerian Treasurer of the Lagos City Council. Among other boys who later became prominent Nigerians were M.N.Q. Sagoe, another eminent lawyer in later years, and Adefarasin, who ended his career on the Supreme Court. It is a curious fact that the early Igbobians first made their mark in the field of Law. Diversification however came in later years. For example, in the set immediately before mine, we had Kwoku Adadevoh, who became an eminent professor of medicine and vice-chancellor of the University of Lagos; Michael Ibru, later to become a legendary businessman; and Ignatius Olisemeka, who later became one of the country's most accomplished diplomats. Outside this set, two other distinguished diplomats were Olujimi Jolaoso and Yinka Olaitan, my classmate.

I found Igbobi quite different from the Grammar School, which was also an elite school in its own right. The main difference arose from the boarding nature of Igbobi, which involved the boys in communal living everyday from six o'clock in the morning to 9.30 at night. This allowed for greater interaction among the boys, and between them and the masters than at the Grammar School; and this, most important of all, facilitated friendships which lasted for a lifetime.

***

My first year was spent savouring this idyllic new life at Igbobi, working hard and playing hard. One game-changing event, however, took place that year. Rumours had gone round the school that the proprietors had appointed a new principal for the school in London, and the boys were naturally curious to find out what kind of man he was, and what kind of principal he would be.

We did not have to let our imagination wander for too long before the acting principal, Mr Norman P. Morris, announced to us the expected date of arrival of the new principal. Mr Morris had thought up a rather unusual and scary way for the boys to receive their new principal.

On the appointed day, all the boys had to play the part of savages, with chalk marks on their faces and bodies. We were then to hide securely in the Senior Block, lying in wait for our guest. Meanwhile, a huge cauldron of water was placed on fire in the garden in front of the Block. As soon as the new principal, accompanied by Mr Morris, came within sight of the cauldron, a whistle would be blown and we were all to troop out in mock attack. Luckily, we were not armed with spears! If the new principal was scared, he did not show it. He probably immediately took the performance for the joke that it was, as a skit on the popular European image of Africa. Surely, our new principal must have read extensively about the school before setting out from Britain.

Without any further ado, we dispersed as previously instructed, to take a shower while the new principal was shown to his lodge. Later, spruced up in our khaki, we made for the Assembly Hall for the formal reception of the new principal. There, we sang lustily, and the principal could not help remarking humorously that he could not believe that those beautiful sounds were coming from the same group which had previously welcomed him to the school.

***

Our new principal, we were told, was the Rev. Reginald B. Parker, a priest of the Anglican Church. Like Mr Morris, he had an M.A. from Oxford, but also a B.Sc. in Chemistry from the University of Manchester. He had come to us from Oundle School, one of Britain's famous public schools. The boys took to him immediately because of his charisma and sense of humour. It was clear from that first encounter that he had come to turn around Igbobi College, which already had the reputation of being one of the best schools in Lagos, and indeed, Nigeria.

A debate inevitably ensued, however, among the boys – and we later learnt, among the staff as well – as to the appropriateness of the weird – and some said, demeaning – manner in which the principal had been received. I do not think that anyone actually asked Mr Morris what he had had in mind in arranging that kind of reception, so we had to resort to speculations. Obviously, Mr Morris could not have sought to create a bad first impression which could have remained with the Rev. Reginald Parker for the rest of his time at Igbobi. The charitable intention to attribute to Mr Morris, many claimed, was criticism of uncomplimentary ideas of Africa held in Europe, knowing full well that the new-comer would almost immediately afterwards be presented with the sharp contrast which would reveal the true picture.

Others, however, not satisfied with this charitable interpretation, questioned the wisdom of creating that kind of first impression at all, at a time that many people were sensitive to such unflattering images of Africa in Europe.

In the end, Mr Morris was given the benefit of the doubt, especially as the motive appeared to have been correctly interpreted by the new principal. Certainly, there was nothing in the new principal's behaviour in the ensuing ten years that he spent at Igbobi to suggest anything but that he loved the school and the boys, and was inspired to elevate the school to the highest possible level.

***

The Rev. – later, Canon – Reginald B. Parker in no time earned the affection and admiration of the boys, to the extent that they spontaneously agreed that the middle initial 'B' in his name obviously stood for Babatunde!

No more than one week after first setting foot on the soil of Igbobi, the new principal was in khaki like everyone else. He always wore, to match, brown shoes and brown hoses; and the boys admired his determined gait – the gait of a man who had come three thousand miles with a mission which he was determined to accomplish. And nowhere better was he admired than every morning when he made his entry into the assembly hall for the opening of the school day. Then, magisterial in his Oxford gown over his Anglican cassock, he would stride down the full length of the aisle and mount the rostrum. Obviously, a new era had dawned at Igbobi. By today's standards, Igbobi was a very small school, with not more than 150 boys altogether, which, I imagine, made the reforming principal's task even easier.

I found that I was thrust into the middle of highly-gifted classmates, in which competition was fierce. Not surprisingly, practically every member of the class later in life created a niche for himself. Ikpehare Aig-Imoukhuede was in the class and already showed his class as a writer with his short stories. But perhaps the most spectacular achievement of the members of the class later in life is shown in the fact that the class produced six professors – three each in the Universities of Ibadan and Lagos, one of the Ibadan professors also serving two terms as vice-chancellor. And this time, medical science predominated. Ladipo Hunponu-Wusu, my classmate and friend from the Lagos Cathedral School days, and now my classmate once again, has distinguished himself as a professor of community medicine at the University of Lagos. Two other classmates – Gabriel Odia and Olu Aina – have also been professors in the same College of Medicine. At Ibadan, Jide Desalu retired as professor of Anatomy, and Patrick Aghadiuno was professor of Pathology before his sad demise. Ayo Banjo retired as professor of English Language and vice-chancellor at the same university.

Other classmates equally distinguished themselves in various professions. Sidney Afonja retired as Chief Judge of Ondo State. Lere Adesina, another lawyer, did a stint in the Nigerian Senate, while Segun Coker, still another lawyer, ended up as the Head of Service of Lagos State. We even produced someone for the military forces – Admiral Oduwaiye, who held high office at the Supreme Military Council.

Other outstanding members of the class included Bayo Bodede, later a gifted engineer who played a prominent part in setting up NITEL; Segun Odulate, a versatile scholar who later went into manufacturing; and Remi Ogunlesi, another gifted engineer, who worked for the Electricity Corporation of Nigeria. We have even made a showing in business, with Bandele Ogutuga rising to the position of president of ICAN, and Bola Oyesanmi holding high office in Insurance. John Sagay ended his career as a federal civil service commissioner.

The boys in my class bonded beautifully and became noted for their hyperkinetic adventures. But they were so academically sound that the principal had the confidence to reduce the school certificate course from six to five years, beginning with our set. The waters had been tested with the set immediately before us, which had sat for the school certificate examination after five years. But those boys came back in their sixth year and them left school in April of that year following their excellent results.

Igbobi had already established a reputable academic standard before the arrival of the Rev. Reginald Parker. What the new principal did was to reinforce that standard through a fine corps of teaching staff. Two features were noticeable during the first two years of the new dispensation. In addition to long-standing members of staff, the school received annually, during their long vacations, a number of undergraduate students of University College Ibadan, who must have been close to their final year at UCI and who turned out to be very stimulating to the boys. Easily the favourite among the students was Olujimi Jolaoso – an old boy of the school – because, in addition to his personal and intellectual attributes, he was a star athlete at UCI. Another favourite was Mr – later, Dr – Alafe Aluko, who taught Mathematics and History and managed to get virtually every boy in my class to make an 'A' in both subjects in the school certificate examination.

The principal himself taught my class Greek, making us read parts of St. John's Gospel in Greek. The expatriate staff, in addition to helping to maintain the high standards, also played an important part in the cultural life of the school. S.S.G Hough, a young Oxford graduate, was a fine pianist who regaled us every morning with piano sonatas in the assembly hall while waiting for the principal to make his entry. Another young Oxford graduate, Mr Moorehouse, was an accomplished cricketer and helped Mr Morris in training the boys at the nets.

Of the older, established, members of staff, the most dreaded – and later, most unforgettable – was Mr Talabi Esubiyi, who had been there from near the beginning of the life of the school. He was the Master of Townsend House, but his influence, and even presence, was felt in every corner of the school. Mr Esubiyi was also personally in charge of the school shop, where he sternly stopped the boys from running up large bills to be settled by their parents.

Boarding life was exhilarating. Rising was at 6.30 a.m. The boys then quickly cleaned up the dormitories, made their beds, went for a shower and got ready for breakfast. Everybody should be in the dining hall within five minutes of the bell being rung. The Master on Duty stood at the entrance, and when the time was up, ordered the door to be shut. Late-comers had to miss the meal. The same procedure was adopted for lunch and supper. Perhaps this was the reason why, in later life, Igbobians are noted for punctuality!

There were, in my time, four Houses. Three of them were named after Church dignitaries: Oluwole, my own House, was named after the late Bishop Oluwole of the Anglican Mission. Similarly, Townsend House was named after Bishop Townsend, one of the earliest Anglican missionaries in the country, while Freeman House was named after Thomas Birch Freeman, one of the earliest Wesleyan (Methodist) missionaries, who in fact was a Black American. The fourth House, Aggrey House, was named after Aggrey of Africa, the great leader from the Gold Coast, now Ghana.

As was to be expected, competition was keen among the Houses, but in spite of the best efforts of the other Houses, Aggrey House always managed to come up tops. It was as if the school authorities had annually foreseen which boys were likely to be very good sportsmen and loaded Aggrey House with them! Oluwole House was middling, but occasionally showed mastery at cricket.

After classes, followed by lunch, came siesta. Every boy had to lie on his bed, and the whole compound was completely silent. Siesta (also called 'rest period') was followed by individual activities on the sports field, after which the boys showered and got ready for supper.

Seating was arranged in Houses in the large dining hall, with a prefect at the head of each table to maintain law and order. At the head of the entire hall itself sat the Master on Duty and the four House Captains, one of whom was also the Senior Prefect. When the Master on Duty did not wish to take his meal, he passed it over to the Senior Prefect, who might share it with his colleagues.

Three meals in particular made the dining hall buzz with extra activity. The first was breakfast, where each boy was allowed to have as many cups of coffee as he wished. This led to competitions on various tables, where the boys competed for who could have the highest number of cups of the beverage. I believe a boy actually managed to have ten cups. He was hailed as the real 'coffee smoker' and was believed to have a refrigerator installed in his throat! The next two favourites were beans and *dodo*. Many boys eagerly devoured their servings of beans, insects and all. And during *dodo* meals, some boys increased their helpings by persuading other boys to give them some of theirs. Champions of coffee, beans and *dodo* were celebrated throughout the school.

Supper was followed by the prep period, during which all the boys went back to their classrooms to do their homework, supervised by the prefects. The day ended with the evening Assembly, after which the junior boys (i.e. Forms 1 to 3) went straight to bed while the seniors went back to their classrooms for a little more stint of prep. General lights-out came at 9.30, and everywhere, again, was silent till the next morning.

But not all the boys had the expected eight hours sleep, for there was a flourishing tradition of 'ghosting' among the senior boys. This was how it went. Shortly after lights-out, particularly at the approach of examinations, the senior boys in the senior dormitory went into the box room and proceeded to shade the light so that it would not be visible to the House Master, who occasionally went around the building to ensure the observance of lights-out. Having shaded the light bulb, the boys then sat or reclined under the shaft of light and went to business reading, and communicating in whispers.

But it was by no means just a swotting session. After reading for a while, the 'ghosts' went into a prolonged break, during which the box-room was converted into a mini-dining room. *Garri* was produced and soaked in water, and lots of sugar and milk added. While this was going on, on one hand, loaves of bread were produced on the other, and tins of sardines opened. A good time was certainly had by all, after which the camouflage was dismantled and the box room returned to its normal state. The boys then stole back to their beds to catch a little sleep before the official rising. Naturally, they were often the last to rise. It certainly says much for the ingenuity of the boys that this practice went on for years without the authorities being any the wiser.

I often wondered what really was the attraction of ghosting: the opportunity to do further reading, or the sumptuous party which it featured. In any case, I found that I was constitutionally not suited for this nocturnal escapade because I must have a good sleep at night. However, I consoled myself with the thought that what I lost by not ghosting I gained from converting the rest period to study time while lying on my bed and watching everyone else in the dormitory sleeping blissfully.

Years later, I could not help marvelling at how, throughout my years at Igbobi, not once did we have a blackout. Not once was our evening prep disrupted for this reason. Similarly, not once did the showers in the bathrooms fail to deliver water.

***

Saturday was a special day. The day began like other days, with the boys rising and tidying up the dormitory. But the tidying up was more spirited on Saturdays because there was always an inspection carried out by the House Master, sometimes in the company of the principal himself. Every boy stood by his bed to show what a good job he had done, with his bed neatly made and the mosquito net duly deployed on the top of the bed.

After the House Master had departed, the House Captain went round to place six pennies on each bed. This represented our pocket money for the following week, and all these pennies were destined to end up in the purses of the two women who operated the '*dodo* shed'.

All the boys trooped to this shed during break between classes to have a quick snack. We queued up while the women made our favourite snack of mashed *dodo*, which the women called 'moss.' Peanuts were also on offer at the shed, but the boys' favourite was always 'moss'.

After lunch on Saturdays, the boys were free to spend the rest of the day as they wished until prep time at night. Some hung around the dormitories while others spent their time in the classrooms. A few others, aiming at breaking records at the next athletics meeting, spent their time on the sports field tracks.

But naturally, the Saturdays that we looked forward to were the open days. On such days, after breakfast, the boys emerged from their dormitories in their gleaming whites and stunning caps, and headed for the gate. The gate was some two miles away from any signs of habitation, and we walked through the kolanut plantation (which gave the school its name) and felt relieved when we sighted the Yaba bus stop, the terminus of the bus service in Lagos operated by J.N. Zarpas, a Greek entrepreneur. Those whose destination was Yaba carried on walking while others, like myself, took the bus at this point. I got off the bus at Ebute-Metta, on Strachan Street (now Herbert Macaulay Street) where my aunt lived and spent the day with her and my cousins. Occasionally, I made a foray into Lagos Island and spent time with my great cousin and his family at Idumagbo Avenue.

All too soon, it was time to return to school. The journey back was more burdensome than the journey out. Whereas the journey out was in droves, the journey back was in dribs and drabs, and this made it seem as though the journey from Yaba bus stop back to school was longer. We did our best to return on time, for at 6 p.m. there was a roll call conducted in front of the dining hall. As we gathered at this point, we could see a few boys racing from the gate to arrive in time for the roll call. Those who were not around to answer to their names were marked down for punishment.

***

One notable innovation brought about by Canon Parker was the devolution of greater authority to the prefects, and the new mystique accorded to the senior prefect, sometimes now referred to as Head of School or Head Boy. The most visible sign of the new order was the institution of the 'order note' for bad conduct, which prefects as well as masters were empowered to issue to errant boys. Since it was generally known that any boy who earned up to four order notes in a term would be shown the gate, this meant that prefects were now wielding enormous powers. Boys were, however, given the right to appeal against an order note issued by a prefect, and prefects were occasionally overruled by the appellant's House Master.

***

Indeed, nothing made the principal more angry than to discover that a senior boy had ill-treated a junior boy. On at least one occasion during my time, such a report was brought to the principal, who immediately called a special assembly. The principal informed us that the senior boy 'had been making life unpleasant for a junior boy'. The senior boy was summoned to the podium and had corporal punishment administered on him by Mr Esubiyi.

Early in 1950, the news floated around the school that the Form Five boys of that year were going to be entered along with the Form Six boys for the Cambridge School Certificate examination. The principal had clearly reached the conclusion that Igbobi boys did not need six years for the examination. But to be on the safe side, those Form Five boys of 1950 were asked to return to school to await their results. Michael Ibru was appointed senior prefect for 1951. When the results were released in March,1951, the principal was proved absolutely right. The boys did excellently well and accordingly passed out of the school at the end of the first term.

A new set of prefects was appointed for the rest of 1951, and I was mildly surprised to find that I was one of them. Besides, I was also appointed captain of Oluwole House, in succession to Kola Olafimihan, one of the stars of his class, who later went on to be a brilliant medical scientist. Ibru's successor as senior prefect was John Sagay, who later ended his career in the Federal Civil Service Commission.

As a kind of preparation for my new responsibilities, I had, in previous years, been chapel monitor and library monitor. At this time, the assembly hall doubled as the Chapel. My duty therefore was to ensure that the hall was in proper shape for the morning assemblies, and for the Sunday services. The second monitor, also from my class, was Lere Adesina, who later practiced law and served as a senator in the National Assembly. For the Sunday services, the seating had to be re-arranged so that we had a choir stall. Whereas the piano was used for morning assemblies, a harmonium was used for the Sunday services. It helped that I was a chorister myself. The school organist was none other than Mr Ade Akomolafe, who was putting his musical training at St. Andrew's College, Oyo, to good use. He was not only organist but also choir master, and conducted the choir practices. One or two of the boys were able to play the piano, and at least one of them, Ajibade, was awarded the Swallowbeck music scholarship to cover his years in school. I understand that, much later, Ayodele Falase also won the scholarship. Falase went on to be the organist of All Saints' Church, Jericho, Ibadan, combining the position with that of Vice-Chancellor of the University of Ibadan.

My position in the library simply gave me the opportunity to browse at will. I recall that one of the books that caught my attention was Josie Leigh's *The Professor*, which I read out of curiosity. The library was well-stocked, and the boys made maximum use of it.

Being a school prefect and house captain was a little demanding. But fortunately, the junior boys were not too troublesome, and my classmates were very supportive.

***

During the year 1951, Major Allen, a British resident in Lagos who had grown to be very fond of the school, established the Major Allen Prize for good conduct. The novelty of the prize was that the entire student population was to decide by vote the winner of the prize. Oviawe, a boy in Form Three, won the prize for the first time, and the runner-up prize – the *Proxime Accesit* – went to me. I recall one of my classmates saying to me that it was no mean feat for a prefect to be voted for massively, especially by the junior boys. Such a prefect could not have been regarded as an ogre!

***

Altogether, my final year in school turned out to be an eventful and memorable one. I was already the school goalkeeper, in a year when the school progressed to the final of the Schools Cup, and I recall the trepidation with which I took my place at the post at Onikan Stadium. Sadly, though not unexpectedly, we lost to the old rival – St Gregory's College. In the end, the school considered I had played my part sufficiently gallantly to award me the coveted football colours at a tumultuous school assembly.

I did not discover any talent in myself for athletics, though I would have loved to be a successful hurdler. However, I had a passion for cricket, which saw me into the school cricket team, in which I was the wicket keeper. Our main rival in cricket was King's College, which had a truly formidable team. I recall Canon Parker once remarking that 'Banjo always plays in the most dangerous position in a team!'

Towards the very end of the year, I found myself walking again proudly to the podium, this time to be decorated by the principal with the cricket colours.

As the year slowly drew to a close, the Cambridge school certificate examination loomed in the horizon, and spells of silence fell over the Form Five classroom. My class was talented, and had indeed sometimes been described as precocious; so there was no doubt that the school certificate results would be very good. The question was whether or not the whole class would end up in Grade 1.

At the appointed time, my class trooped out every morning and headed to the Methodist Girls' High School, Yaba, which was the centre for the examination. I was pleasantly surprised to find that the papers were much easier than I had feared, and when the results were released the following March, I found that I had earned the expected distinction in English Language, and in a few other subjects including Mathematics. That made me feel that I had acquired a balanced education at Igbobi College.

***

I found that Igbobi was a tremendous watershed in my life. It was there that I discovered myself, my intellectual orientation and my modest capacity for leadership. No doubt, I had been fortunate to be there during what has later been described as Igbobi's 'golden age,' and Canon Parker did manage to get the school listed in the Whitaker's Almanac of public schools – the only one in West Africa. That was worlds away from the barefaced philistinism which was visited on the school in the aftermath of the civil war. Even more rewarding for me is the fact that I have kept all the friendships that I cultivated at the school, as the rest of the story will show.

It gives me enormous pleasure to say that my junior brother, Gboyega, also went to Igbobi. He gave a good account of himself and completed the school certificate course in four years. He later read History at Reading University, and obtained a Masters degree from Birmingham University. He returned home to study librarianship at the University of Ibadan, worked in the library of the University of Lagos for many years and is the immediate past General Manager of the Musical Society of Nigeria (MUSON) in Lagos.

***

In December 1951, I went back home to Ibadan, to await the results of the examination, and to consider what next to do with myself. The results turned out to be very good, and I came up in Grade 1. If I were to follow my brother's footsteps, I would have started looking for where to do my 'A' levels in Britain. He had gone to Norwich City College to do his 'A' levels, after which he went to King's College, Newcastle-Upon-Tyne, a college of the University of Durham, to begin his medical course. I decided, meanwhile, to return to Lagos where, naturally, all my friends were. I went to stay with my aunt, and my uncle took me completely as one of his own children; and since I was older than any of them, he granted me great privileges.

***

One day, one of my classmates, Ogedegbe, came to visit me and appeared in the uniform of a customs officer. He told me how much he was enjoying his job and asked if I would like to join him there. I told him the idea of going to work in uniform did not at all appeal to me, and he replied that there were also clerical jobs at the headquarters on the Marina, where I would not have to wear a uniform. Since that would keep me in touch with at least one of my old classmates, I told him I would give a clerical job a try, meaning, of course, to do it for only a few months.

When I told my father about my intentions, he told me that the chief clerk at the Customs headquarters in Lagos was an old student of his; and he sent me to him with a note. On presenting the note to Mr Odugbesan, he asked me to follow him. We went round the large hall where all the clerks were working until we found a vacant seat; and he asked me to sit down and start working!

That was how I came to become a clerk at the Customs Department. Ogedegbe was glad at the development and popped in to see me from time to time. The location on the Marina was particularly convenient for me, for it meant that I could join my uncle every morning in his Chevrolet as he went to work as manager of John Holts nearby.

Soon, I was moved to the Accounts section under Mr Vanderpuye, a Ghanaian, the movement of West African nationals in the pre-independence era being so fluid. This was the section that prepared the salaries every month. The top positions were, naturally, dominated by British expatriates, and I noticed that there were only about six Nigerian names featuring in this category. One of these names was that of Mr Mbamali, a name that was destined to acquire a great significance to my life later.

Meanwhile, I enjoyed my stint at the Customs Department. There were two other recent school-leavers in my section – Ali and Onwukeme – and we had a very pleasant time together, sometimes sneaking into Kingsway Stores which was virtually next-door. It so happened that the Comptroller of Customs at the time, Mr Bishop, had also developed a liking for walking into Kingsway, presumably as a form of relaxation. As soon as we spotted him, we quickly sneaked back to our desks.

One day, Ogedegbe came to see me, and said that he had news which might interest both of us. He produced a newspaper and directed my attention to the announcement in it to the effect that the federal government was about to establish three post-secondary colleges, one in each of the three regions of the country. All three of them would offer 'A' level courses in the arts and science. In addition, the northern college would offer courses in architecture; the eastern college would train engineers; and the Ibadan college would offer courses in administration. But the remarkable thing was that the three colleges were, in essence, branches of a federal college – the Nigerian College of Arts, Science and Technology, humorously described by someone as the Nigerian College of All Sorts of Things! The Ibadan campus was to be the headquarters, for that was where the Principal, the formidable Dr Hart, was to be based.

Ogedegbe suggested we should apply to do our 'A' levels there. I thought it was a good idea, and then I thought, with my 'A' levels, I might be able to join my brother at King's College, Newcastle-Upon-Tyne. I was, however, very disappointed to find that Ogedegbe did not follow up on the excellent suggestion. As for me, I lost no time in finding out more about the new college and then putting in my application.

Early in 1953, I received a letter of admission, informing me that the college would open on 1 October, and describing where in Ibadan it was sited. I went straightaway to inform Mr Odugbesan and to thank him for the experience of the civil service that he had graciously helped me to acquire. Then I got in touch with my dad in Ibadan to appraise him of the new development. My uncle, aunt and cousins were happy for me. They had made my short stay with them very pleasant and memorable. In due course, I was back in Ibadan to make necessary preparations.

3

AN IBADAN INTERLUDE

Back in Ibadan, the first thing I did was to find out the location of this new college. I was staying with my dad in the new premises of St Luke's College, which was at the Molete end of Ibadan. I discovered that the new Nigerian College was situated next door to University College, Ibadan (UCI), off Oyo Road, an area that was, as yet, an undeveloped end of the sprawling city of Ibadan. The Nigerian College was to be fully boarding, but my dad had presented me with the gift of a Raleigh bicycle to mark my performance in the School Certificate examination, which now made it inexpensive for me to visit home whenever I wished.

The fees at the college were extremely low but, in contrast, the facilities were impressive. The campus was built around a sports arena, which made it possible, whenever a soccer or cricket match was being played, for some students simply to stand in the veranda of their hostels and watch. The rooms in the hostels were most comfortable, with single occupancy. Even before the first day of operation, the laboratories were ready and well stocked, as was the library.

We soon discovered that we were sharing lecturers with UCI. For example, to teach us Latin we had Ian Bowman from UCI. He was very impressive, and I thought he spoke Latin as if it was his second or third language, as he took us through Cicero's *"Pro Milone!"* By the end of the first session, he had so captivated me that I was fully determined to read classics at university.

His residence was not at all far from the boundary between the two institutions, and I would occasionally walk through the footpath, which we had christened 'techno-varsity road', to have discussions with him. I discovered that he was a graduate of the University of Glasgow, Scotland, and I determined that that was the university I would apply to after my 'A' levels. He promised that at the appropriate time, he would assist me with the application formalities.

Moving in the opposite direction, two of my lecturers in due course ended up at UCI. One of them was Ellen Cain, the young and attractive graduate of Oxford, who taught us English Literature of the romantic period. She ended up on the staff of the English Department in UCI. The other was Dr J.C. Anene, the only Nigerian to teach us. He taught History, and we all thought he was an engaging speaker of the English language. Dr Anene ended up as professor of history at UCI. The head of the English staff at the Nigerian College was Dr Wright, a New Zealander, and to teach us Chaucer was Mrs Oruwariye, who told us that her mother was English but her father Ghanaian. She was an excellent teacher who would not proceed until she was sure that every member of the class was on board. Many years later, I got to know her husband, Dr Oruwariye, who had a flourishing medical practice in Oke Ado, Ibadan.

We were curious to know what the cuisine would be like, but were very pleasantly surprised to find that both in quantity and quality, it was excellent. We had waiter service, and could have as many helpings as we desired. I thought perhaps we were being pampered because we were the pioneer students of the college, but perhaps the authorities had simply borrowed a leaf from UCI where, we found, the fare was similarly generous. At any rate, the standard remained high during my two years there.

It was, naturally, up to us students to establish a communal life, which we were conscious might become a tradition for this fledgling college, but it did help that we were next-door to UCI and were aware of what was going on there. The first four extra-curricular activities to emerge were dramatic presentations, soccer, cricket and dancing.

The students in my class decided to engage in dramatic presentations. I do not clearly remember now, but we might have been influenced by the activities next-door, where UCI was putting up dramatic performances of a very high standard, some of which we went over to watch. Our performances were, of course, no match for the sleek ones at UCI. Still, we did what we could, and kept our fellow-students happy. One performance which appeared to catch the imagination of the audience was that of the play, *Nix Nought Nothing*, a fairy play in Joseph Jacob's anthology, *English Fairy Tales*. Our production featured, among others, Christine Clinton and Subomi Balogun, both of them my classmates. It went down very well and we were encouraged to carry on.

With cricket, we were lucky to have among us, old students of Igbobi College, Government College, Ibadan, Government College, Umuahia, Government College, Ughelli and Christ's School, Ado-Ekiti, where the game of cricket had become established. I naturally resumed my position behind the wicket, and my former classmate at Igbobi, John Sagay, occasionally delivered some good runs. We were not strong enough to challenge the team from UCI, but we enjoyed ourselves and provided a diversion for our fellow students, some of whom watched from the veranda of their hostels.

Soccer was developed at the same time; and this time, I had a rival between the posts. One of my contemporaries was

Dejo Oyelese, who had already developed a reputation as the goalkeeper of one of the clubs in town. I believe he was the better of the two of us, but since we needed two goalkeepers for internal matches, both of us had a lot of practice. Oyelese later graduated into one of the leading clubs in the country.

Dancing was a different matter altogether. Here, everyone enthusiastically participated. It should be noted that what we engaged ourselves in was strictly ballroom dancing. We were fortunate that one of us, Fred Odunze, who eventually qualified as a medical doctor, had had very good training in ballroom dancing. He was a willing coach to the rest of us. Odunze was a delight to watch as he executed the quickstep, the slow fox-trot, the waltz, the rumba and the tango. Music was supplied for the most part from the records of the British Victor Sylvester and his famous band. Highlife had not yet really taken hold in the country, though we were aware of the occasional appearance of the Ghanaian E.T. Mensah at UCI under the auspices of a fledgling Sigma Club. But there were no Nigerian highlife stars. We had regular hops which were very well attended, and we were even occasionally joined by some members of staff and their wives.

***

Academic work started in earnest. I was delighted to find that I had three other Igbobians in my class, doing the same combination of subjects. John Sagay had been the senior prefect in my final year at Igbobi, and was one of those who had come to spend their holidays with me at Ibadan on a number of occasions. He eventually read history at UCI and Cambridge. Segun Coker, another classmate at Igbobi, had spent the short spell after Igbobi in the Nigerian Broadcasting Corporation and turned up at the Nigerian College with a good collection of gramophone records which we listened to in his room. Subomi Balogun had finished one year after us at Igbobi, but had so effortlessly blended with us that the general belief was that all four of us had been classmates at

Igbobi. A close friendship, indeed, developed between me and Subomi, leading, several years later, to his being the best man at my wedding. The friendship has remained as strong as ever.

Naturally, all four of us Old Igbobians bonded closely at the Nigerian College, and often indulged in the Igbobi rallying cry: 'Up IC!' which practically everyone in the Nigerian College thought they heard as: 'Four, Five, Six!'. The quartet of us were therefore generally referred to as 'the four, five, six!'

In the typical Nigerian fashion, we also instituted religious worship: for the Muslims on Fridays, and for the Christians on Sundays. I recall that the first time I ever saw Professor Kenneth Dike was when he came from UCI to conduct a service for us in the common room of our college. I was struck by the combination of erudition and piety.

We must have been about twelve in my class, with three girls, all of whom later in life got married to very prominent Nigerians. Christie Okoli (whose senior brother had been my senior at Igbobi) got married to Chinua Achebe, no less! Bimpe Abimbolu married the author and former university administrator, Vincent Ike, who later became a traditional ruler in Anambra State; and Christine Clinton was married to the literary scholar, Professor Ben Obumselu. All three of them had moved over to UCI to take their first degrees, as did most of the boys in the class. One of us, Fakayode, later became a judge in Oyo State.

The quality of our preparations for the 'A' levels of the University of London was exceptionally good, a fact which was forcibly brought home to me during the examinations when I had no particular difficulty, an experience which, I am sure, was shared by all of my classmates.

Meanwhile, with the help of Mr Bowman, I had perfected my admission formalities to the University of Glasgow, to the point of being actually offered admission before my 'A' level results were out. By the time these results were out, I was actually already in Glasgow.

I had had the assurance from my dad that he would be responsible for my university education. He had written a very successful text book titled *A West African Teacher's Handbook*, published by the University of London Press. The book was widely sold throughout English-speaking Africa, and even in the West Indies, as I found years later during my sabbatical at the Cave Hill campus of the University of the West Indies in Barbados. There I was amused to hear someone ask me whether I was the author! With handsome royalties from the book, my dad was able to give that assurance.

We were treated like undergraduates at the Nigerian College, but did not form a student union. We however did have cause to meet together from time to time, for which purpose we needed to have a leader. Ossai Agyeman from Ghana was chosen for this role, and he made a good job of it. Looking back now, I consider it remarkable that an institution which was not a university had opened its doors to students from outside the country, a practice which even the present-day teeming universities in the country could profit from.

***

Once the examinations were over in May, 1955, we turned our minds to considering what next to do with our future. Most of my classmates had applied to UCI, and I learnt later that they had been successful. I made my plans in early September to secure a flight to London, where I expected to be met by my brother. The British Council in Nigeria in those days had a programme in Ibadan for students intending to study in Britain. I attended and found it very helpful. At the end, they obtained from us our travel plans. They then actually promised to arrange for us to be met by their staff at the airport in London, and for transitional accommodation to be arranged for us in London before we went off to our various universities. After saying my farewells in Ibadan, I set off for Lagos on the first leg of my journey. My uncle, aunt and cousins were all excited about my impending journey. I stayed with them for a couple of days.

The BOAC flight to London was scheduled to leave Ikeja on the mid-morning of 21 September, 1955, and so, fairly early in the morning, accompanied by my aunt and a couple of her friends, I was on my way to Ikeja. At the airport, we found other passengers waiting, among them, people like me going to Britain to study. We waited to be asked to check in, but nothing happened for a long time. When, at the scheduled time of departure, we still had heard nothing, we naturally became anxious.

Then, unofficial information, theories and speculations started filtering through to us. We gathered that the plane to take us should have arrived at Ikeja the previous evening with the passengers from London, but that it had not shown up. We thought it strange that, if the flight from London had indeed been postponed, we should not have been so informed as soon as we had arrived in the morning. Throughout the whole day, no official announcement was made. When in the end it was made, it was to ask us to go back home and return to the airport the following morning. Distress was clearly visible on every face, and we wondered, in particular, how those passengers who had come to the airport from outside Lagos were expected to manage.

It was at my auntie's place later that evening that we first heard of the mind-blowing tragedy that had occurred, as related by the radio. The flight from London had taken off from London all right, but had crashed en route in Libya, with the loss of everybody on board. I felt horrified and numb. Some people, thinking to cheer us up, speculated that if the aircraft had made it to Lagos, it could very well have crashed on the way back to London; and that only intensified my horror. Once we were back home, my aunt went immediately into passionate prayers, in which, I could well believe, she was engaged the entire night. I myself had a fitful sleep that night, wondering what the next morning might bring.

When the list of the victims of the crash was released next morning, it turned out that the Orimolusi of Ijebu-Igbo was one of them. This brought, for me and my family, a new personal dimension to the tragedy, and to my aunt's bewilderment, for the Orimolusi was a relation whom I had known very well. While we were at Oyo, he had, before his coronation, been working at the Baptist Hospital, Ogbomoso, and had occasionally visited us. There were people, however, who were confident that he could not possibly have perished in such a gruesome accident. They believed that he must have been saved miraculously, must have landed on his own safely in Libya, and would ultimately find his way back to Nigeria and to his beloved Ijebu-Igbo. I hoped so with all my heart, though I could not understand how such a feat could have been accomplished. Of course, sadly, that speculation in the end came to nothing.

We arrived at Ikeja next morning, now fully conscious of the risks of air travel. We passengers were in a fix. We were afraid our flight might be postponed again, or even cancelled outright; and yet, in the circumstances, we dreaded boarding a flight that day. We waited in solemn contemplation, discussing in hushed whispers among ourselves.

Then suddenly, we were jolted by the crackle of the public address system, followed by the announcer's voice asking us to check in, in preparation for departure. There were tearful farewells as we disappeared into the departure area, saying silent prayers to ourselves. Solemnly ascending the steps into the aircraft, we quietly settled into our seats.

The cabin crew, sympathetic to our predicament, did their best to lift our spirits; and indeed, a couple of hours into our journey, we had become as cheerful as could be expected, taking care not to refer to the events of the previous day.

Samuel Ayodele Banjo, author's father

Author's father as a Vicar

Parents' wedding, 1930

Parents at St. Andrew's College, Oyo

A family picture

Form III, 1949

Igbobi College Staff, 1949

Form IV, 1950

1950 - Dancing Club

At Nigerian College, Ibadan

At the Nigerian College of Arts, Science and Technology, Ibadan, 1954

At Ikeja Airport, 1955

Father's grave at Ijebu-Igbo

4

SOJOURN IN GREAT BRITAIN

We landed in London on the late afternoon of the same day, and were all eager to find out what London looked and felt like. As the plane descended to land, the aerial view was truly breathtaking. Once on the ground, I could not help noticing the businesslike manner in which work proceeded, and the prevailing quietness. I cleared immigration and customs without any difficulty, and emerged into the public waiting area within the airport complex. As the British Council in Ibadan had instructed us to do, I looked around for someone bearing a placard indicating the British Council. I went up to him and he introduced himself. Having checked for my name on the list he was carrying, he asked me to follow him.

Outside the airport building, there was a bus waiting. Once we were all assembled – about six of us – we were informed that some of us (including myself) would be taken to the British Council hostel at Queen's Gardens, while the rest would be taken to another British Council hostel at 1, Hans Crescent.

My initial reaction on stepping out of the airport building was one of amazement. I was aware that it was autumn, but did not expect that the weather in London could be this balmy, having left Lagos with the mindset of going into a frighteningly cold country. Instead, this was very pleasant weather indeed. Besides, although it was already about eight o'clock in the evening, it was still broad daylight. I concluded there must have been a gross exaggeration about the British weather; but as it turned out, I had to wait just a few more months to face the howling chilly winds of Glasgow. For the moment, I thought London was at its best. I did not have to rush out first thing next morning to get myself a warm overcoat. That could now wait until I joined up with my brother in Newcastle.

As we left the airport and drove towards Bayswater, I was impressed with the well-paved roads, the sets of traffic lights and the massive grey buildings.

Next morning, our British Council friend was on hand to take us to the shops and allow us to do some sightseeing. We even called at Hans Crescent, where we found, as at Queen's Gardens, students and visitors from practically every part of the Commonwealth.

After a couple more days, we were ready to disperse to our various destinations. I was seen to King's Cross railway station by an official of the British Council, where I boarded the train for Newcastle-Upon-Tyne. As I settled down to enjoy the entrancing British countryside speeding past me, my heart was full of gratitude to the British Council for the support I had enjoyed from it all the way from Ibadan. I imagined what an unthinkable challenge it would have been if I had had to face the journey all on my own. This favourable first contact with the Council was to be repeated for decades in later years.

When, a few hours later, I arrived at Newcastle railway station, I found my brother waiting for me on the platform. We had a joyful reunion and he led me out to his car. When we arrived at his flat, I found a familiar face in Sam Oduntan (now a retired professor). He and my brother had been classmates at the CMS Grammar School in Lagos, and were now medical students living in adjacent flats. I regaled them with news from Nigeria; how, in particular, Western Nigeria seemed to be forging ahead with development.

The next morning, my brother took me to Jackson the Tailor, where I ordered three suits and later picked up a Barracuda topcoat. It was a trifle cooler in Newcastle than in London, but still pleasant. I spent the next two days sightseeing and trying to get into the mood of living in Britain.

Ready for the final phase of my journey, I packed my increased baggage, and my brother saw me off at the railway station, where I boarded The Flying Scotsman for Glasgow. The view from my window seat on this train was even more breathtaking, and the speed at which we were going justified the name of the train. I sat back and started to contemplate what lay ahead of me; what life in one of Britain's ancient universities would be like; what, in particular, living in a hall of residence of the university would be like; and how long it would take me to settle down. My dad had told me he would arrange for my monthly allowances to be remitted from his account in Barclays at Ibadan to any branch of Barclays of my choice in Glasgow. As it turned out, however, Barclays did not operate in Glasgow, or anywhere in Scotland, for that matter. I found instead that the British Linen Bank operated in association with Barclays Bank, and so that was to be my bank for the next four years.

Glasgow

My reverie was cut short as the announcement came through that we were entering Glasgow Central railway station; and I heaved a huge sigh, more of anticipation than of relief. It occurred to me straightaway that from this point onwards,

I was on my own: no familiar face waiting for me on the platform, no welcoming placard. I made my way out of the station and hailed a cab. I asked to be taken to McBrayne Hall on Park Circus Place. The cabman knew exactly where it was and, about twenty minutes later, deposited me at the front door of a massive grey building. As I got out and looked up, I saw, over the front door, the university's coat of arms with the legend: *Via, Veritas, Vita,* affirming the religious foundation of the university.

Paying off the cabman, I climbed up the steps and pressed the door-bell. Moments later, the door opened, and I saw a maid in full uniform. She looked at me, and then at my luggage, and asked me to come in. She led me to the Warden's study, where I met the Warden, Dr Ritchie who, I later discovered, was a senior lecturer in German at the university. Having made me feel welcome, he asked that I should be shown to my room on the first floor. I quickly discovered that there were already two other Nigerians in the hall. One of them was Timi Morgan, reading engineering, and the other was Seni Sikuade, who had been a friend from way back in Aroloya, where he had worshipped with his father and the family. Seni and I, of course, immediately bonded. He was reading medicine.

The tradition in the hall was that freshmen were put in double rooms, and might move into single rooms in their second or third year. I was paired with a Scottish student, but before we had got to know each other very well, trouble erupted with another African student who had similarly been paired with a Scottish student. The African student, Shayiwe Riba, was from South Africa and had refused to get along with his roommate. I was approached and asked if I would agree to share a room with him, as he had apparently refused to share with any British student. I agreed, eager to save the situation, and ended up sharing a large and comfortable room with Shayiwe. I must say that I found his behaviour embarrassing, even after he had told me his story.

For the first time, I learnt of the horrors that Africans endured in South Africa under the apartheid regime. Relating them to me made him extremely angry, and he told me that he had come to Glasgow to study medicine purely as an insurance. He was looking forward to returning home to join fully in the war against the agents of apartheid. When I reminded him that he was at Glasgow University on a scholarship granted by Oppenheimer, one of the prominent apostles of apartheid, that made him even angrier, as he retorted that his father had died a miserable death in one of Oppenheimer's mines.

This incident gave me an early revelation of the Scottish character. As soon as they discovered that they had a difficult student on their hands, the hall authorities could easily have asked him to vacate the hall and perhaps go and look for digs in town. But they did not. Rather, they treated his petulance with patience and compassion, an attitude shared by all the students in the hall. One curious fact about Shayiwe, however, was that in spite of his seeming dislike for Europeans, he had a Swiss girl friend who visited him from London regularly!

It has to be said that Shayiwe and I spent two pleasant years as roommates. In our spare moments, we talked about each other's country, and it was clear to me that we were having a totally different colonial experience in Nigeria. We also discussed English studies and medicine, thereby broadening each other's perspectives. After two years, each of us moved into a single room, and I saw less of Shayiwe, except occasionally in the Green Lounge, where hall members gathered, waiting to be summoned into the dining room.

The day after my arrival in the hall, I went through Kelvingrove Park into the university precincts dominated by the magnificent Gothic spire on Gilmorehill. As I walked round, I could breathe, simultaneously, antiquity and modernity. I had heard, before coming up to Glasgow, of such eminent scholars who had adorned the university as, in the humanities, Adam Smith, the father of modern economics, and David Hume, the philosopher. On the science side, there were such names as Joseph Black, in Chemistry, and James Watt, the inventor of the steam engine. I was told that these four men in fact made the university sparkle in the eighteenth century and were, in fact, close friends. I stepped with awe into the Hunterian Museum, and looked round the magnificent library, where I was destined to spend much of my waking hours in the next four years.

The University of Glasgow (*Universitas Glasguensis*) is one of Britain's ancient universities. Established in 1451, it is the fourth oldest English-speaking university in the world, after Oxford, Cambridge and St. Andrew's; and the second oldest in Scotland, after St. Andrew's. The 500th anniversary had been celebrated four years before my arrival. The Vice-Chancellor was the philosopher Sir Hector Hetherington, who had been appointed in 1936 and served till 1961.

I had been briefed in Nigeria that even after very good 'A' levels in three subjects, one had to do four years for the first degree which, however, ended with an M.A. This degree was awarded in three classes, without the conventional division of the second class into upper and lower.

When the university opened a few days later, I was invited to see my academic adviser. He was an avuncular old academic who instantly put me at ease. After briefly talking about Nigeria, we got down to the subject of my proposed course at the university. He seemed impressed with my 'A' level results, but then dropped the bombshell. If I intended to take a degree in Classics, where was my 'A' level result in Greek? That made me feel slightly dizzy, and I explained that my only contact with Greek had been at school, and it had not even been offered for 'O' level there. The old man fixed me with his gaze for a brief moment, but long enough to make my heart start racing. What to do, now? Then he smiled and said that I had two options (which I prayed did not include going back where I came from!).

The first option, he said, was to spend the first year at the university bringing my Greek up to scratch. That would mean spending a total of five years for the degree. I immediately said to myself, and then to him, that that was not an option. I was already making enough financial demands on my father by choosing to study at a Scottish university. I waited impatiently for the second option. He studied my credentials again, and looking up, said, 'You've got a very good result in English; why don't you switch to an Honours degree in English, to save yourself having to spend an extra year?' (or words to that effect). He assured me that I would still be able to take Latin as one of my subsidiaries. Though it meant a fairly radical change in my original plans, it did not take me any time to agree.

I thought the Scottish system of university education had much to recommend it. For an Honours degree in English, for example, I had to offer three subjects in my first year and, naturally, I chose English, which was now to be my major, Latin (called 'Humanity' at the university) and History. In the second year, while retaining my major, I had to pick two new subjects, and I opted for Moral Philosophy and Political Economy. In my last two years, I had to concentrate on my major. That way, I thought the four years would have been well spent, deepening my knowledge of my major, but at the same time making a broadly educated man of me.

My first attendance at a Humanity lecture was, indeed, memorable. The lecture was delivered by the professor and head of department himself, Professor Christian J. Fordyce, a very formidable man. We waited for him in the large lecture hall, and I was not very surprised to find that I was the only African there. Professor Fordyce walked magisterially into the hall, threw his mortarboard stylishly on the table, surveyed the assembly in front of him (disdainfully, I thought), and then addressed us, gathering his academic gown around him. What he had to say struck fear into the heart of each of his listeners. Looking round at us, he said, slowly but firmly, that the pattern over the years had indicated that one-third of us would pass the examination at the first attempt in May; another third would pass at the re-sit in September. The remaining third would have to repeat the course or look elsewhere. Then he launched into the lecture, reading the Latin set book to us like his second language, and reminding me of Ian Bowman.

I listened with a mixture of fear and admiration, wondering which third I would end up in. As it happened, I was among the first third. My great interest in the subject, and Ian Bowman's excellent teaching at Ibadan, had mercifully paid off.

My experience at the English lectures was remarkably different. The lectures on Shakespeare were delivered by the Regius Professor, Peter Alexander, the famous Shakespearean scholar well-known for his complete works of Shakespeare. It was a delight to listen to him and experience his deep scholarship and subtle humour. The poetry lectures were delivered by Edwin Morgan, who himself later became an outstanding poet – in fact, the first poet laureate of Scotland.

***

At the end of that first year, I looked forward to classes in Moral Philosophy. My father, after all, had been a graduate of philosophy. As it turned out, I thoroughly enjoyed the course. As for Political Economy, I was fascinated by the ideas discussed and the new perspectives that they threw on my understanding of society and how it works.

The day after my first exploration of the university precincts, I took the tram down Sauchiehall Street to Forsythe's, to get myself kitted. There I collected the university blazer, tie and scarf. In coming years, appropriately dressed, I walked down Sauchiehall Street feeling, as in the old song, that Glasgow belonged to me!

In my third year, I entered the junior honours class, and for the following two years, operated within an intimate group. For the literature courses, I had a tutor, Dr Davies, to myself. Dr Davis often told me that she always looked forward to receiving my essays because they contained perspectives different from my colleagues', who, she said, always wrote from the same British tradition. I submitted my essays through the letter box at her home, and later discussed them at her home over cups of tea.

But I found the language courses more exciting, covering, as they did, the history of the language from Anglo-Saxon to early and late Middle English. This was followed by a few lectures on Modern English; but this was before modern linguistics fully came into its own in Britain and the United States. *Beowulf*, at first sight, did not look like English to me; but I soon got used to it and enjoyed the epic narrative. We traced the transition of the language from Old English, through early middle English to Chaucer. Along the way, we studied Scottish English texts, with Robert Burns given his rightful prominence.

The language classes were particularly enlivened by Dr Blakely. His classes were highly interactive, and everyone was at ease. But here again, we also had the great fortune of being taught by the famous Old English scholar, Professor Norman Davis, a highly inspiring teacher. When I left the university in 1959, Professor Davis left to take up the Merton Chair of English at Oxford, one of the most prestigious at that university. I retained contact with him from Nigeria and went up to Merton College on a few occasions to visit him. When I had my first Ph.D student in Anglo-Saxon at Ibadan, Professor Davis graciously agreed that I should send the student to him at Oxford for six months.

***

The student union at Glasgow was very lively, and the student union building, very imposing, was daily a beehive of activities. I did not hang out much at the union building. But I did look in during the cricket season to update myself on fixtures, as I was a member of the university's second eleven. I did not play football for the university, but was the goalkeeper for my hall team. Also, I looked in on weekends to witness the marathon debates in the union building. The chamber was a replica of Westminster, and students streamed in day and night, and simply took their seats on the side for which they wished to speak. Some of the speakers I listened to were quite impressive, but I always watched from the gallery and never ventured to take my seat on the benches.

I was around when a new Rector (Lord Rector) was to be elected. As the election was undertaken by the student body, there were vigorous campaigns in the union building. Lord Butler, a Conservative Party leader, emerged winner, and I remember there was a riotous reception for him in the union building afterwards. Students of Glasgow had elected Rectors from every walk of life in Britain and beyond, and I thought it was a remarkable tradition to choose Rectors in this way, for the Rector chaired the University Court (the equivalent of governing councils in other traditions). Equally remarkable, to me, was the General Council chaired by the Chancellor, which comprised all alumni of the university. I have received, without break for sixty years, notices of meetings of the Council, as well as minutes of every meeting. One was really made to feel that one was part of the university for the rest of one's life.

***

I did have some exposure to the social life of Glasgow. I took an early opportunity to ride on the Glasgow Underground. I had been told that it was the third oldest underground in the world, after London and Budapest. The train went in a circle, stopping at fifteen stations. After that one trial, I never again had need to travel underground but stuck to the trams.

I was a fairly frequent patron of Glasgow Theatre Royal, and once saw a phenomenal performance by Sir Laurence Olivier in the lead role in Ibsen's *Master Builder*. Back at home, I had been captivated by Sir Laurence's performance as Hamlet in a film version of the eponymous play by Shakespeare.

At the beginning of my second year, two old classmates of mine at Igbobi arrived in Glasgow, and although neither of them was in the same hall with me, we naturally saw a good deal of each other. Ladipo (Ladi) Wusu, my friend and classmate since primary school, was one of them. He was a great lover of classical music, and so he and I frequented the St. Andrew's Halls (since replaced by the Glasgow Royal Concert Hall), where we enjoyed concerts, oratorios and Italian opera at reduced student tickets. I also regularly went to the avant garde Cosmo Cinema, also at reduced student tickets. My other old classmate was Patrick Aghadiuno. Both Ladi and Patrick had come to read medicine. All three of us went practically every weekend to the British Council Centre off Great Western Road, where we met students from practically every part of the world.

Another Nigerian, Ladipo Daniel, was admitted to the hall in my third year. He too had come to read medicine, the favourite course for Nigerians at Glasgow. He and I attended the Eucharist service at St Mary's Anglican Cathedral every Sunday morning. The Anglican chaplaincy of the university was based at St Mary's Cathedral, where we were well looked after by Father Sessford. There was an added bonus for us in attending this early-morning service. At the beginning, we had informed the Hall Matron, Miss McKenzie, of our intentions, and wondered whether our breakfasts could be reserved for us in the hot plate in the dining room. She readily agreed. But we found that after service, we could go down to the basement of the cathedral to have a full English breakfast. When we informed Miss McKenzie of this, she said she would keep our breakfasts for us, anyway. That was how it came about that we had two breakfasts every Sunday!

Indeed, the catering in the hall was excellent in quality and quantity. We had waiter-service in the dining room at breakfast, lunch and dinner. Then, from about nine o'clock throughout the night, food was laid out in the supper room for us to help ourselves at any point during the night. Obviously, this came in very handy on nights that I went to the theatre, cinema or St Andrews Halls, or when for any other reason, such as working on my essay or preparing for examinations, I had to stay up late.

As all students seemed to do, I took holiday jobs at Christmas and in the summer. The Post Office needed hands to help them cope with the huge Christmas mail, and were happy to take on students for a couple of weeks or so. It turned out to be a very interesting experience for me. We had to start delivering mail from early in the morning till sometime in the afternoon. The most enjoyable day was Hogmanay (New Year's Day). Every home I went to early in the morning had a surprise waiting for me. The members of the family were very excited on catching sight of me, and they would rush to the door in obvious pleasure to give me gifts of cakes and cookies.

When I returned to the hall after my first Hogmanay experience, Nigerians who had had a similar experience in the past explained that I had experienced my 'first footing'. When I asked what this meant, they explained that there was a custom in Scotland which made the Scots believe that if the first person they saw in the new year was an African, they would be the beneficiaries of good luck throughout the year! I must have been the purveyor of good luck to quite a few families during my four years in Glasgow.

It struck me that while we were reading of negative attitudes to Afro-Americans in the United States, here it was quite the opposite. African students in Glasgow got invited to Scottish homes, and I was even once invited to one of the stately homes, where I was overwhelmed by the simplicity of the family in the midst of opulence. Throughout my four years in Glasgow, all I ever encountered was an unfeigned and quiet welcome.

For summer vacation jobs, I got together with my close friend, Sina Ojo, who was reading engineering at Queen's University, Belfast. I had, during my first summer, worked on Renfrew Street in a warehouse. There had not been much to do, and it must have been largely an expression of the company's corporate responsibility. I spent the best part of my time chatting to my boss and helping myself to large quantities of tea.

Next summer, Sina and I decided to take a job in a fairly rural area in England, where we were employed in the operations of canning peas. There were quite a number of students involved, and we were all accommodated on site in one long dormitory. We were woken up early in the morning and, after a quick breakfast, went to clock in.

The reason why Sina and I were doing this job was so that we could raise funds for a holiday on the continent of Europe. As soon as the job was over, we went to obtain French and German visas. We were going to travel by train, and I asked Sina if he did not think that we needed Belgian visas as well, as the train would traverse that country. He thought that since we were not going to get off the train in Belgium, we should not need visas for that country. That turned out to be a huge mistake, as we were to find out later.

We arrived in Paris to spend a few days, and after a lot of sight-seeing, embarked on the second stage of our journey, which was to take us to Germany, confident that, as in Paris, we would secure accommodation at the first available university student hall or hostel. We had a pack of Whot cards with us, with which we were whiling away the time. Then we arrived in Charleroi, Belgium. The door of our carriage opened and a couple of policemen came in, checking passengers' visas! Sina and I looked at each other, and although I had a very elementary knowledge of the French language, pretended to have none at all. We were ordered off the train and taken to the office. The policemen discussed our case with their superiors and decided we had to be put on the next available train back to Paris. After about a couple of hours, a Paris-bound train came along, and we were escorted into it. At this stage, it became clear that we were into a greater adventure than we had bargained for!

We had to evolve a plan very quickly. At the first station outside Belgian territory, we got off the train and took another one heading north to Lille, where we knew there was a university. We secured accommodation there, and early next morning found our way to the Belgian consulate where, without any fuss, we procured our visas. Then we headed straight back to that last railway station before Belgium, and got on the train in our second attempt to get to Germany. This time, there was no problem, and we arrived near midnight in Dusseldorf. We were quite famished, and as no one could tell us how to get to the university, we tried, at least for the first night, to find lodgings. But try as we would, we had no success. The door was slammed on our faces a couple of times. We therefore decided to go back to the railway station and bed down there for the night. It was still, and the streets were already deserted. Then suddenly, we heard the faint and distant sound of singing; and as we walked on, found a solitary pub where the singing was coming from. We entered, and prayed that we might find something to eat.

It turned out it was also some kind of restaurant, which had obviously closed for the day. Nevertheless, we sat down at a table, and after a while, a middle-aged man approached us and asked us where we had come from. We told him we were Nigerian students studying in Britain. At that, his eyes lit up. He told us he had been a refugee in Britain during the last war and had received very kind treatment there. He asked us where we were staying, and we replied that that was the problem. We were looking for somewhere to spend the night, but meanwhile, were very hungry. It turned out he was the owner of the establishment. He provided us with some snacks and told us he had just one spare room, upstairs, if we would not mind sharing it. We gladly accepted the offer, and were amazed to discover later that it was for free.

We bade our kind host goodbye in the morning and went our way. We looked around Dusseldorf with its scars of war, and then took the train to Cologne, where we saw the damage that had been wreaked on the cathedral during the war. Indeed, evidence of war damage was still visible in a number of places as we went sightseeing. After a few more days, we returned to London the way we had come. We had had an interesting vacation, to say the least, and now, Sina returned to Belfast, and I to Glasgow.

The following summer, Sina and I chose to work in an army barracks, again south of the border. We were employed in the kitchen to operate the huge dish-washer and, naturally, we had a lot to eat. We were accommodated in the barracks, but saw very little of the soldiers, just as they could not have known of our existence either. Sina and I went on long walks and felt very relaxed. This time, we did not plan any excursions into continental Europe.

***

A high point of my stay in Glasgow came about when, one day, I left the library at lunch time and headed to my hall for lunch. As I went on, I noticed a car, parked outside the hall, which did not look like one belonging to any of my fellow residents. It was a Vauxhall, and momentarily reminded me of Canon Parker, who had ridden one like that at Igbobi. As I drew nearer, I saw the disc 'WAN', showing clearly that the car was from Nigeria. I quickened my steps, entered the hall and made straight for the lounge, where I was sure to find my old principal. We were indeed happy to see each other. We had been told while at school that Canon Parker spent his home leave visiting his old pupils in British universities, and I was flattered that he had come to see me. After briefly exchanging pleasantries, I took him to the warden's study and introduced the two men to each other. As it was already time for lunch, the warden invited us to join him at his table in the dining room.

After lunch, I told Canon Parker of my two former classmates who were also in Glasgow and said that, on their behalf, I would like to invite him out to dinner in town later. He readily agreed, and as soon as I had seen him to his car, I got in touch with Ladi and Patrick, who were excited at the thought that Canon Parker was in Glasgow. We decided to take him to one of the swankiest restaurants in town and communicated the address to him.

The evening went merrily, and at the end, I asked the waiter for the bill. As he was about to hand it to me, Canon Parker took it from him, and in spite of our protests, settled the bill, telling us, when the waiter had left, that we could not have afforded the amount from what he suspected were our monthly allowances. This was a kind of anti-climax for us, for we had intended the dinner as a kind of very modest payback to an excellent principal.

***

Sometime in my penultimate year at Glasgow, I received a letter from my step-mother asking me how Moyo Sagoe was settling down in England. I replied to say that I had not seen Moyo, but that there was a chance of my seeing her in the summer. Moyo had lived with our family in Ibadan for years, and had, in fact, become part of the family.

The British Council was organizing a conference for overseas students in Britain to take place in southern England that summer, and I had indicated my wish to attend. Moyo was training at a hospital in Hereford, so I could take advantage of being in the neighbourhood to see her. I wrote to her to inform her of my plans, and she promised to make hotel reservation for me. However, she added that she would be on duty when my train was due to arrive at Hereford, but that she would send one of her colleagues to meet me at the railway station.

On the conclusion of the conference, I took the train to Hereford, totally unaware of how memorable the journey would turn out to be. As the train pulled up at the station, I alighted, looked up and down the platform and my eyes caught a stunningly beautiful female figure in Nigerian outfit. We walked up to each other, and she confirmed that she had been sent by Moyo. We left the station and she took me to the hotel reserved for me. She introduced herself as Alice Mbamali, and the surname immediately rang a bell. That was the name of one of the most senior officers of the Customs department in Lagos during my stint there. It turned out that she was his daughter. What a small world! Once I had settled in, she took me, as Moyo had instructed her to do, to the famous Hereford cattle market. At the end of the short excursion, she took me back to the hotel, where I waited to be joined by Moyo. Moyo and I talked about old times, and then she left, saying she would not be able to see me in the morning as she would be back on duty, but that she had ordered a taxi to pick me up and take me to the station.

I sat back in the train for the long ride back to Glasgow, still unaware that I had just made a life-changing journey. I planned, once I was back in Glasgow, to write to my stepmother to inform her that Moyo was well and happy in Hereford. Of course, I would write to Moyo herself to thank her for the arrangements made for my visit. Then I thought I ought to write to Miss Mbamali to tell her what a pleasure it had been to meet her.

Next day, I promptly wrote and despatched the letters. The postal system in Britain was, I knew, exceptionally good, but still I was surprised that within twenty-four hours, I had received a reply from Miss Mbamali. From that point onwards, correspondence between us regularly crossed the border between England and Scotland.

***

As my final year opened, there were two overriding thoughts on my mind. The first, naturally, concerned my coming final examinations – nine three-hour papers to be taken in the course of one week. One of our lecturers had warned that it was going to be as much a test of physical as of mental readiness. He had advised that in the weeks leading up to the examinations, we should take long walks in the early evening, and go to bed early. I stuck to this advice religiously.

The second thing was what to do with the degree, once I had got it. I had little difficulty in coming to the conclusion that I should go into what I regarded as the 'family profession', which was teaching. I wrote to my dad about this decision, but told him that I was going to apply for a government scholarship to do the postgraduate certificate course in Education at the University of Leeds. I do not recall now why it had to be Leeds, but after four years of Scottish education, I wanted to have an English experience. I also thought that, this time, my dad should be relieved of the financial burden. Perhaps sub-consciously, I also reckoned that Leeds was nearer to Hereford than Glasgow was!

I applied to Leeds and was offered admission, but not to a hall of residence. I thought it might even not be a bad idea to try living in digs, for a change. However, I would cross that bridge when I got there. The urgent matter, for the moment, was to design a strategy for passing my examinations, and passing them well. For all I knew, I might have been the first African ever to be in this situation, and I decided to give it my best. I was encouraged by the remark once made by Dr Blakely to our group that, for all he knew, Banjo might be the first member of the group to become a professor.

***

The final examinations came and went, and while waiting for the results, I decided that I would take a holiday during the summer and go to Barcelona, in the company, this time, of my Igbobi classmate and life-long friend, Bandele Ogutuga, an accountancy student in London. At the same time, I decided to explore what possibilities were open to me by way of employment back home. I planned to go down to London and find out from the Nigeria Office, which was being run by the British government.

When the results came out, they showed that in our honours class of about twenty, one of us got a first, more than twelve, including myself, made a second class, and the rest passed in the third class. I was happy, and immediately finalised my arrangements for a holiday in Barcelona under the auspices of the national student union, of which I was a member. But first, I went down to London to have a reunion with my friends, Subomi Balogun, Bandele Ogutuga and Gbenro Ajayi, all of whom shared a flat on Fellows Road; and they all felicitated with me.

I went up to Nigeria Office and told them my mission; and an English lady came to attend to me. I told her I had just graduated from Glasgow and was wondering what positions were open to me back in Nigeria. She asked to see my results, and as I had already graduated in June, I showed her my diploma, all written in Latin. She seemed very impressed, and asked me to give her a minute while she disappeared into an adjoining room. When she returned, she placed a form in front of me and asked me to fill it out. When I told her I would not be able to take up a job for another year as I would be at Leeds University, she told me she would keep in touch.

I firmed up my holiday arrangements, and on the due date took the train from London which would take me through France to Spain. Bandele was to join me a few days later. My accommodation in Barcelona had been arranged by the student union while I was still in Glasgow, but I was slightly taken aback at the reception desk when I was asked whether I was Mr Banho. When the gentleman showed me my name on the list, I realised, for the first time in my life, that the letter 'j' was pronounced in Spanish as 'h'. So, I was Mr Banho while in Barcelona, and must not forget that!

When Bandele arrived two days later, we headed to the Costa Brava simply to take a look at the history-laden Mediterranean sea in all its splendour. The weather was different from anything I had experienced in the previous four years. It was the closest I had been to being back at home.

Life in Barcelona was at a much slower tempo than it had been in Glasgow or London. The whole city seemed to shut down after lunch while Barcelonans had their siesta. Then at about eight o'clock in the evening, it erupted into life as everyone seemed to pour into the Ramblas, just window shopping or taking a stroll in the cool of the evening.

After two thoroughly enjoyable weeks, we returned to London, Bandele by air, and I by train. By the time I returned to Glasgow, the hall was nearly completely deserted, as almost everyone had gone away for the summer vacation. I packed up and headed to Leeds, where accommodation had been arranged for me with a landlady. My landlady and her husband lived alone in the house, and told me that they had made arrangements with the university for three student lodgers. I was obviously the first to arrive. I was installed in a spacious and comfortable room, and the landlady was particularly solicitous of my comfort. From the first night that I arrived there and every night afterwards, I had a mug of steaming hot cocoa drink delivered to my room as a nightcap. The landlady explained that since I had come from Nigeria, where cocoa came from, she assumed that I must be very fond of the drink. I made no effort to disabuse her of the idea, and enjoyed the drink.

About six weeks later, the couple called me to their sitting room and, in a mournful tone, informed me that the university had not sent them any more lodgers. As it would be unprofitable for them to continue with only one, they regretted to inform me that I had to look for another accommodation. I could see their point, and asked to be given one week to sort myself out. I went to the student union notice board to find out what sorts of accommodation were on offer. This time, I decided to go for a flat and see how I would cope. It had to be within walking distance of the university, and I found one on Blackman Lane – what a name! I went to check it out and found that the twin flat to the vacant one was occupied by another Nigerian, Charles Effiong, a medical student. I took the flat and settled in. I had never done any cooking in my life, and so decided to have all my meals at the university, and find a way of surviving on Sundays. As it happened, Charles was an excellent cook, and he put me through my paces so that I could look after myself on Sundays.

The friendship which I struck up with Charles was destined to be renewed back home at the University of Ibadan, where he became the honorary paediatrician to all my children. He became a professor at Ibadan, and later, vice-chancellor of the University of Calabar, at a time that I myself was vice-chancellor at Ibadan.

***

The University of Leeds, a redbrick university established in 1831, and a member of the prestigious Russell Group, was one of the leading universities in Britain. I settled down to classes, where I found Professor William Walsh particularly inspiring with his lectures on the philosophy of education. He was such an elegant speaker of the English language, and cut the figure of a thespian. Most of the course, however, was conducted through individual tutors, and I had a very agreeable one.

Leeds, though a major city of England, was smaller than Glasgow, and the university was correspondingly smaller. Nigerian students appeared few, and so, unlike at Glasgow, there was no association of Nigerian students that I was aware of. However, I had the pleasure of running one day into someone who had been my classmate at primary school in Oyo, Alarape Busari, who was studying printing technology. Seun Solarin, who had been my junior at Igbobi, and Frank Okoisor, who had attended St. Gregory's College, Lagos, were also there, both of them studying dentistry. And there in Leeds was the ubiquitous British Council, which had a flourishing centre that attracted foreign students. The pleasant lady in charge was Mrs Dalton.

I settled down to my studies and, of course, kept the line to Hereford quite busy. Then, true to her word, the lady from Nigeria office in London got in touch. She informed me that the French government had offered four scholarships to Nigerian graduates to acquire French at the University of Besancon, France, and wondered whether I would be interested. She said the French government was doing this to help Nigeria to build up its diplomatic service on the eve of the country's independence. It was going to be a three-month immersion course.

I found this an attractive proposition, as it would help me to improve on my rather rudimentary knowledge of the French language. As for the possibility of eventually going into the Nigerian foreign service, that was not an unattractive prospect either. I replied to express my interest, but also immediately wrote my dad to inform him of developments. He replied to say that going into the diplomatic service was not such a bad idea, but hoped that I would not be posted abroad straightaway, having already been away from home for five years. He thought it would be good for me to return home for a while first. I decided to think about it, but thought I should concentrate on my postgraduate course first, and then take a decision towards the end of it, when it would be time, if I so decided, to prepare to leave for France.

As part of the course at Leeds, I was attached for short spells, first to a local primary school, and then to a comprehensive secondary school. The primary school gave me an insight into the careful attention given to pupils in England in providing them with a sound foundation for the later tiers of education. My stint at the Leeds comprehensive school was, however, an eye-opener, as it exposed me to the full range of abilities among English teenagers. Each class in the school had six streams or more, and I was made to teach sample streams.

The ability displayed by the boys in the upper streams was incredible. Nothing that they were taught seemed to be new to them. The classes were truly interactive and a source of pleasure to any teacher. The other end of the streams, however, was a near nightmare. The boys appeared menacing, and it was clear that they had no interest whatsoever in learning anything. One morning, as I opened the door of one of such classes, I was horrified by what I saw. The furniture in the classroom had been moved to the walls in a circle, and two boys were slugging it out, to the loud cheering of the rest of the class. I gently closed back the door and went to make a report to the principal (or headmaster), who asked me to leave the matter to him. He had not seemed much surprised.

Boys in these lower streams obviously went to school because they were compelled to do so by law until they reached a certain age. As soon as they reached that age, they simply dropped out unceremoniously. I understood that the police occasionally came to the school to pick up boys for crimes they were suspected to have committed.

I knew that the comprehensive school idea was a subject of fierce political controversy between the conservative and labour parties of Britain. The conservatives, naturally, opted for grammar schools, which admitted pupils of superior ability only. The labour party, on the other hand, seemed to be opposed to anything that smacked of social stratification. The conservatives would appear to have won the argument. What was at issue was the tension between quality and access in any nation's education policy, which inevitably triggered ideologically-based arguments. The tension would appear to have persisted throughout the world, especially the developing world.

My year in Leeds ended successfully, and I was now a qualified teacher. Now I had to face the question of my immediate future — to head back home, or to go on to the university of Besancon in France.

5

A FRENCH INTERLUDE

By the time I finished at Leeds, I had made up my mind to go to Besancon, but without necessarily committing myself to entering the diplomatic service immediately thereafter. I therefore checked out of my flat in Leeds and went down to London to complete all the formalities at Nigeria Office. Among the group of four Nigerians to make the journey to Besancon were Donatus Nwoga, who had just graduated in English from the university of Belfast, Northern Ireland , and Gbolahan Abisogun, a former student of Queen's College, Lagos, who had just taken a degree in English from Cambridge University. We were seen off at the railway station by Jide Alo, who had been my classmate at the Nigerian College, Ibadan, and had gone from there to read History at University College, Ibadan. Interestingly enough, Jide eventually married Gbolahan.

Donatus and I bonded immediately, a situation aided by the fact that both of us were sent to live with the local commissioner of police, who lived with his wife on top of a hill which was accessed by a cable car. On his return home, Donatus went to teach at the University of Nigeria, Nsukka, where he blossomed into a formidable literary critic and became a professor. Gbolahan eventually became a high official of the federal ministry of education. She had withdrawn from the course in Besancon after only a few weeks, and returned to London.

The French-speaking West African students at the University of Besancon were most hospitable to us. They gave us a big welcome party where they made us feel home-sick by playing a lot of highlife music.

We had classes from the morning till early evening every weekday with the same instructor, and in a darkened room with a wide television screen which provided the necessary audio-visual support.

***

I thought the course at Besancon was an extraordinary one, showing the capacity of the French to teach their language effectively to foreign learners. They seemed to have perfected the methodology for an immersion course, and Besancon seemed to have acquired the reputation for most effectively delivering such a course.

Day in, day out, we listened and repeated - *Ecoutez... Repetez apres moi* rang in our heads all day long. Shut off from the real world outside, we stayed locked into the make-believe world of M. Thibaut. The staging and sequencing of the course material seemed perfect, and the selection of vocabulary material most appropriate. The result was that after about a month, we had started developing some self-confidence in the use of the language.

At weekends, we were back in the real world; and we made the most of it. On Saturdays, we would go to our favourite restaurant for lunch, and would listen to one another as we made our orders in French. When we had finished eating, we would delay the waiter for as long as possible while we practised our French, such as it was, on him or her! The dividends of the course were quick to manifest.

By the end of the second month, we had developed enough confidence to go into grocery shops to make purchases, usually of fruits. There was, however, one hilarious occasion when we entered a shop and, after looking round, one of us, fixing his gaze on apples, confidently asked the shopkeeper for some *pommes de terre*; whereupon, to our colleague's amazement, the shopkeeper presented him with some potatoes! We had, of course, been taught that *pommes* meant 'apples', and our colleague had simply assumed that what he had asked for was the long form of *pommes*. There were regular soirées during our stay in Besancon, and soon we were merrily singing some French songs with full understanding.

At the end of a most profitable time, the group returned to London and then dispersed. As far as I know, none of the Nigerians in the group eventually entered the Nigerian foreign service, but I am also aware that in subsequent years, more groups of Nigerians were sent to Besancon.

I returned to London with two things uppermost on my mind. One had to do with arrangements for my return home to Nigeria. But even more important was an engagement party which Alice and I were looking forward to having before I returned home. At this point in time, Alice had two more years to spend to complete her course in nursing and midwifery at Hereford and Birmingham, and we thought it would be nice to have our formal engagement in London and then the wedding when Alice returned home.

The engagement party was held in my friends' flat at Fellows Road, and Bandele, Subomi and Gbenro were most cooperative. A small group of friends gathered at the flat to celebrate with us and wish us well.

Then I was ready to make the final arrangements for returning home. There was, however, one bigger party for me to attend before setting sail on the MV Aureol for Lagos. 1 October, 1960 was Nigeria's independence day, and the Nigeria Union of Great Britain and Ireland had booked the Royal Festival Hall in London for the celebration. Nigerians came from all over Great Britain and Ireland, many of them in their Nigerian outfits, which added great colour to the occasion. I ran into a number of old friends, who I had not even been aware had been in Britain. It was even much bigger than the typical Nigerian party, full of laughter, fun and highlife.

A Homecoming

A few days later, I took the train to Southampton to embark on the MV Aureol. Some of the passengers, like me, were returning home after various years of sojourn in Britain and were looking forward to seeing what transformations independence would bring about in coming years. The passage was smooth, and it was awe-inspiring just looking at the endless expanse of the Atlantic Ocean for several days on end.

At last, we arrived in Las Palmas in the Canary Islands. We had been fed by fellow Nigerians with stories about the islands, most of which were by no means flattering. We were allowed to disembark and walk around on *terra firma* for a change. We were immediately besieged by dubious-looking men playing hide-and-seek with the local police while trying to sell obviously smuggled goods to us. I was taken in by one of them, who purported to be selling expensive fountain pens. I thought I should purchase four to present to my friends back home. But alas, every one of the four pens had disintegrated before we got anywhere near Lagos!

From Lagos I went to Ibadan and had a happy reunion with the family. My father was still at St. Luke's College. After resting for a couple of days, I found my way to the Western Nigerian ministry of education situated in the beautiful

A French Interlude

Western Regional Secretariat. There I was told that I had long been expected. Apparently, they had earmarked a post for me as education officer in broadcasting. Since I had not turned up, that post went to someone else, and another post was then earmarked for me as education officer at Queen's School, Ede. I was told the story of what had happened to that posting several years later by the principal of the school at the time, Mrs Oredugba. She told me that the first question she had asked the ministry on being notified of the posting was whether or not Mr Banjo was married. When the answer was negative, she had insisted that she did not want a young male graduate education officer in her school! She had not added whether she had tried to protect me or her girls!

At the ministry, I was taken to the office of the establishments officer, who all but said to me: 'There you are, at last!' He then told me that I had been posted to a teacher-training college somewhere with the magical-sounding name of Abraka.

"Where?" I asked in disbelief.

"Abraka," he repeated.

"But I thought I was going to be employed in the Western Region," I explained.

"Yes, Abraka is in the Western region," he affirmed.

At this stage, I noticed that there was a large map of Nigeria hanging on the wall behind him.

"Would you be kind enough to show me where it is on the map?" I implored him.

Without as much as turning round to look at the map, he said, "I don't know!"

He then sent for a driver who apparently had ferried many an education officer to Abraka before in the line of duty, and asked him to locate Abraka on the map for me. The man pointed straight at a region in the Niger Delta. I quickly imagined how many miles separated Ibadan from Abraka, and it dawned on me that I was in for an adventure. I was given a week of grace to get ready to go.

***

I spent that one week looking round Ibadan, and trying to feel the pulse of the country generally. I thought Ibadan had not changed dramatically as a city, but one or two indicators of development caught my attention. There were two state-of-the-art roads joining Mokola to the lovely Western Nigerian Secretariat complex: the first, from Mokola, was Queen Elizabeth Road, constructed to mark the British monarch's visit while I was away; and the other was Parliament Road, which branched off Queen Elizabeth Road and led to the regional House of assembly, located in the same complex as the secretariat. If this was a signal for the construction of modern urban roads in the largest city in (West) Africa, I thought it had to be applauded.

The attempt to develop a new Ibadan seemed already to be taking shape in the form of Bodija estate. It was good to see a clear departure from the old (colonial) idea of government reservation areas to an estate housing owner-occupiers.

Not far from Bodija, a parkland campus of University College Ibadan had recently been occupied by the college, following a move from the former temporary quarters. This new campus promised to be the jewel on the crown, not only of Ibadan, but of the whole of Nigeria. Apart from being aesthetically pleasing, it was also already showing signs of being a citadel of learning and research quickly attracting the notice of the world. The first generation of Nigerian professors was already in incubation there.

On the other side of Bodija from UCI was a new University College Hospital adorning that area of the city. The college of medicine of UCI had initially been accommodated in the premises of Adeoyo hospital, which had been made famous by Sir Samuel Manuwa, who had truly become a legend. It was commonly said that when he died, his brain was going to be preserved in a museum! The new premises now appeared to rival UCI itself in beauty and modernity.

The omens thus seemed propitious as Nigeria set out on its journey into political independence. Particularly pleasing was the fact that a solid foundation seemed to have been laid for the country in the form of three Regions headed by extraordinarily competent leaders. The Western Region, in particular, was extremely lucky in having a man of Chief Awolowo's learning and foresight as its first premier.

During the negotiations in London for Nigeria's independence, in which all the regional leaders had participated, Chief Awolowo had made a point of getting in touch with every Nigerian student in Great Britain and Ireland. He had sent each of us a postcard which contained his portrait, and on the back of which he had sent us inspiring messages which fired our hopes for an independent Nigeria.

Even during the lead-up to independence, Chief Awolowo had begun to show his total dedication as a leader. He had embarked on far-reaching and ennobling projects, such as free primary education, the construction of a world-standard stadium, and the first television house in Africa. Other notable structures, such as Cocoa House, were to be added soon after independence. His party, the Action Group, had already focused on education, health and full employment.

The Eastern Region was led by the charismatic and erudite Dr Nnamdi Azikiwe, who was well-known throughout Africa. He was later succeeded by Dr Okpara, a medical doctor who tried to keep abreast of developments in the Western Region.

In the North was the formidable figure of Ahmadu Bello, Sardauna of Sokoto and scion of the Sokoto caliphate, a man who combined in himself both political and religious authority, and therefore had an overwhelming following in his Region.

The three leaders were of an unexceptionable stature and competence, but that did not mean that all the problems of the country were set to be solved. The disparateness of the country was symbolized in the three great leaders themselves. The orientation of the Northern Region had been eastwards, and although that of the Southern Regions had been westwards, the Western Region had taken its inspiration largely from Britain, while the Eastern Region had turned more to the United States of America.

Indeed, within five years, cracks had begun to emerge; mistrust, petty jealousies and vindictiveness had begun to set in; and before the celebration of the seventh year of its independence, Nigeria was to embark on a costly and needless war with itself. More than fifty years later, the ability and willingness to forge a strong nation out of the disparate parts would still be lacking, and so, the drift would continue.

6

In the Delta

Anyway, buoyed by the prospects of the moment, I headed to the Niger Delta, wondering what might be in store for me. I set out from Ibadan in the morning and, passing through Benin City and Agbor, went through a maze of villages – Umutu, Obinomba, Obiaruku – until I arrived at Abraka. It was a rural village, and the only sign of modernity seemed to be the government teacher-training college, to which I was immediately almost totally confined.

I was led to my quarters, a sparsely-furnished one-bedroom bungalow with a paraffin-operated refrigerator. Obviously, I was destined to live a camp life here. As quickly as possible, I got myself a househelp, since Charles Effiong had by no means done such a wonderful job on me.

The morning following my arrival, I went to make my presence known to the principal of the college, S.F. Edgal, a classics graduate of University College, Ibadan. I found him to be a likable man, and when he got to know that I did play lawn tennis, he was very happy; and so practically every afternoon, he and I were to be found on the college tennis courts. He was very good – much better than I. I got to know that, like me, he was living alone. He was a grass-widower whose wife was following a course of studies in Britain. There were very good tennis courts at Kwale, a few miles from Abraka, and also one or two very good players; so occasionally, we would go to play at Kwale. Apart from anything else, it gave us the opportunity of playing doubles.

The students – some of them older than I was – were very earnest. While following the prescribed course, a few of them were also studying for their 'O' levels by the side. I recall one of such students, Tony Momoh, who eventually graduated in law and became an important politician in the country. There being little else to do, I gave them a lot of my time inside and outside the classrooms.

Not having a car of my own was already a bit of a handicap. I therefore made time during my first two weeks to go to Benin to order a car. I was sure of a vehicle advance from the college which I would pay back on very generous terms. I looked around in Benin, and the only car to my liking was a Borgward Isabella, jointly manufactured by Volkswagen and Mercedes, and marketed by the German-owned Western Nigerian Technical Company. It was a two-door 'sporty' car which caused me a bit of amusement each time I drove to Ibadan on holidays as I got spoken to in Edo language because of the registration number of the car!

I settled down to the routine, looking forward to a game of tennis every afternoon. On my first holiday, which was Christmas, 1960, I went to Benin to pick up my car. I then spent a night with a very old friend whom I had first met in my boyhood days in Ibadan, Idowu Giwa-Amu. He had, in the interval, read law, and was later to become the Attorney-

General of Bendel State. It was already past lunch-time by the time I left Benin for Ibadan, and I remember my dad being astonished to see me at such a late hour, for it was already past 10 p.m. But I had had quite a pleasant drive, for Nigerian roads had not yet become veritable death-traps, and the car was in mint condition.

Now that I was mobile, I took immediate steps to visit Alice's mother, who was domiciled in Sapele, further into the delta. I was very well received and was able to meet the extended family. I was instantly introduced to Itsekiri pepper soup.

Just as my new world was beginning to make sense to me, Edgal called me to his lodge one afternoon and, wearing a long face, told me I had been given marching orders from Ibadan. I was to proceed to Government College, Ughelli, a well-known top boys' school.

> "But I've been here for only six months!" I almost protested, thinking as much of the tennis afternoons as of my students.
>
> "Well," said the principal, "I'm told the English results in the school certificate examination at Ughelli, just released, have been pretty bad, and they want you to go there and make sure that that never happens again."
>
> "I hope that won't turn out to be a tall order." I answered in resignation. "When do I have to move?"
>
> "As soon as you're ready," replied Edgal. "Good luck!"

I returned to my residence and looked at all of my worldly possessions. I had had to buy a bed as well as a few items for the sitting room. I wondered if I would have to move all of that to Ughelli. I was told that all my personal belongings would be sent to Ughelli after me. So, off I went. The adventure thickened.

***

The campus of Government College, Ughelli, looked quite different from that of the Government Teacher Training College, Abraka. It was an expansive, well laid-out campus with well-maintained structures and well-tended lawns; and I did not fail to notice that bang in the middle of the premises were two well-maintained tennis courts, which further lifted my spirits.

This time, I was driven straight to the residence of the principal, 'Nick' Carter, a former major in the British army. He was a serious-looking man, and I immediately suspected that he would be a strict disciplinarian, which indeed he was. But the other side of him was evident whenever he led the college to cheer on our boys whenever there was an external match. At such times, you could hear his voice miles away. He obviously held the school very close to his heart. He told me the reason for my being posted to Ughelli, and I promised to do my best. I asked him if, by any chance, he played lawn tennis, but he said no. There had to be someone around who did, I thought.

Government College, Ughelli was one of Nigeria's elite boys schools. Founded in 1945, it quickly became famous as much for the academic standards as for its prowess in sports, especially under the principalship of V.B.V. Powell, a great sportsman who had been the first principal of Government College, Ibadan, before going to Ughelli. One of my esteemed classmates at the Nigerian College in Ibadan in the 1950's had been Godwin Adokpaye, an old boy of Ughelli. We products of Igbobi at the college had shared fellow feeling with him. Godwin went on to take a degree in Classics from University College, Ibadan, and subsequently to be a captain of the oil industry in Nigeria.

I was assigned the very first three-bedroom bungalow just inside the gates of the college. The building had just been completed and I was to be the first occupant. My next-door neighbour was a young Englishman, Alan Fergusson, who was the Latin master. Like me, he was single, but alas, he played no tennis! However, he was an avid reader of English literature, and we spent long hours together discussing literature or the fate of the world. Alan told me that he was a direct descendant of Lord Lugard, who had cobbled Nigeria together in 1914. That, in fact, was why he had decided to come and work for a few years in Nigeria.

The school was, as was to be expected, very well staffed, and the boys had been very carefully selected. Old boys of the school were to be found in the topmost positions in academia, the civil service and industry. Years later, I was to run into Oyewale Tomori, who had been one of the most outstanding of my students at Ughelli, at the University of Ibadan. In the course of time, he had become a very distinguished professor of virology and subsequently, president of the Nigerian Academy of Science. Before my time, of course, the school had produced academics of the calibre of Obaro Ikime, professor of history at Ibadan, and J.P. Clark, Nigeria's first professor of English. Gamaliel Onosode, another old boy, had read Classics at Ibadan and had then gone on to distinguish himself in the private sector.

I found a pleasant mixture of ability and motivation among the students, and teaching them was a pleasure.

A few months after I got to Ughelli, Carter left the school, and who was to replace him but S.F. Edgal! Thus we were able to renew our afternoons on the tennis courts. There was good camaraderie among the teaching staff, and I quickly settled down, making sure that the boys did a lot of writing and reading, as well as discussions in class. Soon, it was time again for the school certificate examinations, and when the results came out a few months later, the English results were outstanding, with quite a sprinkling of 'A's.

One of my senior colleagues with whom I immediately bonded was Lamidi Sofenwa, a Latin master. Sofenwa's wife was the matron at the government hospital in Warri, not far away, and so I spent many Saturdays going with Sofenwa to visit and to have a good lunch.

Just as I was beginning to suspect that the good English results might earn me a long spell at Ughelli, signs of the gypsy nature of my employment appeared in the horizon. As a result of what looked like jiggery-pokery among the political leaders, the decision to create Midwest Region started to be discussed. Originally, the minority groups in the south and the north were going to be granted their own states, but in the event, only Midwest Region in the south was earmarked for creation. This created some acrimony in the Western Region, to which Midwest had hitherto belonged.

Return to Ibadan

It was not long before we started hearing of repatriation in both directions. Finally, the fate of the four Yoruba education officers at Ughelli briefly hung in the balance, before we were told to prepare to go back to what was left of the Western Region. Two of us, Lamidi Sofenwa and myself, were sent to Ibadan to resume at Government College there. Being a senior education officer, Sofenwa was immediately assigned accommodation in the college. I was asked to wait until mine, which incidentally was next to Sofenwa's, would be ready. Mrs Sofenwa was still in Warri; so Sofenwa graciously offered to accommodate me until my place was ready.

***

Government College, Ibadan, founded in 1929, was not all that different in character from Government College, Ughelli; which was hardly surprising as the two schools had shared a common proprietor. What was more, the same education officers did tours in the two schools, as well as in other government secondary institutions. For example, V.B.V. Powell had headed both schools at different times while, in less than two years, I had already had Abraka, Ughelli and Ibadan under my belt.

In due course, I moved into my own accommodation and proceeded to settle down. The fact that home was only half an hour's drive away in Molete, added to my sense of well-being. Also, Ibadan was, of course, much bigger than Abraka or Ughelli – indeed it was the largest city in West Africa, with numerous features of modern living.

The staffing at Ibadan, as at Ughelli, was excellent, and the boys lively and intelligent. I more or less continued what I had been doing at Ughelli and was pleased to see how responsive the boys were. The school had produced, and was destined to produce, illustrious Nigerians, including an Oba of Benin, who had gone from Government College, Ibadan, to King's College, Cambridge; academics of the quality of Muyiwa Awe, another product of Cambridge; Mololu Olunloyo, a First Class Honours graduate and winner of gold medal from the ancient University of St. Andrews, Scotland; and, of course, Africa's first Nobel Laureate in Literature, Wole Soyinka. It also has to be said that one star who emerged from one of the classes that I taught at the time was Femi Osofisan, who in later years became a prize-winning dramatist and essayist.

I was assigned two extra-curricular duties, namely, as housemaster of Swanston House and as the coach for cricket. I had observed that there were no tennis courts in the premises and was forced to give my racquet a long rest. As for cricket, Government College, Ibadan, had one of the strongest school teams in Nigeria. I recollected my own days at Igbobi, when the teams from the two schools exchanged visits. We were intrigued then to find, whenever we came down to GCI, that their boys wore shorts without pockets, and that made them the butts of our jokes. Mololu Olunloyo, a member of the GCI team, was noted – and feared – for his ferocious bowling.

But if Government College, Ibadan, was famous for anything in those days, it was for its dramatic productions under the direction of its energetic principal, Derek Bullock, a graduate of Durham University in England. In these productions, the school collaborated closely with St. Anne's Girls school, Ibadan, under its own principal, Chris Groves. It is hardly surprising that Bullock and Groves eventually married each other. I thought one big effect of the dramatic productions on the tone of the school was that the boys, more perhaps than the boys from other schools, were pleasantly articulate.

Being in Ibadan enabled me to participate in a number of out-of-school activities, such as serving as an examiner in English for the West African Examinations Council, participating in dramatic efforts by a group in town based at the British Council Centre and being involved with some other British Council-related programmes, in which I interacted closely with their English Language Officer, L. Moody.

Meanwhile, Alice had returned to Nigeria, and we planned our marriage for the middle of 1963. She had secured employment at the University Teaching Hospital, Ibadan, where, incidentally, her senior brother, Ernest Mbamali, was also a senior lecturer in orthopaedics. I had known Ernest since his days at St. Gregory's College, Lagos, and now, we became specially close.

Alice and I went to Onitsha to formally seek Alice's father's permission for our marriage. As Ajie of Onitsha, he received us in the company of other chiefs and was most gracious. He did warn us, however, that as Ajie, he would not be able to attend the wedding personally, but would come to visit us afterwards. He added that Professor Chike Obi, as Alice's cousin, would give her away. We returned to Ibadan and fixed 8 June, 1963 for the wedding. My father consulted Bishop Odutola of Ibadan and obtained his consent for the marriage to take place at St. James' Cathedral, Oke Bola, Ibadan. Thereafter, we went, for a session of counselling, to the Venerable I.G.A Jadesimi.

8 June dawned, and all was set for the wedding. My best man was none other than my very close friend, Subomi Balogun. He had returned to the country and started a brilliant legal career which was to lead him to the position of the most celebrated Nigerian banker. The joining was performed by Bishop Odutola, who was assisted by the Venerable Archdeacon Jadesimi and a number of other clergymen. Alice's three siblings were present: Felicia, Ernest and Theresa, while the bride was given away by Professor Chike Obi, at that time teaching at the University of Lagos. He was a terrific human being and a model Nigerian. From the date of the wedding, he developed the habit of introducing me to people as 'the Ijebu man who stole my cousin'!

On my side, the only absentee was my younger brother Gboyega, who was still pursuing his studies at the University of Reading in England. My indefatigable and loving elder brother, Bayo, was, however, very much around making sure that everything went according to plan.

Reception was in the hall of St. Luke's College, Molete, where my father was still principal, and the master of ceremonies was no less a personality than Rev. Canon Alayande, whom we regarded as a member of the family. My father had asked him to play that role, which he did in his inimitable manner.

By 2 p.m. the reception was over. Alice and I were taken back to my quarters at Government College and, as we had planned, transferred ourselves immediately into our Borgward Isabella. I took the wheel and we drove straight to the Hotel de la Plage in Porto Novo, Dahomey (now Benin Republic), to begin our honeymoon.

We had a hilarious experience as we drove into Porto Novo city centre. Not having been used to street lights in Nigeria, and also considering the excitement of the day, I drove straight through the red light and immediately heard a furious whistling behind me. I then observed a gendarme on a scooter giving us a hot chase. I drew up and then suddenly realised what I had done. The gendarme approached me pouring out French at a speed which made it a bit difficult for me to understand, but I did understand what he was on about. All the same, I pretended not to understand a word of French, to draw his attention to the fact that we were tourists. Thereupon he took another look at the registration of the car and exclaimed in an interesting Yoruba accent: "Do you speak Yoruba?" I answered in the affirmative, and with an increased glint in his eyes, he continued in Yoruba, "You have broken the law. Bring something." I thought I had misheard him; but yes, he was there in the open, and without even bothering to lower his voice, asking me for a bribe!

He noticed my discomfiture, and then quickly asked where we were going. I told him and he asked us to follow him. And that was how we arrived with an outrider, no less, at the hotel. He took our bags out of the boot and took them to the reception. At that point I gave him 'something'. After all, he had worked for it!

It felt good to be in a French-speaking environment again and to discover that, after three years, I had not completely forgotten all the French that I had learnt in Besancon. Alice watched as I insisted on speaking haltingly to people in French. However, whenever there was a complete breakdown in communication, I easily retreated into Yoruba. Then Alice could join in, as she herself spoke fluent Yoruba.

The Oyo empire had once extended to Dahomey, and Yoruba, along with Fon and Fulfulde had remained one of the country's national languages. The European powers had simply cynically, late in the nineteenth century, shared the same ethnic group between two powers, as they had done in other places at the Berlin conference, thus complicating Africa's development problems.

We spent much time at the beach, and wandering round the shops. We were also able to look in at an arts exhibition displaying the indigenous arts of the area.

Honeymoons do not last forever, and we finally had to be back in harness. I had to begin a new life which, among other things, consisted in twice daily runs between Government College and the UCH. At this point, also, I had to dispense with the services of my househelp, Okon, who had graciously agreed to go with me from Abraka to Ughelli, and then from Ughelli to Ibadan. The boys, in school, seemed to have been taking note of my change of status and gleefully offered their congratulations.

***

Now a married man, I had to think seriously about what I intended to do with the rest of my life. What were the prospects in the ministry of education? In due course, I might be promoted senior education officer and, after that, what? As it happened, I was indeed promoted senior education officer the year after I arrived in Ibadan. I thought the prospect, sooner or later, would, however, be to be consigned to a desk job in the ministry of education, perhaps even shunted into the inspectorate division of the ministry, which might not be totally to my liking.

University College, Ibadan was at this point on the threshold of becoming an autonomous institution, having been a constituent college of the University of London since 1948. I wondered whether it would now expand enough for me to gain a position there in the English department. This was almost a pipe dream, however, as I was aware that I would need postgraduate qualifications to stand a chance. In the meantime, I devoted my full attention to my boys in GCI, conscious of the fact that there were only very few schools in Nigeria to offer comparable job satisfaction.

At the same time, I sustained an interest in the activities of the British Council at their centre in the Dugbe area of Ibadan. About a year after I started work at Ibadan, the Council's English language officer, L. Moody, with whom I had bonded very agreeably, told me of a joint plan by the British and American governments to be executed by the British Council and the American State Department. The idea was to offer scholarships which would be tenable for the first year at the University of Leeds, England, and for the second year at the University of California at Los Angeles (UCLA). The year at Leeds would lead to a specially designed Postgraduate Diploma in English Studies, while the year at UCLA would lead to a Masters degree in Linguistics. Moody told me that the first scholarships were to be offered to two West Africans and wondered whether I would be interested. I thought it was a very good idea, and it did not take me much reflection to express an interest. This, after all, might well prove to be the route to a position at the University of Ibadan which had just won its autonomy.

Early in 1964, Moody informed me that I had been recommended to the British Council in London for one of the scholarships. If successful, I would have to proceed to Leeds in October of that year. I started to get mentally oriented to that possibility, and so when a few weeks later Moody informed me that the recommendation had been successful, I was mentally ready for my second sojourn at the University of Leeds. I immediately set about securing a two-year leave of absence from the government of Western Nigeria, and Alice did the same with the University Teaching Hospital (UCH). For logistical reasons, we decided that I should go ahead in October while Alice joined me in December. This meant that Alice would have to return to the Nurses' Home at the UCH for three months.

McBrayne Hall, University of Glasgow, 1957

Brother's wedding day in Newcastle with the bride Valery and cousin, Bisi, 1957

Honours English Class, Glasgow University, 1958

McBrayne Hall, University of Glasgow

Alice in Glasgow

In front of McBrayne Hall

Miss L. Bown's Seminar, Cowley Manor

McBrayne Hall, Glasgow

Partying in Glasgow

M.A. Glasgow, 1959

Dr Bayo Banjo on his graduation day

At Besancon, France, 1960

Sir Hector Hetherington
Vice Chancellor, University of Glasgow

Glasgow University

With Alice

Engagement in London, 1960

At Loch Lanond, Scotland

With Ladipo Hunponu-Wusu in Dublin

G.T.T.C, Abraka, 1961

Wedding day, Ibadan, 1963

Wedding, 1963

At Leeds University, 1964

With the Deans, UI

7

From Leeds to UCLA

On arrival in Britain, I first stopped at the British Council offices in London, where I was further briefed about the programme. The British Council would be responsible financially for my year at Leeds, while the State Department would do the same during my year at UCLA. The following day, a British Council official was assigned to take me to the shops to acquire warm clothing; and the following day, the same official saw me off at the railway station.

It was an advantage that I was already familiar with both the city of Leeds and the university. This time, however, I did not have to look for lodgings as accommodation had been reserved for me in the ultra-modern Bodington Hall, which had been built since my earlier time at the university. One pleasant surprise for me was to discover that the warden of the Hall, Brian Annan, was an Edinburgh graduate who, as I learnt later, had taught for two years in the English

Department of University College, Ibadan. He was happy to see me, and to relive his Ibadan years.

Bodington Hall was a huge hall of residence which accommodated students from different parts of the world. Apart from students from Europe, there were a few from India, Pakistan and East Africa. Among the students from Kenya was James Ngugi, who later became a celebrated writer and whose first novel, *The River Between*, was in fact launched in the course of that year, to the delight of all African students at the university. Ngugi had arrived the same year as myself, and was following an M.A. course in English Literature.

The School of English at the University of Leeds had already acquired a reputation in various branches of English studies such as English linguistics, English literature (including African literature of English expression) and drama. There was also a huge lexicographical research going on then under A.P. Cowley who, incidentally, had also previously taught in Nigeria. But by far the most iconic personality at the School of English at Leeds at this time was the legendary Norman Jeffares, with whom I was to interact in later years.

The course designed for me and my Sierra Leonean colleague was with a language bias, which turned out later to be lucky for me. We had only a few literature courses, which we shared with students, such as Ngugi, who were doing a straight M.A. course. The language section was under the supervision of John Spencer, who had spent three years on the staff of the English Department at University College, Ibadan. He was a very pleasant man and very effective teacher. He was assisted by Michael Gregory, a very engaging speaker and striking personality. We saw very little of Terry Mitchell, the professor of English language, except at the Inaugural Lecture which he delivered while we were there. Spencer and Gregory introduced us to the modern science of linguistics, and in particular to taxonomic syntax. It was quite a revelation for me. I was enthralled by the sheer intellectual beauty of Halliday's Scale and Category Theory of Grammar. The syntax sessions were complemented with a course on taxonomic phonemics.

As the first term drew to a close, I had to look for a suitable flat in the vicinity of the university for Alice and myself. Luckily, I was able to find one, and so, a couple of days before Alice's arrival, I left Bodington Hall and settled down in the flat. As soon as Alice, in turn, had settled down, we made enquiries at St. James' Hospital, which was Leeds University's teaching hospital, about the possibilities of a job for her. She was offered one immediately, and as she had done all her training in Britain, had little difficulty fitting in.

Leeds had changed very little during my four-year absence. The British Council Centre was still the magnet for foreign students, and indeed Mrs Dalton was still in charge there.

As it turned out, it was a busy time for both of us – with Alice working at the hospital, and I working on a project which was to be part of the examination for the postgraduate diploma. Soon enough, it was May, and the examination took place. I then later turned my mind to the impending year at UCLA while waiting for the results. When they were released, I had cause to be happy, for I was one of the two students in the class to be awarded the diploma with distinction. We arranged accommodation for Alice in the nurses' hostel while I concluded my travel arrangements.

In 'The City of Angels'

This was my first time ever to travel to the United States, and there was much for me to wonder about. Even though Britain and USA spoke the same language (though not entirely), I wondered how much the two countries really had in common culturally. Even Winston Churchill, whose mother, incidentally, was American-born, had been credited with the remark that the US and Britain were two countries separated by a common language! I expected the US, from all I had heard and read, to be a more prosperous and more adventurous society. On making enquiries, I was told that I was lucky to be going to Los Angeles, for two major reasons. The first was that the climate was quite mild, with hardly anything severe enough to be described as winter. The second reason was that California was one of the most racially stable states in the US.

With Alice comfortably installed in the nurses' hostel and expecting our first baby, I proceeded on my journey to Los Angeles in the summer of 1965, a long journey made more harrowing by the refusal of Pan Am to serve any form of refreshment for long hours, presumably because they were already operating the Los Angeles time. That did little to foster my enthusiasm to see the country and live in it. At long last, we landed at the Los Angeles airport. UCLA had been kind enough to send Bowden, one of the professors in the department of English, to meet me and take me to the International Student Centre in town. Bowden informed me that I would have to stay at the centre for some time while a suitable apartment (yes, apartment, not flat) was found for me. I checked in, thanking the kind professor very warmly.

At dinner time, I went down to the dining room, where I met a few other residents, a couple or so of them from Africa. I later went to bed and then, in what seemed to be the middle of the night, woke up feeling wide awake. I looked at my watch, which I had already changed to LA time, and then it struck me that my body clock was still operating the British summer/Nigerian time. I got out of bed and walked to the corridor, and then suddenly heard the door slam behind me. I turned round, tried to let myself back into the room but found, to my horror, that the door was indeed locked. I looked round, and there was an eerie silence everywhere. There was no way of seeking help, and so I went downstairs to the lounge where, indeed, there was nobody to be seen. For five hours I sat down, praying for the day to break. When at last it did, I was helped back into my room.

***

I had asked the professor how far the centre was from the university campus, and he had responded that the university was just in the next block. I was glad that I was already virtually on campus. But I was in for a shock.

I had given myself some fifteen minutes to get to the campus and find the English department. After breakfast, I went out into the street and turned left, as I had been asked to do, and there, indeed, was a block of offices. I scrutinized it and found no signs of its being part of a university. I moved on to the next block and similarly drew a blank. After trying two more blocks, I had to seek for help and was told that the university was just after the next set of traffic lights, which by now was close by. I walked on, crossed the intersection, and there, indeed, was the famous UCLA. On my very first morning in the United States, I had been introduced to my second Americanism: a block, in the US, means the distance between two sets of traffic lights.

I walked into the attractive campus and found my way to the department of English, where I had a brief meeting with Professor Clifford Prator. From him I learnt that my business at UCLA really had more to do with the fledgling department of linguistics. I subsequently attended a few of Prator's classes and found that, unlike my experience in Britain, he was a hard-liner who thought his British counterparts were being too liberal in encouraging varieties of English to develop outside Britain, particularly in the former colonies. I was surprised at this and felt that if Prator's argument was pressed to the logical conclusion, even Americans should be speaking exactly like the British. He would probably have responded by saying that American English was based on native English exported to America and allowed to follow its own line of development there among native speakers of the language. But should the language, exported admittedly in different circumstances, to other parts of the world, where it became a second language, not be allowed similarly to follow its lines of development in the new habitations? As it turned out, this was to be a major subject of debate among Nigerian linguists for the best part of the following decade.

***

It was among the very vibrant linguistic scholars that I had my intellectual home. Those were the early days of Noam Chomsky's transformational-generative theory of grammar. The linguists at UCLA were at the cutting edge of the development of this theory. The group was brilliantly led by Robert Stockwell, of whom it was believed that not a single day dawned without his being on the telephone with Chomsky, who was based at the Massachusett's Institute of Technology (MIT), discussing the theory. Among other notable scholars in the group were Barbara Hall-Partee and Paul Schachter.

Also at UCLA at this time was the incomparable phonetics scholar, Peter Ladefoged. Ladefoged's phonetics laboratory was a sight to behold. In the course of his research he did unimaginable things to his own vocal tract. Ladefoged had taught for a year at University College, Ibadan in the department of English before the establishment of the department of linguistics at the college. There he had built up a model phonetics laboratory. Such was his fame that in the production of the film *My Fair Lady* in Hollywood next door, he was hired as a consultant to advise on how to bring the heroine from Cockney to received pronunciation.

In due course, I moved out of the international student centre into an apartment on Gayley Avenue, near the university campus. Westwood, where the university was located, had not yet become a city of shiny skyscrapers. In fact, it was still referred to as Westwood Village. The shopping centre was not extraordinary, though it attracted the occasional stars from Hollywood and Beverly Hills, whose sightings caused considerable stir in the neighbourhood.

Within a couple of months of my arrival in Los Angeles, a historic event occurred. One Nigerian I had quickly become very friendly with was Ade Dekalu, whose senior brother, Akin, had been my classmate at the Cathedral school in Lagos. On the evening of August 11, 1965, Ade called me on the telephone and asked me if I was aware of what was going on in town. When I said that I had no idea, he asked me to step into my fourth-floor balcony and look towards the city centre. When I did so, a saw a huge conflagration in the horizon; and when I asked Ade what it was all about, he said: 'Watts is burning!' I did not know what to make of this, but Ade then explained that there was intense rioting going on in that part of town by the African Americans. I recalled instinctively that I had been told that California was immune from racial tension; but here I was, more or less in the middle of perhaps the first major riot in the state.

Things must have been simmering beneath the surface for some time, and now the African Americans had broken out in rebellion, for this upheaval had been triggered by the arrest of an African American for drunk driving. The tension in the entire city of Los Angeles was palpable. The media reported that within twenty-four hours of the outbreak of the disturbance, the gun shops in the city had sold out their wares.

Where I was staying in Westwood was predominantly a 'white' area and I instinctively felt a little insecure. I had actually just concluded arrangements to move from Gayley Avenue to Sepulveda Street, a little more distant from the university. I now began to wonder whether I would not have been much safer where I was. All the same, I decided to move.

***

Soon after my arrival at Los Angeles, I had bought myself a jalopy, a two-stroke engine DKW sedan. Within a few days of moving to Sepulveda, I noticed that I was being trailed by police patrol vehicles. The police were presumably wondering what I was doing in such a neighbourhood. They trailed me consistently as I drove back home from the university. Then one day, as I stopped at a petrol/gas station near my residence, the operator, an African American, who had been talking to me about his dream of coming to establish a ranch in Nigeria, told me that the police had been making enquiries about me. He had told them that I was a postgraduate student from Nigeria. That information presumably made them decide that they had been barking up a wrong tree, and I stopped seeing them through my rear-view mirror.

Two more incidents of this sort forcefully brought home to me the difference between living in Britain and living in the United States. I had a friend living in a block of apartments in town, and I drove there from time to time. On one occasion in the evening, I drove there as usual, parked my car in the nearby parking lot and started walking to the entrance of the building. I then suddenly heard running steps behind me and, before I knew what was happening, felt a firm grip on my shoulder while the light from a torch was shone on a policeman's badge. I was completely bewildered, but before I could utter a word, I heard the policeman say that someone had been seen trying to tamper with one of the cars in the parking lot. Mercifully, before I could find the words to ask what that had to do with me, another policeman shouted from the parking lot to say that the suspect had been caught. But still, the policeman asked me what I was doing there. On being told that I had come to see a friend, he asked for the friend's name and went with me to the lobby of the building to check the names of the occupants and, finding the name I had given him there, unceremoniously turned round and left. Not a word of apology.

The third instance involved me and my friend, Ade. Ade was planning to move out into a new apartment, and had asked me to join him 'flat hunting.' Now, Ade had a glossy red Plymouth convertible in mint state. He set back the hood and we set out on a pleasant late afternoon.

After we had been on the road for about fifteen minutes, Ade suddenly said to me, 'Ayo, we're being trailed.' He said he had been watching the car through his mirror, and had twice slowed down to see whether the car would overtake us; but it did not. Ade had been in the United States for many years, and I told him he was perhaps being oversensitive. He said he was sure we were being followed, and then made a random diversion from the main road. Indeed, the car was still behind us. It was already getting dark before we found a 'To Let' sign in front of a building. Ade parked and told me confidently that by the time we came back from making our enquiries, the police car would be parked firmly behind ours. I was alarmed to find that he was absolutely correct. As we drew close to our car, two policemen came out of the patrol car, approached us and asked for the particulars of the car. Ade was angry and ready for a confrontation, but I told him, in Yoruba, to leave it to me to handle the conversation.

Ade showed them the particulars, which they read with the aid of their torch light. Then they moved round and opened the bonnet of our car and examined the engine, again with the aid of the torch light. Then they asked for our ID's, and I calmly told them that we were not in the habit of carrying our passports around. They were visibly surprised and asked us where we were from. I told them Nigeria and invited them to come to my apartment to examine our passports. At that point, they completely lost interest in us, slammed shut the bonnet, returned to their car and drove off. Again, not a word of apology.

I think Ade was lucky that I handled the conversation. Ade had acquired an American accent, and the officers would have assumed straightaway that he was an African American and probably given him a rough treatment before I could get a word in edgeways.

In spite of these incidents, however, I had a happy and fulfilling time at UCLA. The staff of the linguistics department were truly inspiring. They introduced me to Chomskyan linguistics, which I found as fascinating as the Hallidayan model, in spite of their different orientations. Halliday had presented an excellent surface mapping of natural language, but Chomsky was concerned with explaining how 'an ideal speaker-hearer' of a natural language is potentially able to utter (and understand) all the sentences of his mother tongue. There were, at the beginning, those who protested, arguing that the Chomskyan theory had hardly anything to do with linguistics. But the model quickly gained traction, and I was personally glad to be armed with both models as they both gave me enormous intellectual satisfaction. Indeed, I had a bonus towards the end of my time at UCLA. The Linguistic Society of America had decided to hold that year's summer school at UCLA, and both Halliday and Chomsky were to give courses!

I quickly applied to attend and looked forward to seeing these two intellectual giants in action. Whenever they gave their classes, there was hardly any standing room in the lecture hall. Not just postgraduate students, but staff from other universities crowded the lecture hall. Chomsky was gentle and soft-spoken, whereas Halliday emitted much greater energy. There was no doubt that we were listening to the last word in each of the theories.

Halliday's theory was, however, undergoing a transition before our very eyes. From purely taxonomic concerns, he was already developing a 'systemic functional grammar' which, like transformational-generative grammar, posited three 'components' (in Hallidayan terms, 'strata', comprising the semantic, phonological and lexico-grammar strata, and the choices available to ideal speakers).

***

I did a little sight-seeing around California. I went to Nepa valley and came away with free bottles of wine. I went up north to San Francisco, where a sister University of California was located at Davis, and I saw the magnificent Golden Gate Bridge. In Westwood itself, I was lucky to be there when Miriam Makeba came to perform. She was on stage with just one guitarist, and together they produced enchanting music.

One of the highlights of my stay was when, on 30 October, 1965, I received the thrilling news that I had become the father of a baby girl born at St James' Hospital, Leeds, England. I was delighted and gave her the name, Olubunmi, which was one of my brother Bayo's middle names. Alice's mother sent the Itsekiri name, Alero, to give a proper balance.

During my last six months, I was largely preoccupied with the preparation of my dissertation. I engaged the services of typists to get the work put into proper shape. Then suddenly one afternoon, I received a letter from Desmond Maxwell, the then professor and head of the English department at the fledgling University of Ibadan. I had never met him before, and wondered what the letter could be about. Maxwell had written to say that he had heard from the British Council of my outstanding performance in the recently concluded postgraduate diploma course at Leeds. He said that the department of English at Ibadan was planning to broaden its offerings to include a strong showing in English language. Indeed, they were planning to offer students in the department the choice of emphasising either literature or language. In view of this, he wondered if, at the end of my year at UCLA, I would be interested in joining the staff of the department to help in building up a strong language section. I could not believe my eyes. A prized job at the University of Ibadan falling on my lap, just like that? I wrote back to say that I was indeed very interested. Maxwell wrote again and expressed his pleasure at my acceptance. He then asked me when I was planning to return to Nigeria via Britain; and when I wrote back to tell him, he suggested that we should meet in one of the waiting rooms at Victoria railway station, London.

I completed my dissertation and finished the examinations. Shortly after, the results were released, and I had earned an M.A. Linguistics of UCLA. If the result of my meeting with Maxwell in London turned out to be positive, then I did not need any more to wonder what to do with the rest of my life.

Having previously booked my passage home through New York and London, I made my way to the airport revelling in my extraordinary good luck. I simply left my faithful jalopy parked in front of my apartment and left. I had just had a most rewarding two years; and now, I was presented with the prospect of a lifelong profession.

***

Arriving in London, I made for Victoria station and nervously searched the waiting rooms. Maxwell himself was on the lookout for me, and we finally guessed each other's identity. We found a quiet corner to sit in, and began our conversation which, by the end of it, had turned out to be an interview for the post of lecturer at the University of Ibadan! He appeared satisfied and told me when I got home to go to the university and collect my letter of appointment from the registrar.

I made my way to Leeds, eager to meet my family. Bunmi was already some nine months old and doing very well. I briefed Alice, not only about my year in Los Angeles but also about the prospects of a job at the University of Ibadan (UI). She could now look forward to going back to UCH, Ibadan, but then we wondered what the implications of a job at UI would be for me, as I had only recently been promoted senior education officer by the government of Western Nigeria. We decided to cross that bridge when we got there. We also decided that I should go ahead first, and two months later, after everything would hopefully have been settled at UI, Alice and Bunmi would join me. Meanwhile, we had heard disturbing news of the coup d'etat and counter-coup in Nigeria and wondered whether things were under control.

I left for home via London, and just how well things were under control was indicated when we were told that we would go on to Accra first, apparently to monitor the situation in Nigeria before going on to Lagos. From Lagos I made my way to Ibadan and decided, for the time being, to lodge with my brother, Bayo, at his Ring Road Jokotola Lodge residence.

***

I spent some two weeks with my brother, Bayo, and his wife Valerie, during which time I tried to settle back into the country. First, I had to seek release from the services of the ministry of education of Western Nigeria. When I reported at the ministry, I was advised to go and see the chief inspector of education. There I was surprised to discover that the ministry had made no arrangements whatsoever for my future, in spite of the fact that I had informed them of my expected date of return to Ibadan. All the chief inspector had to tell me was to go and review a book on English language recently published by D.W. Grieve and let him have my review.

Since the ministry apparently had no plans for me, and I was not bonded, I was encouraged to go straight to the University of Ibadan to pick up my letter of appointment. The registrar, Nathaniel Adamolekun, was temporarily away from his office following an epic disagreement with the vice-chancellor, Kenneth Dike. The acting registrar was Oduaran, and I was ushered into his office. When I explained why I was there, he told me that the letter of appointment was indeed ready, but that the government of Western Nigeria had written to block the appointment, saying I was still in their services. How they had got to know of the impending offer of appointment by the university I did not know. It appeared they had their spies.

Infuriated by this dog-in-the-manger situation, I thought I should have a word with my father, who had retired from St

Luke's College and was now an Anglican archdeacon based at the old and famous St Peter's Church, Aremo, in Ibadan. I explained the situation to him and said that I seemed to have no option but to resign my appointment with the ministry of education. I then went into his study and used his typewriter to prepare my letter of resignation. I immediately headed back to the university and asked to see Oduaran again. I told him that I had resigned my appointment with the ministry of education and handed him a copy of the letter of resignation. The spot that he was, he took the letter from me and then handed me my letter of appointment. Thereafter, I went to the chief inspector's office and, attaching my letter of resignation to my review of Grieve's book, deposited the two documents with the chief inspector's secretary.

From reports reaching me, the chief inspector was poised to wage war over this matter, and I wondered what was his special interest in the case. Having been told that Professor Ade Ajayi of the university's history department and Chief Adeniyi Williams, director of works of the same university, were members of the Western Nigeria Public Service Commission, I went to see Ade Ajayi, an iconic Igbobian, who told me that he could not understand the attitude of the Western Nigerian government, which seemed to delight in preventing Western Nigerians from taking up jobs at the centre, only to turn round to complain that the Region was being discriminated against in matters of federal appointments. While I was with him, he rang Adeniyi Williams, who shared the same views. They then promised to keep an eye on the situation.

Indeed, the chief inspector did cause the permanent secretary of the ministry of education, Augustus Adebayo, to be hauled up before the Public Service Commission. He was asked to explain why he had failed to effectively block my appointment at the university. He must have so effectively defended himself and been so robustly supported by the duo from the university, that the Commission not only sanctioned my withdrawal from the state civil service but caused a letter to be written to the university to say that it had agreed for my services to be transferred to the university, thus preventing a break in service. I suspect that this episode smoothened the way thereafter for people seeking to transfer their services from the state to the centre.

***

That hurdle having been successfully scaled, I moved into the accommodation allocated to me at the top flat of 10 Amina Way on the campus of the university. The following morning, I made my way to the Department of English in the Faculty of Arts. I was hugely impressed with what I saw. It was clear that the University of London had maintained at Ibadan the same scrupulous care over facilities, and that the University of Ibadan, in its four years of autonomy, had kept up the standards. I was shown to my room, Room 67, which, incidentally, I kept, not only for the entire twenty-eight years of my career at the university, but also since my retirement, having been made a professor emeritus.

I found that a very senior professor had also been appointed at the same time with me to establish the language programme in the department. He was Professor Harold 'Fritz' Whitehall. Originally an Englishman, Frits had had a spectacular career in the United States and was, among other things, the author of the scholarly introduction to *Webster's Dictionary*. He was to turn out to be the supervisor for my Ph.D. thesis.

I then discovered that I was the only Nigerian or even African on the academic staff of the department. Ibadan at this time had the policy of sending the best graduating students abroad for higher degrees, and two Nigerians had been sent from the English department to Oxford under this scheme. It was expected that they would return to join the staff of the department, but then the civil war broke out in 1967, and Ibadan lost both of them to Nsukka. Predominance of expatriate academic staff was a common feature in all the departments of the university at this time, but the university had put in place a vigorous staff development programme which paid dividends as time went on.

The parkland campus was delightful, with impressive architecture and lush green lawns. It was altogether a perfect setting for prolonged meditation; and sports facilities were also adequately provided. It was a fully residential university, with all students and staff suitably accommodated. The student Halls were not just hostels, they were Halls of Residence, run on the model of the ancient universities of Britain. Each Hall was headed by a Master, who was invariably a professor, and the day-to-day administration was in the hands of a Warden, who was a senior member of the academic staff. There were formal dinners, attended by the Warden, and also occasionally by the Master. Within a year of joining the university, I was invited to be involved with hall administration. Professor Ade Ajayi, who was the Master of Nnamdi Azikiwe Hall, invited me to be the Assistant Warden, while Billy Dudley was Warden. I later succeeded Dudley as Warden. Almost ten years later, after I had become a professor, I was appointed Master of Mellanby Hall.

I settled down at my Amina Way flat while awaiting the arrival of Alice and Bunmi, who were travelling back home on board the Aureol. Within a fortnight of starting work at the university, I had obtained a car loan on generous terms from the institution, and had bought what everyone else seemed to be buying at this point in time – a Peugeot 404, a very light-footed car indeed. I was thus able to drive up to Apapa wharf in Lagos to bring my family. This was, however, in the days before the Lagos-Ibadan expressway, and so, I had to travel through Sagamu. Fortunately, traffic on the inter-city roads had not yet become nightmarish.

We settled down in the flat and employed a nanny. Alice then went back to UCH to report her return and was asked to resume immediately. We then adopted a routine. Depending on Alice's duty hours, I took her to the UCH and picked her up later in the day. Eventually, she settled for the outpatients department, which was, indeed, more family friendly. At any rate, Bodija market had not yet at this time interposed itself between the university and UCH, and the run took only about fifteen minutes.

We gradually integrated ourselves into the cosmopolitan university community and, from time to time, visited the bookshop, the staff club, the arts theatre and the zoo. As time went on and the family grew, I had to make the runs to the staff school, and much later, to the International School, both of them located on campus. By this time, luckily, Alice had acquired her own car.

Fritz Whitehall and I got on at first sight. He was, of course, some thirty years older than I, but his writings at this time included a body of poetry; and he had written a tertiary textbook on the *Structural Essentials of English Grammar* which had proved popular in the US and which we were happy to adopt in Ibadan. His background was in taxonomic syntax of the immediate constituent mode, and he encouraged me to introduce small doses of Hallidayan and Chomskyan linguistics.

The English curriculum was revised to make every student take some core courses in literature and language while deciding to emphasize either. The meeting point was literary criticism, which is at the heart of the main competence that every graduate of English seeks to acquire. For this important course, the department decided that every student in the department should be exposed at tutorials to a literature and a language tutor. Copies of poems were handed out to students, who first met at language tutorials (given by Fritz and myself). Here, a stylistic analysis of the poem was carried out, enabling the students to see what the poet had done with the language to achieve all the effects that he had managed to achieve. Obviously, this kind of treatment should precede any other kind of literary criticism which the students encountered with their literature tutors, whether sociological, psychological, Marxist, psycho-analytic, etc. The theory of stylistics was, of course, additionally taught to students emphasizing language. To reinforce the primacy of speech in all students, they were all made to take, in their final year, an examination in spoken English.

The rest of the language emphasis covered synchronic and diachronic study of the English language, as well as the sociolinguistics of the English Language in Nigeria. As earlier remarked, one of my early postgraduate students, Oyewole, actually took his Ph.D in Anglo-Saxon.

We were happy with the new curriculum that we had put in place, and all went well for the first few years. But then gradually, it became seriously undermined by over-enrolment of students, and a consequent breakdown of the much-cherished tutorial system. When eventually the Faculty of Arts gave in to the blandishments of the course system, the damage was complete. The deleterious effect on student performance cannot be overemphasized, for where students had been writing altogether about three essays a week for their tutors, they ended up writing none at all. One long essay at the end of the session – the so-called 'project' – is hardly a substitute for constant writing of essays.

The department had, from the beginning, maintained very high standards. As at the late sixties, it had produced, in thirty years, only two First Class honours graduates – Molara Ogundipe and Dan Izevbaye – and we had even done better than the department of History, which had produced none. Our results were underwritten by external examiners, but there was one occasion when we were obliged to give in to the external examiner in the person of Norman Jeffares from the University of Leeds. I recollect the occasion vividly because I happened to be sitting next to Jeffares at the departmental examiners meeting. I noticed that he had come in with a pile of answer booklets which he neatly placed in front of him. He remained quiet throughout the meeting and, as usual, no first class was awarded, though it was unanimously agreed that one candidate came pretty close to it. At this point, Jeffares pointed to the pile of booklets in front of him and said: 'This is a first class!' As we already felt that that was, indeed, the best performance in the bunch, we all acquiesced without any debate. And that was how Biodun Jeyifo became the third First Class honours graduate of the department of English.

Jeyifo has gone on to fulfil the promise that he made at this examination. He has turned out to be a formidable academic, plying his trade at Obafemi Awolowo University, and subsequently at Harvard, USA. He has also been running a weekly column on the pages of *The Nation*, in Nigeria. After Jeyifo, the department lapsed for a while again into its dearth of Firsts. Now in recent times, in contrast, a trickle of Firsts has been recorded. It needs to be stated that Jeyifo's predecessors – Molara Ogundipe and Dan Izevbaye – also turned out to be distinguished professors, bringing honour to the department.

I was pleased to have Peter Young join us in the department in my second year. Young, an Englishman from Oxford, had been my classmate at Leeds during the Diploma year, and had afterwards gone to the University of Sierra Leone, where Eldred Jones, the doyen of African scholars in English Literature, supervised his Ph.D in African Literature. This consolidated the friendship between Young and myself. He later left Ibadan for Kristiansand, Norway, the home town of his wife, Siri. Through his influence, I have paid two visits to Kristiansand, once as a Visiting Professor, and Peter and I have been in continuous contact from his years in Ibadan.

As soon as I started work in the department, I registered for a Ph.D on a part-time basis, and Fritz Whitehall was appointed as my supervisor. I decided to work in the area of contrastive linguistics in pursuit of my interest in language universals, comparing aspects of the syntax of English and

Yoruba. I submitted the thesis in 1969 and had A.C. Rowlands of the University of London as my external examiner, and Ayo Bamgbose as internal examiner. Following a successful defence, the degree was awarded in November, 1969, and I now felt like a full-fledged academic.

Now I had to settle down to the real work, which was publications. 'Publish or perish' was the mantra, and everyone was trying to be as productive as they could be. For this reason, lecturers' rooms in the faculty remained occupied till early, and even sometimes late evening. There was as yet not an abundance of local journals to publish in, but this need was gradually supplied. Journals became quickly established in History, Religious Studies and English, but an attempt to provide a faculty-wide journal was made from the department of English with the publication of *A Journal of Humanistic Studies*. An admirable bumper edition came out in 2017.

The pressure to publish has driven some academics to publish in nondescript journals of doubtful quality, but the Appointments and Promotions Committee of the university has remained very vigilant. This led to the assumption that, to earn promotion, a good proportion of one's publications must appear in internationally recognized journals outside the country. In this way, high standards have been maintained.

I took my first step on the promotion ladder in 1969 when I became Lecturer I, followed by the next step in 1971 when I was promoted Senior Lecturer. In 1973 I became a Reader and, finally in 1975, became a Professor of English Language. With this achievement, I felt my life ambition had been fulfilled, but of course I had to remain active in research and publication to justify the leadership role that this promotion had conferred on me.

A band of scholars in English studies was building up at this time; in fact, it was the era of the first generation of such scholars. Prominent among them were Ayo Bamgbose, Bisi

Afolayan, S.H.O. Tomori and Biodun Adetugbo. I was happy to be numbered among this group.

Earlier in 1966, the Nigeria English Studies Association had been formed and now provided an outlet for the vigorous research that was going on among English scholars in the country. The association was actively supported from all parts of the country and enjoyed the goodwill of the British Council in the country. It had ambitious goals, for while it organized learned conferences for its members, it also held workshops for teachers of English at the secondary level of the education system. It was my honour and privilege to serve as the president of the Association for ten years, 1968 to 1978. For many years, the Association published the highly-regarded *Journal of the Nigeria English Studies Association*.

Two factors eventually militated against the regular holding of the workshops. The first was the lack of support by most state governments, which were unwilling to sponsor their teachers for this purpose. The academics were prepared to give their time freely, but participating teachers had to be aided to make the journey to Ibadan, the venue of the workshops, and they also needed to be helped with accommodation.

To make matters worse, university calendars were becoming unpredictable, and it was becoming increasingly difficult for the academic staff for the workshops – and even the venue – to be available, as the long vacation was steadily disappearing from the calendars of universities, only to return later, on the arrival on the scene, several decades later, of the private universities. An opportunity of the university system making a significant impact on the lower tiers of the education system was thus lost.

Nevertheless, the next few decades were a period of intensive activity by linguistic scholars in the country. The Nigeria English Studies Association was able to nestle in the bigger regional body – the West African Linguistics Society, in which Ayo Bamgbose was a prominent member, serving as

Secretary/Treasurer for a number of years before becoming president. The meetings of the society took us to various parts of West Africa, and a camaraderie developed among the scholars on the sub-continent. The Society published an authoritative journal on West African linguistics. Another regional association was the West African Modern Language Association, in which literature was stressed more strongly than language. That too took scholars to the different West African countries, and I served as president for a number of years.

At home in Nigeria, I was also able to relate to the Yoruba Studies Association, which was based at the university and which embarked on a number of laudable projects, including a glossary of technical terms within the larger concerns with the development of a Yoruba meta-language.

At the same time, I was able to collaborate with scholars abroad. I was Associate Editor of *English World-Wide*, published in Amsterdam, Holland. On the invitation of Oxford University Press in Britain, I produced the *Oxford Primary Dictionary*. I also participated in the production of the *Longman Primary Dictionary*. I was, for ten years, a contributing editor to the *Annual Bibliography of English Language and Literature*, which was published by the Modern Humanities Research Association of Britain based at Oxford University. For seven years, 1975 -82, I was a founding editor of the *Ibadan Journal of Humanistic Studies*, a journal which is still going strong. I was also Vice President of the International Federation of Modern Languages, 1982 - 1990.

Thus I was kept busy right from the beginning of my career, and the tempo of research and publications activity was only reduced during my eight-year tenure as the vice-chancellor of the university. At the same time, I was gradually being drawn into university administration. The first step in this direction was taken when I was appointed Sub-Dean to Ayo Bamgbose in 1970. This gave me an insight into the workings of the faculty ever before I was appointed acting head of the

English department in 1972. The following year, the post of professor in the department was advertised and I applied. However, I was not successful, as Michael Echeruo, from University of Nigeria, Nsukka, was appointed to the post. Michael thus became the first Nigerian, and alumnus, of the department, to be substantive head of the department. He had graduated from the department in 1960.

In 1973 I applied for and was granted study leave, which I spent at the University of Leeds. While I was there, I received communication from the University in Ibadan informing me that it had been decided that I should be interviewed for the post of Reader. An interview panel was set up at the University of Leeds, with Norman Jeffares presiding. This time, I was successful.

My family joined me in the latter part of my leave, which was spent in London, and we were provided accommodation by the University of London. I took the opportunity to purchase a Volvo saloon car from the manufacturers in Sweden. I crossed a very rough North Sea to pick it up from the factory in Goteborg and drove all the way from there to Kristiansand in Norway to spend some time with my friend Peter Young and his family. Kristiansand was a small city and I was impressed by the immaculate planning and by the very high standard of living there. Peter himself was preparing to travel to Oxford, England, for his summer vacation, and so, after a couple of weeks, we left Kristiansand in a convoy. We parked our cars on the ferry and crossed over to England. In due course, Peter and I parted ways, he branching off to go to Oxford while I went on to London.

Having arranged for the car to follow us on a cargo boat, the family, after a few more weeks in London, took a passenger boat to return to Ibadan, via Lagos. By this time, the family was complete: Ayotunde had been born on 5 September, 1967, twenty years after the loss of my mother; Ayoyinka had arrived on 7 January, 1969, ten years after my graduation from Glasgow; and Ayodapo had followed on 29 April, 1971, twenty years after my passing out of Igbobi. All these names had been given by my father, whose own name was Ayodele. On account of the growth of the family, we had moved, in 1969, from the flat on Amina Way to a house on Sankore Avenue. This house was subsequently expanded with the addition of an en suite bedroom on the first floor, and a study on the ground floor.

We settled back in Ibadan, and two years later, in 1975, I was made a professor of English Language by the university, in succession to Fritz Whitehall. The department prospered under the headship of Michael Echeruo, a distinguished literary scholar and poet, but he had to leave to take up the post of pioneer Vice-Chancellor of Imo State University. By this time, I myself had been elected Dean of the faculty in 1977, in succession to Lloyd Thompson of Classics, thus entering the next phase in my involvement with university administration. Indeed, in my second year of deanship, I was elected chairman of the Committee of Deans, which placed me close to the apex of the administration of the university. My Sub-Dean in the first year of my deanship was Odunuga of Modern European Languages, and in the second year, Ijagbemi of History.

The faculty had already evolved a system and a culture. Faculty Board meetings were held with predictable regularity, and serenity prevailed in the faculty precincts. Indeed, the culture included the manner in which, since the beginning of the university, Deans of Arts had been elected. They were elected unopposed because no one really ever put himself or herself forward for the post; rather, faculty members decided among themselves whose turn it was to be Dean, principally on the basis of seniority, and approached the candidate with the offer.

As a matter of fact, I had, in 1977, been looking forward to the substantive headship of my department, which would have given me the opportunity of further strengthening the language offerings in the department, among other things. But Obaro Ikime, whose turn it really was, was in a similar predicament. He was eager to infuse more life into the department of History. I was, in the end, obliged in the circumstances to take up the deanship.

Lloyd Thompson handed over to me immediately after the last meeting of the Faculty Board for the session, as he was due to travel out of the country the following day. I found, to my great relief, that running the faculty – the oldest in the university – was like operating a well-oiled machine.

As dean, I was not entitled to succeed Echeruo as head of department, and the position therefore went to Dan Izevbaye, another outstanding literary scholar.

The tradition of seamless tradition from one Dean to the next in the faculty unfortunately broke down in 1981. I was on sabbatical at the University of West Indies at Cave Hill, Barbados at the time but was kept in touch by colleagues back home about the extraordinary event at our faculty. Two candidates had actually put themselves forward for the post. The senior candidate was Obafemi Kujore of Classics, but Solomon Unoh of Language Arts had decided to offer him a challenge. I thought tradition would prevail, but was somewhat surprised that Unoh won the day. From that time onwards, it was nothing surprising to find the deanship contested for in our faculty. There is, of course, nothing wrong with the democratic process of election. It was just that the faculty had been used to what might perhaps be described as a more civilised way of choosing its Deans – one which did not lead to any fragmentation or polarisation of the faculty. The sad part is that such fragmentation or polarisation had a way of outliving election times and undermining the previous solidarity in the faculty. Unoh was succeeded by Bodunrin of Classics.

***

I did find time for recreation, from the beginning of my appointment at the university. Predictably, my main recreation was lawn tennis. On the courts attached to the staff club, I came in contact with truly superior players. They included, believe it or not, Oba Olateru Olagbegi, the Olowo of Owo then temporarily domiciled in Ibadan. For his age and status, the oba was remarkably nimble on his feet. Other outstanding players included Mark Nwagwu of Zoology, Tunde Yoloye of Education and Isidore Okpewho of my own department. These were clearly a cut above me in performance, and I did learn from them. Expectedly after each session, I dropped in at the staff club to cool off, even though I was never a strong club man.

I also played some cricket. The cricket culture was still strong at the university, and among the staff with whom I participated were Harrison of the College of Medicine, Thompson of Classics (a Bajan, no less) and Ukoli of Zoology. I took turns at wicket-keeping with Harrison. There was an Indian team in Ibadan at the time, and indeed, the last event I participated in on the very last day of my vice-chancellorship in December 1991 was a match in my honour between the Indian team and the UI team.

I also socialized in a number of ways. I worshipped regularly at the Chapel of the Resurrection, where the Eucharist service, and sometimes even the Mattins, lasted exactly fifty-five minutes every Sunday. Those were the days before the spread of Pentecostalism. My routine later every Sunday was to listen to some of my collection of classical music before lunch, and then, in the early evening, to go with Alice to visit my brother Bayo at his Jokotola Lodge on Ring Road. There, I got together also with my sister Tokunbo, and brothers Gboyega and Kunle. We sadly lost Kunle in 1989; and Gboyega, when he had transferred to Lagos, joined the group whenever he was in Ibadan; so it was usually my brother, my sister, Alice and myself discussing family affairs, including the estate in Ibadan of our late mother.

Later, after I had become vice-chancellor, I was invited, by virtue of my office, to join the Ibadan Dining Club, a men's club, while Alice joined the female counterpart. The Ibadan Dining Club was founded in the 1950's by an elitist group in the city of Ibadan. Membership at the beginning comprised Sir Olumuyiwa Jibowu, a highly distinguished Justice, Mr Justice R.A. Doherty, Mr S. Ade Ojo, Clerk of the Legislative Assembly, the legendary Chief S.O. Adebo, Head of Western Nigeria's Civil Service, and Professor Oladele Ajose of the then Faculty of Medicine of the University of Ibadan. The Dining Club grew in later years to include prominent civil servants, academics and businessmen, and for some time, had a quota for prominent non-Nigerians.

The two clubs – men's and women's – met together for the annual gala night in November of every year. The female club became moribund a few years ago, but the annual gala night has continued, with members' wives in attendance.

***

I had gone ahead by myself to Barbados in January, 1981, living with a landlady, Mrs Hinds, an arrangement that had kindly been made for me by my collaborator at the University of West Indies, Cave Hill, Richard Allsopp. Mrs Hinds was a secretary at the university. When Alice and the children joined me in the summer, we moved into a commodious house and acquired a car. A fairly detailed account of our stay in the West Indies is contained in my earlier publication titled *In the Saddle* (published in 1997 by Spectrum Books Ltd), and need not be repeated here. Suffice it to say that we had a very pleasant stay. The population of the island at the time was below 300,000, and I reckon that up to a third of that number were tourists from Europe frolicking in the blue Caribbean and driving around very barely clad in tiny vehicles.

But just as tourists were flocking to the beautiful island, there was also a steady stream of Bajans, as the citizens of

Barbados are called, out of the country, principally to Canada. The reason for this was not difficult to discern. There was a high level of education on the island, and no prospects of adequate employment.

The campus of the University at Cave Hill, Barbados, was one of the three campuses of the university, with headquarters at Mona, in Jamaica. The third campus was at St. Augustine in Trinidad. In spite of the small size of the Cave Hill campus, I found that the library was very well stocked, and I spent many profitable hours there. On one occasion, I was surprised to find the legendary Sir Arthur Lewis consulting the library.

My plans to visit the Mona campus fell through in the end, but I did manage to visit the St. Augustine campus. The trip to Trinidad enabled me to see the contrast between Bajans and Trinidadians. Where Bajans were relaxed, quiet, and easy-going – and could even be described as laid-back – Trinidad and Trinidadians reminded me more of home. Of course, Trinidad was a much bigger island, but more crucial was the fact that it was, like Nigeria, an oil-producing country. Economic activity was therefore more boisterous, and the traffic and noise of the city centre contrasted with the quiet of Barbados and reminded me of Lagos.

The population of Trinidad was visibly more racially mixed than that of Barbados; but what was particularly significant for me was the appearance of ethnic segregation. This feature was brought home to me forcefully on my arrival as I was driven from the airport to my hotel. It was mid-afternoon, and as we drove along, we would see Indian children streaming out of a school, and later, Trinidadians of African origin streaming out of another. It occurred to me then that the nation of Trinidad was still very much in the making.

***

While in Trinidad, I got a surprise telephone call from all the way in Tobago, Trinidad's tiny twin island. The caller was

Senator Elder, who had spent a number of years as a Fellow at the Institute of African Studies of the University of Ibadan, where he had been noted for his addiction to danshiki, which he wore throughout his stay at Ibadan. He told me that he had come to know that I was in Trinidad, and had an important message for me from his country's Senate. I wondered what that message might be, but before I got round to asking him, he said that the Senate would be glad if I could pay a visit to Tabago, even if for only one day. I checked my diary and found a suitable day, and we both agreed on the date.

As this was not on my original itinerary, I could only spare one day for the trip. Fortunately, flight time was going to be no more than a few minutes. On the due date, I took the morning flight and booked to return on the afternoon flight. This turned out to be the most scary flight I had ever experienced. The craft was a tiny propeller plane, and it flew so low that I could see the shimmering Caribbean sea all the way. Indeed, at landing, I had my heart in my mouth as it appeared we were going to land in the sea. In the nick of time, however, the undercarriage made contact with firm ground. The island was too small to have the normal size of airport, or to operate jet liners.

In the arrival hall of the airport was a delegation of four led by Senator Elder to welcome me. All four of them were members of the Senate. As it was nearly lunch-time, I was driven, after necessary introductions, to what appeared to be the grandest hotel on the island, where I was treated to an exotic lunch of seafood. All the time, my curiosity grew as to the explanation for this extraordinary treatment.

After lunch, Senator Elder broached the mission of the delegation. Apparently, he had had a very happy experience at Ibadan and had completely identified himself with the country. On his return to Tobago, he had related his experience to Senate and suggested that the obvious connections between Tobago and Nigeria, especially the Yoruba, needed to be fully exploited. His studies had shown him that the Yoruba had supplied more original settlers on the island than any other African group. Senate had consequently mandated the delegation to ask whether I would be available to come to Tobago to act as a consultant in the efforts to design a fitting cultural policy for the island.

I was dumbfounded, while a mixture of surprise and appreciation welled within me. When I finally found my voice, I thanked the delegation for this honour they sought to do me, personally, and to my country. Obviously, I had to think this out in the right frame of mind. Elder came in immediately to say that they realized, of course, that there were necessary procedures to go through, but that if I was comfortable with the idea, they would have to contact the Nigerian Government and ask it to spare me to work with them on terms that would be agreeable to both parties. I thanked him for saying that, but my own concern was, predominantly, what this would mean for the plans I had been nursing to join my colleagues in the Department of English at Ibadan to further work on our curriculum. I began to feel a sense of conflict.

All five of us further brainstormed on the matter, at the end of which I gave a tentative consent. After that, our discussions turned to other matters, notably Trinidad/Tobago relations. Some strong feelings were expressed that the oil which was boosting the economy of Trinidad in fact partially came from Tobago. When I asked how that was possible, I was told that there were strong suspicions that some of the oil was being siphoned from Tobago to Trinidad! After all, only a tiny strip of the ocean separated the two countries.

After a very enjoyable afternoon, I was taken back to the airport and returned to Port of Spain, Trinidad. I concluded my business with colleagues at St. Augustine and, after a few more days, made my way back to Barbados, stopping over briefly at beautiful St. Lucia on the way.

Back in Barbados, it was also time to slowly wind down my business. The last few days were taken up with sessions of recorded interviews between me and some officials of the university, which the university intended to keep in its archives. My stint at Cave Hill had turned out to be a most refreshing period, researching mostly, but also doing a little bit of teaching. And, of course, the beaches always beckoned.

It had been very pleasant working with Richard Allsopp, and very rewarding sharing friendship with Trevor Thompson, originally a Jamaican, and my compatriot, Iz Osayimwese, who had been similarly at Cave Hill from the University of Ibadan with his family. His wife was, in fact, a Bajan.

I left Barbados with my family and was seen off at the airport by a sombre-looking Trevor Thompson, who had confided in me a few days earlier that he had decided to return to his university job in Britain.

***

It was summer, and we arrived in a sun-bathed London festooned with all manner of decorations. The city was gripped with excitement in anticipation of the wedding of Prince Charles and Lady Diana. We stopped over for a few days in London, and while we were there, my eyes caught an advertisement by one of the agents of Mercedes cars. They were offering to sell a very barely-used car which had only been used for a demonstration drive in Italy and had had only a few kilometres on the odometer. I decided to check it out. As part of our sightseeing in London, the whole family went in search of the address of the agent.

We found the place, and the manager gladly let us have a look at the car. It looked like brand new, even smelt like it; and the price seemed very reasonable. As I had enough resources in my royalties account in London, I concluded the negotiations with the manager. The car was to be taken to Southampton and shipped on a cargo boat to Lagos.

We ourselves left London a few days later by air. From Lagos, we drove straight on to Ibadan.

***

We went straight from Lagos to Ibadan on 28 July, 1981, and did all the necessary clean-up in the house. Next morning, I went to the Central Porters Lodge and found, not surprisingly, that my pigeon-hole was full to overflowing. I deposited all the mail in my Room (67) in the department and went back home to take another couple of days' rest before fully going back to work.

Within four days of my return to Ibadan, I received a letter from Vice-Chancellor Olayide, which I could not say was totally unexpected. He had offered me the headship of English which, of course, I immediately accepted. The following day, I moved base to the Head of Department's office, where I continued reading my accumulated mail. To be able to clear my desk as quickly as possible, I spent long hours in the department, and got accustomed to being the last person to leave the faculty at night.

It was on one such evening that I heard an almost startling knock on the door. My surprise rose from two considerations. In the first place, I did not expect that it was already generally known that I had returned from sabbatical and installed myself in the Head of Department's office. The second was that it was too late in the day, anyway, to receive a visitor.

I summoned in the caller, and he turned out to be Professor Taiwo Kolawole of the Faculty of Medicine, who had been my junior at Igbobi by three or four years. That increased my surprise. Taiwo Kolawole, seeing me surrounded by masses of paper, decided to go straight to the point. He began by narrating how he had traced me to my present office, and then broached the reason for his surprise visit. He brought me up to date with some of the recent happenings at the university, and said that the university was looking for a new Deputy Vice-Chancellor, as Afolabi Toye, who had held the office since the beginning of Olayide's tenure, had accepted the vice-chancellorship of the University of Ilorin, a federal university located in Kwara State. I momentarily wondered what that had to do with me. Then Kolawole really startled me by saying that he had come to me from my brother Bayo's residence, where he had gone to seek my brother's assistance in persuading me to stand as a candidate for the post.

I thought immediately that poor Taiwo had embarked on an impossible mission. Was this his own personal idea, perhaps as an Igbobian? He said no, that he was expressing a pervasive wish in the university. I was, naturally, sceptical about such a claim, but let it pass, for I thought I had a stronger counter-argument. How was he sure that Olayide would feel comfortable, having as his Deputy the man who had been a close runner-up in the election which produced him as Vice-Chancellor? Taiwo said he was absolutely sure Olayide would welcome the idea. Then I produced what I expected to be the clincher: Olayide had only a few days previously appointed me the Head of English. Surely, nothing could have been farther from his mind at that point in time than the prospect of my succeeding Toye as Deputy Vice-Chancellor. But Taiwo was not to be beaten off. He maintained that in spite of that appointment, he was absolutely sure that Olayide would be happy to have me working with him. Again, I was sceptical.

I suspected what was going on in my mind, subconsciously, was that I now had three choices open to me. The prospects of Tobago remained in the background; the headship of English was now a reality; and now comes this idea of vying for the Deputy Vice-Chancellorship.

Taiwo then dropped the surprising idea that he was prepared to arrange for Olayide to come over to my house to tell me himself that it was his wish that I should succeed Toye. I saw the earnestness on Taiwo's face and accepted the plan.

At home later that night, I recalled a letter which I had received towards the end of my time in Barbados from Segun Odunuga of Modern European Languages, a close colleague, which informed me that Toye was about to leave for Ilorin, and saying what a wonderful idea it would be if I could succeed him. I had assumed that that was merely a friendly wish.

Before Taiwo left, we had fixed a date and time when Olayide would come over to the house. I discussed the situation that had arisen with Alice, who was as mystified as I was. I told her that arrangements had been concluded between me and Taiwo Kolawole, whom she knew very well, for Olayide to visit us, and we decided all we could do was to watch further developments.

On the due date, at about seven o'clock in the evening, Olayide indeed walked through the door, accompanied, not by Kolawole, but by Segun Odunuga. As he walked in, he broke the ice by asking: 'Where is my beer?' The beer was duly produced and he poured himself a glass, while Odunuga did the same. An atmosphere of conviviality was generated, aided, no doubt, by Star beer. When Olayide thought it was the right moment, he turned to me.

> "Ayo," he declared solemnly, calling me by my first name for the first time ever, "there is no one else I would wish to be my deputy but you."

I was somewhat jolted by this performance and had to think very quickly how to respond. I thought it was no use going again over the argument I had had with Kolawole, as I was sure Olayide would have heard all about it. An idea which Alice and I had discussed earlier then forced itself into my mind at that moment. It was simply this: that if I continued to reject these overtures, people might assume that my real problem was that I was a bad loser refusing to have anything to do with the winner. And nothing could have been farther from the truth than this. I thereupon thanked Olayide for his kind gesture and gave my consent.

The three-cornered conundrum was already resolving itself. Tobago was receding farther into the background; the headship of department was threatened; and the deputy vice-chancellorship was emerging as the likeliest prospect.

The scene now had to shift to the Senate of the university. According to regulations, the vice-chancellor presents a list of two to Senate to choose one from and recommend its choice to the Governing Council of the university, which then makes the appointment. Up till that time, it was unknown for Council to reject the recommendation of Senate.

By the time the meeting of Senate for this purpose is called, of course, everybody knows the vice-chancellor's preference, and tends to vote in accordance with it. To do otherwise would be an unthinkable slap on the vice-chancellor's face. This does not mean that the vice-chancellor's preference is returned unopposed. By no means, there are always people who consider that they have sufficient reason to scuttle the vice-chancellor's plans, but they are usually in a small minority.

As expected, Olayide called a meeting of Senate for the purpose of electing a new Deputy Vice-Chancellor. The meeting was held on 26 October, 1981, and although my sabbatical was technically over, I decided to absent myself from the meeting. Later in the evening, and for days afterwards, I was inundated with congratulatory messages, and the weight of my new responsibility began to dawn on me. Given so much goodwill, this was a job, I thought, I had to handle with every sense of responsibility.

Different theories to explain this development were now being offered to me by different well-meaning members of the academic community. Some of them told me outright that they thought Olayide was getting too powerful and had surrounded himself with a formidable kitchen cabinet. My mission, they suggested, was to moderate things and restore the old academic traditions of the university. Others thought that I had been co-opted to launder the image of the current administration. As such, they warned, I should be careful to preserve my credibility.

In the final analysis, however, only Olayide himself could say why he was so eager to have me as his deputy. After all, he could quite easily have chosen a member of his kitchen cabinet. It was evident that he and I had quite different personalities, and maybe that could have served as a kind of attraction for him. To emphasize his eagerness, Olayide wrote me a letter the very day after the meeting of Senate, asking me to assume office immediately, and adding that he had obtained the executive approval of the Pro-Chancellor and Chairman of Council for his decision.

I then contemplated how my plans had been radically altered in the space of a few weeks. I had hardly settled into the head of department's office before I was obliged to go back to Room 67. I was succeeded in office as Head by Dan Izevbaye, an outstanding literary scholar and fine gentleman. Surely, in his hands, the department would continue to prosper. Even without my expressing the wish, he let me retain the ownership of Room 67, and I subsequently agreed that the room should be left free for the use of visiting professors in the department; and that was how it was used until I was reunited with the room in 1991, after my long tenure as Vice-Chancellor.

***

The tradition of having a Deputy Vice-Chancellor was fairly recent at the University of Ibadan, and the first holders of the office had operated from their departmental rooms. Later, it was considered necessary for the DVC to have an office within the main Administration Building, which was much later to be formally named Tekena Tamuno Building, in appreciation of Tamuno of History's contributions to the development of the university as Vice-Chancellor, 1975-79.

The main Administration Building was, at this time, a one-storey building, with the Vice-Chancellor's office at one end of it. When Olayide was elected DVC in 1975, he became the first holder of that office to move into the Building, and occupied the other end, with the administrative staff occupying the space between him and the VC. That made me the second DVC to operate from that office. The DVC's complex consisted of the DVC's Room and a secretary's office. The Building has since been expanded, with another floor added on. Earlier still, the staff itself had been expanded, with two Deputy Vice-Chancellors instead of one. A third DVC was later to be added.

I assumed duty on 1 December, 1981 and, arriving at the Administration Building, went to pay my respects to the VC in his office before being shown to my own office at the other end. My secretary, Mrs Fagbenro, was a pleasant lady who, as I discovered later, was one of the most efficient administrative members of staff around. She helped me to break in into the office without any hiccups.

At the end of that first day, I inevitably had to reflect on the events of the day and ask myself what kind of future I thought lay ahead. Olayide had welcomed me heartily, and this encouraged me to hope that we would have a good working relation together. But what about the kitchen cabinet? Would they be happy to see someone who was obviously an 'outsider' occupying the number two position? What kind of influence would they possibly have on Olayide? The intriguing thing, for me, was that a number of the members of the kitchen cabinet, judging from the names I had heard mentioned, were also people that I would have thought were my friends who remained friendly. How would they manage to square the circle?

An early indication was given when I noticed that no attempts were made to draw me into the cabinet, and yet it was claimed – and indeed I had evidence – that practically all decisions relating to the university were first taken at meetings of the cabinet. I concluded that members of the cabinet were happy for me to remain an outsider. In any case, I was ever so grateful that no attempts were made to draw me in.

One effect of the cabinet idea was that it had encouraged, I was told, the formation of an opposition, which allegedly also met regularly to insist that things should be done properly, and which, consequently, constituted itself into a thorn in the side of the government. This parallel between the governance of a country and that of a university alarmed me, and I hoped that stories had been exaggerated. At any rate, the so-called opposition, most of whom happened to be close to me, made no approaches to me to be a fifth columnist! I was in uncharted waters.

I asked myself: Why a kitchen cabinet of the kind being described here, anyway? From its very beginning, the University of Ibadan, like all other reputable universities we know of, was governed by a committee system which guided and aided the vice-chancellor in making decisions. Ad hoc committees are something else entirely, being a common feature of all well-run organizations, including universities. But ad hoc committees are meant to report to statutory committees as the process of decision-making, in the specific case of a university, winds its way to Senate and Council. But I had never heard of a permanent, all-purpose ad hoc committee – a veritable contradiction in terms.

Up to this time, I had had very little contact with Olayide although, curiously enough, we had been employed by the university in the same year and even to boot, had been, for a brief period, next door neighbours in the Amina Way flats. He was in Agricultural Economics, and I soon heard him being referred to as a very brilliant scholar, which he proved by rapidly becoming a professor. He had drawn a coterie of admirers to himself, and it soon became clear that he was in love with power. Only nine years from the date of his appointment, he had been elected Deputy Vice-Chancellor to Tamuno, and it was rumoured that he was gunning for the Vice-Chancellorship which, indeed, he achieved in 1979, since Tamuno did not desire a second term.

Looking back now, I must say that, on the whole, we had a civilized relationship. I did what was required of me by the regulations to the best of my ability, but not once did the VC ever invite me to his office for any kind of brainstorming – I supposed that would already have been done with the kitchen cabinet. Only once did relations get really strained between us, on an issue in which, while briefly acting for him, I took what seemed to me a perfectly justified position. But one of the kitchen cabinet members was adversely affected and the VC really lost his temper with me.

Following this, I was told he came under great pressure from members of the cabinet, some of whom, I gathered, told him that his deputy was getting too big for his boots and had to be carefully watched. This episode is related in greater detail in *In the Saddle*, 1997.

***

As Olayide approached the end of his tenure in 1983, trouble was brewing in Council. The Pro-Chancellor and Chairman of Council was Dr Christopher Okojie of Uromi fame, who was said to be the national treasurer of the ruling political party in the country. It was also generally believed that Olayide was, himself, a member of that same party, which made him very well connected. What brought about the rift between them was not known for sure, but it was speculated that Okojie was finding Olayide's lust for power unbearable. Rumours on campus had it that the quarrel was taken to Chief Adisa Akinloye, one of the top officials of the ruling party who, very conveniently, lived in Ibadan. Apparently, Akinloye could not do anything to settle the quarrel, because the bad blood continued. Okojie decided to bide his time, knowing that, ultimately, he had powers to determine Olayide's fate.

Okojie's opportunity came when Olayide was coming to the very end of his tenure. The campus was agog with speculations. Olayide had a right, according to the regulations, to have a second term of three years, as against the first term of four years, if Council so recommended. But would Okojie let him have it?

At the next meeting of Council, I was, one might say, a ringside observer, as the Pro-Chancellor was sitting, as usual, between me and the Vice-Chancellor. After Council had disposed of the scheduled business of the day, the Pro-Chancellor turned to the Vice-Chancellor and told him at that point to excuse himself from Council. Members of Council looked at one another in wonderment. There was absolute silence in the Council Chamber, while all eyes were riveted on the Pro-Chancellor.

Once the Vice-Chancellor was out of the Chamber, the Pro-Chancellor dipped his hand into the inner pocket of his jacket and brought out a letter. In a sombre tone, he announced that he had received a letter from the federal government, which he proceeded to read. In it, Council was given the following two options: renew Olayide's tenure for three years in accordance with the regulations; but if Council felt unable to do so, start the procedure for the appointment of a new vice-chancellor.

The silence persisted for a few more seconds, and before any member could think of what to say, the Pro-Chancellor went on: "My firm advice to Council is this: In response to the first option, Council should say yes, it had no objection to Olayide having a second term. In response to the second option, Council should say it was prepared to begin the process for appointing a new Vice-Chancellor, and had no objections to Olayide being one of the candidates."

The Pro-Chancellor's deft move must have surprised everyone, but surely, no one lost sight of the ambivalence of the course of action Council was being led to take. Expectedly, the ambivalence was discussed. Council had been asked to make a choice between two options, but the Pro-Chancellor's proposal would, in effect, mean that it was choosing both options! It was unimaginable that Olayide would submit himself to this humiliation of competing for the vice-chancellorship all over again. However, the Pro-Chancellor felt strongly that there was no real ambivalence in the position he was asking Council to take. According to him, Olayide's chances of continuing as vice-chancellor were not being foreclosed; but surely, according to him, Council had a right to determine the manner and circumstances in which he could continue.

In addition, the important question was raised by members: if Olayide were to be chosen as the best candidate after the proposed interview along with other aspirants, would he then be entitled in the future to another second term, which in effect would be a third term!

It struck me at that point that Olayide had hardly anybody fighting for him on Council, a fact that might have been anticipated by the Pro-Chancellor. Clearly, Council was about to choose the second option without being too brutal about it. It must have been clear to members that while Okojie remained as Pro-Chancellor, Olayide had but very slim chance of continuing.

This development instantly generated a new wave of activity on campus. I was, myself, coming up to the end of my two-year appointment as Deputy Vice-Chancellor, and some members of the community began to make their own calculations. They expected that the DVC would have to man the university while the arrangements for the appointment of a new vice-chancellor were underway. Frantic attempts were therefore now being made to elect a new DVC who would then be acting VC, and who would stand a strong chance of emerging as the new VC. As for me, I felt sure that no one had ever served two terms as DVC, and so, I would happily return to Room 67.

Perhaps the government of the country, as proprietor, had got wind of what was going on for, one day, out of the blue, I received a letter from the Secretary to the Government of the Federation saying that the government had decided that "...you, Professor Ayo Banjo should act in the office of Vice-Chancellor until a new vice-chancellor is appointed." The letter had been copied to the Registrar and Secretary to Council (and Senate), who immediately drew the attention of the two organs of the university to it. I was to act, not by virtue of being the DVC, but in my personal recognizance. Of course, if I had not been DVC such a letter would very likely not have been written to me; but there it was, my name, and not my office, was mentioned in the letter. At this point, the frenetic efforts to get a new DVC elected simply fizzled out.

8

THOUGHTS ON THE NIGERIAN UNIVERSITY SYSTEM

Establishment of Universities

My acting appointment turned out to be for only one year. I believe there were sceptical members of the community who were anxious to see how Banjo was going to run a university without a kitchen cabinet. But in reality, I managed to do so, not only during the one year of acting, but indeed for the succeeding seven years. There was no magic about it. The regulations and traditions of the university made it unnecessary to meet in conclaves anywhere, and the openness was generally appreciated.

The story of the next eight years of my service at the university has been told in some detail in *In the Saddle* (op cit.) and it is unnecessary to repeat it here. But having gone through that experience, followed by the Pro-Chancellorship, subsequently, of three universities, I believe it would be appropriate at this point to comment on certain features of the university enterprise in Nigeria as I saw them.

The enterprise started on a propitious note in 1948 with the foundation of University College Ibadan, which of course metamorphosed into the University of Ibadan in 1962. The most striking feature of the event of 1948 was that the College was planned and mentored for fourteen years by one of the greatest universities in the English-speaking world: the University of London. It was planned to be on the same level with the Colleges of the University in the city of London itself. We are not surprised, therefore, that within the first ten years of its foundation, the College had begun to make its mark in the world, and was working at the cutting edge of research in a number of disciplines.

Staff were recruited from all over the world, and in the circumstances more than ninety-five percent of the academic staff were expatriates, to start with. Ultra-nationalists might have complained that this was an alien institution trying to make English ladies and gentlemen of Nigerians. But this was an inevitable phase, and the College itself had started in earnest a vigorous programme of staff development. The best graduating students were sent for postgraduate studies to the best universities, not only in Britain, but in other parts of the world. At the time of writing this, in 2018, the pendulum had swung to the other extreme, and Nigerian academic staff would be of the order of ninety-eight percent in the university. When this fact is taken in conjunction with the other fact that many of the universities, especially the new ones, do not have a single non-Nigerian student, there is, indeed, cause for alarm for, as Niyi Osundare poetically observes, the 'universe' seems to have been taken out of the 'universities' in Nigeria.

The lesson to be learnt from the origins of the University of Ibadan is that of careful planning and meticulous mentoring. It appeared for some time that this lesson had been taken to heart when Ibadan was made to mentor the Universities of Jos, Ilorin, Port Harcourt and Calabar although, with the exception of Jos, the mentoring was rather informal.

The Vice-Chancellors in these other universities went out from Ibadan and simply developed the institutions in the image of Ibadan.

But this was more than could be said for most of the universities which were established in the 1970's and 1980's. No careful planning seemed to have been done, and the idea of mentoring was not considered at all. All the universities thereafter would appear to have followed the same pattern, with the result that many of the private universities are having to weather the storms of inadequacy of finance and staffing, calling to question the worth of the degrees being awarded.

The National Universities Commission was established to keep an eye on the overall orderly growth of the university system. But although the Commission clearly acts for the proprietors in the case of the federally established universities, its relationship to the State universities is, at best, ambiguous. As for the private universities, once licenses are given to the proprietors, the Commission seemingly considers its task accomplished. Thus the Commission controls the number of private universities but does nothing to guarantee their standards. I have had occasion to recommend that any new university established in the country should be made to sign a memorandum of understanding (MOU) with one of the 'first generation' universities to underwrite the standards in the new university and to play an active role until the first set of graduates is produced. The news coming out of some of the new private universities is by no means cheering, and it would be good if something could be done to help them without encroaching on their independence.

Recruitment of Academic Staff

The provision of academic staff of the right quality and in the right numbers is one of the major problems of the entire system. The new universities are having to depend on attracting staff, including retired staff, from the older universities. They cannot get enough from there while, at the same time, the staff in the older universities have become depleted. There are anecdotes of how some new universities seeking accreditation deceive the NUC by presenting staff moonlighting from other universities without the NUC being any the wiser.

When the country had a much stronger currency, the older universities were able to employ academic staff from other parts of the world, and Ibadan, in particular, enjoyed financial support from the British government for its British academic staff serving in Ibadan, through the British Expatriate Supplementation Scheme (BESS). This scheme was terminated as soon as the British government considered that Nigeria, now an oil-producing country, should be able to look after itself. There is a serious problem here which calls for an imaginative solution as many new universities have found, apparently to their surprise, that there is no way of running a university solely with students' fees, and even hoping to make a profit at the end of the day.

Student Enrolment

Student enrolment has been burgeoning over the years, further complicating the universities' problems. As has often been emphasized, the problem is not that too many students are enrolled in relation to the national population, or that there are too many universities. Rather, the problem, which borders on quality, is a systemic one. It has to be understood that the origins of this phenomenon lie at least partly in the adoption of the 6-3-3-4 system of education delivery. This system has made it possible for all pupils after their Senior Secondary course to routinely take the Joint Admissions and Matriculation examination in a bid to enter a university, instead of being guided into other tertiary institutions more suitable for them. Poor performance in these examinations shows quite clearly that a large number of the pupils are not qualified to take the examination in the first place. Embarrassed by the situation, some universities have drastically lowered their cut-off points and opened the floodgates. Unless they do so, they may find, ironically, that they cannot find enough intakes into their universities, as the number of universities has been increasing apace.

This development has thrown into sharp relief, the problems of enrolment into the universities. To fill the increasing number of vacancies created by the growing number of universities, standards have to be compromised, at least in a number of universities. The problem was even further complicated, at one point, by the discovery of sharp practice at JAMB itself, aided and abetted by candidates' parents. It is encouraging, however, that as I write this, wholesome fresh air is being let into JAMB operations by a new leadership which, if sustained, is bound to sanitize the whole admissions procedure. Over and above this, however, is the problem of universities admitting far more students than they know they can possibly cope with.

A still more fundamental problem is that the only way of securing a satisfactory future for the products of the secondary system, as widely believed by parents, is to have them enrolled in universities. Not much confidence is shown in the other tertiary institutions because of the country's awful reward system. Other countries have been able to produce happy and successful professionals from their technical colleges, but Nigeria has not been able to make other tertiary institutions attractive to school leavers, and yet there is a crying need for the active participation of the products of such institutions in the country's development.

Every year, we are confronted with woeful results in the JAMB examinations, and this leads me to wonder whether any empirical comparative research has ever been undertaken into the admission of students into the universities through the JAMB examinations rather than largely (if not exclusively) through 'A' level qualifications. The facts at the moment would strongly suggest that the latter route is far superior to the current one.

This observation would require some elaboration. The first university institution in the country, University College Ibadan, admitted students only through 'A' level qualifications. It is, in fact, arguable that the establishment of UCI prompted the provision of the Sixth Form in the country's elite secondary schools, so that holders of the Higher School Certificate (HSC) could join holders of the London 'A' level certificates in vying for entry into the new College, and subsequently, the University of Ibadan.

In order not to exclude schools without Sixth Form classes from sending their products direct to the university, the University of Ibadan established the concessional entrance examination, from which it selected students for four-year programmes, as against the three-year ones for the 'A' level entrants. This was obviously regarded as a transitional measure until, with the expansion of Sixth Forms in the country, four-year programmes would no longer be necessary; and this is exactly what happened in the 1970's. Because the university conducted its own concessional examinations, these examinations were found to be not only relevant but also reliable.

It should be noted that the preliminary year into which entrants from the concessional examinations were admitted was not, strictly speaking, a university year, but rather a Sixth Form compressed into one year. Real university work started in the second year of such students, when they joined new 'A' level entrants. Obviously, concessional entrants formed a very small proportion of the entire student population and were quickly assimilated. It is debatable whether university academic staff really enjoyed teaching this category of students, either.

The question naturally arises as to which is intrinsically better: having direct entrants with the London 'A' levels (or the Higher School Certificate) coming to do three years for a first degree, or having concessional entrants who have to spend four years for the first degree. In other words, do direct entrants in the long run perform better in the degree examinations than the concessional entrants? I believe a research was conducted into the problem by a member of the Education Faculty of the university of Ibadan, and no significant difference was found. Of course, as previously stated, the concessional entrance examinations were highly predictive.

The picture has changed since the introduction of the 6-3-3-4 system of education delivery. Under the previous dispensation, all secondary school students took the School Certificate examination (the equivalent of the London 'O' levels) in their fifth year. The best of the products of this examination were then creamed off into the two-year Sixth Form. At present, on the other hand, all pupils spend six years (3-3) in secondary schools, and then all proceed to try to enter university. Direct entrants have all but been eliminated. This has, of course, altered the culture of the university.

It is equally important to bear in mind the quality of schools from which JAMB candidates come. Secondary schools have mushroomed since the 1970's. Some of them are very good, but most are deplorable. Given such a situation, it is hardly surprising that many students attempt to cheat at the JAMB examinations, and there are allegations that marks are sometimes bought outright! The truth of the matter is that, since the Second Republic, successive governments throughout the country have placed an enormous emphasis on access, to the detriment of quality, and it is precisely the wrong time for the universities to be fed with the products of such a system. The situation bears hardly any relation to the old concessional entry system when the selection was very carefully undertaken from much better schools.

In addition, the Sixth Form is a foretaste of the university, with its provisions for individual study and ample time for prolonged meditation. As a result, the products are eased gently into the universities, which turn out not to be completely alien to them. Besides, entrants to the university from Sixth Forms are inevitably one year older than under the current system. Taking 11-plus as the usual age of entry to secondary schools these days, a pupil arrives at the university at the age of 17, and indeed, many have been known to arrive a year younger. These entrants bring their secondary school culture, which it may take two years to wean them out of.

In the light of all this, it is advisable for the country to go back to the old system of 6-5-2-3: six years of primary, followed by five years for 'O' levels, which in turn is followed by 2 years of Sixth Form, the products of which then enter university more mature in age and intellectually than what we have now. The first degree in universities would then take three years.

It is recognized that there is always resistance to change, and there are those who argue that the current system has not been tried long enough. The evidence staring us in the face, however, is that things seem to be going from bad to worse, and we need not wait for a complete disaster. But then, how do we go back to the previous system?

This question cannot be answered without seeing the necessity for a root and branch reform of the entire education system in the country. First of all, we need to upgrade the secondary school system – and this, of course, in turn calls for the upgrading of the primary school system. Once the upgrading of secondary schools is seriously pursued throughout the country, schools will arrive at different times at the stage of establishing the Sixth Form. There are schools which are ready to go ahead straightaway, but it must be admitted that the majority of schools will come on board at different times. The important thing is that all secondary schools in the country should aim eventually at ending with a Sixth Form.

At this stage, we can borrow from the history of the University of Ibadan and temporarily provide a two-track route into the university. In this regard, there are two possibilities. Do we, as was done at Ibadan, allow each university (and there are now some three hundred of them) to set its own concessional examination, or should we, borrowing the JAMB idea, provide for a centrally set concessional admission (not matriculation) examination? The case for a centrally set examination would seem much stronger. But this centrally set examination must earn the respect of every university, and the Joint Admissions Board which results from JAMB, would continue to work very closely with the universities, dealing mainly with problems arising from multiple admissions to universities.

A word about the implications of upgrading the secondary schools in order to restore high standards to the universities. Secondary schools need to have, at the minimum, respectable libraries and laboratories. But more important, they must have respectable and highly-motivated teachers – teachers who are capable of teaching right up to the Sixth Form, thus raising the standards of the entire school. Such teachers have, of course, to be well paid.

The reform being advocated is enormous, and naturally calls for the outlay of huge sums of money. There was a needless argument a few years ago as to whether UNESCO was recommending, for developing countries, the allocation of 23 percent of their national budget to education. Recently, the United Nations itself has emphatically recommended a minimum of 20 percent. The current percentage in the country is less than 15 percent, and if we sincerely wish to declare an emergency in the education sector, we should think of exceeding even the minimum being recommended by the United Nations. Western Nigeria did it in the 1950's.

Financing the Universities

The humongous factor underlying the problems besetting the university system today is, of course, finance. There are three categories of proprietors of universities in the country: the federal government, State governments and private agencies.

These agencies, in turn, can be classified as either corporate bodies, largely religious in complexion, and private individuals.

Federal universities are tuition-free, and the proprietors have also divested themselves from supporting hall accommodation, while at the same time putting a cap on what universities may charge for accommodation. The result is that the halls have become, for most part, an eyesore. While existing universities are poorly funded, more federal universities are being established. The idea seems to be that every State should have a federal university.

The question of tuition-free education in the federal universities has often been debated, especially in view of the fact that the other categories of universities, even including State universities, do charge tuition fees. One way, and perhaps the only way, in which the practice in the federal universities can be justified will be if it can be proved, indeed, that the best candidates for university education are continually creamed off into these universities. They can then be regarded as being on national scholarships. But it has not been proved that this is the case. After all, students do fail in these federal universities or obtain third class degrees, while some private universities have been awarding first class honours degrees. Admittedly, this raises the question of comparative standards, which is another problem altogether. In any case, the more rational course would seem to be to award scholarships to deserving individuals in all universities, while others, even in federal universities, should pay for their tuition. We are now talking of a country where many parents pay about a million naira annually for their children's school fees at secondary school. Modest fees, augmented with bursaries, should be charged in federal universities to boost the institutions' internally generated revenue and ensure acceptable standards.

In candidates' order of preference, state universities come next to federal ones and are under their shadows. They charge fees which are lower than in the private universities and appear to enjoy less autonomy than their federal counterparts. They would appear to be firmly under the control of the State's Commissioner for Education. Whenever the Academic Staff Union of Universities (ASUU) conducts negotiations with the federal government, which is the proprietor of only the federal universities, academic staff from state universities tag along, only for their own proprietors, the State governments, to have severe difficulties in providing the funds to back the agreements with ASUU.

The private universities are *sui generis*. The federal government had liberalized ownership of universities to save itself the trouble of rapidly providing more universities in the country. It had been expected that corporate bodies, especially religious organizations, would come in, harking back to an earlier period in the nation's history when primary education was in the hands of the government and such religious bodies. But to many people's surprise, individuals came forward to obtain licenses for starting universities.

The general belief is that private universities are business concerns. It is thus hardly surprising that the highest level of fees are charged at these universities. It is possible that some individuals went into the venture without realizing the full financial implications. While a few of them are doing well, perhaps the majority face daunting problems, in spite of the high fees that they charge. They find it difficult to recruit staff of international standard because of the financial state of the country, and thus have to rely, to a great extent, on retired and moonlighting staff from older universities. Some of them are, in fact, owing their staff several months' salaries.

It is perhaps too early to pass judgement on these universities. However, it is instructive that they are, as a body, appealing to the federal government to be given a share of the fund (TETFUND) for tertiary education which is dedicated exclusively to the public universities. Some people would argue that the proprietors of private universities usually have no assurance of financial support from the government when embarking on their project, and therefore have no right to expect, as of right, any subvention from the government. However, in the history of education in this country, voluntary agencies at one time routinely received grants from the government in support of their schools. This, obviously, was in recognition of the fact that education was an important function, indeed the responsibility, of the government, and that the agencies were helping the government to discharge its responsibilities.

Following the same line of reasoning, a good case can be made for at least a token financial support from the government for the private universities. As previously argued, there is no justification for students in federal universities enjoying tuition-free education while those in private universities pay heavily.

Over and above this, however, a clear case can be made for allowing all universities in the country, without discrimination, to have access to research funds from the federal government. Exceptional academic staff, wherever they may be employed in the country, should be able to have financial support for their research. This is common practice in many countries.

I have had occasion to recommend a scheme whereby all stakeholders participate in funding university education in the country. Under this scheme, the proprietors of a university would bear the lion's share of the costs, while all tiers of government (with the possible exception of local government, which only exists in name) should contribute, and the students themselves should make a contribution unless they are on scholarships. Bursaries should also be available to aid indigent students. This scheme may appear complicated but it ensures equity and, hopefully, a more reliable source of funding for all the universities in the country.

***

The letter of appointment which I had received from the Secretary to the Government had indicated that the appointment was with effect from 1 December 1984. This meant that the appointment had not been backdated to 1983 when the acting appointment had taken effect.

Having previously been deputy vice-chancellor, I had come into the new office with some firm ideas of what I would like to accomplish. The first was to improve the telecommunication system in the university. The telephone exchange in the university had started off with more than thirty extensions, but by 1984 only one or two were working. When I approached the relevant minister, I was assured that our problem would be solved as part of the bigger plans for the country for telecommunications. I must say that those plans never materialised before I left office seven years later. The university in the end had to wait for the dawn of mobile telephones.

Next, I set my sights on solving the problems of water supply. Water from the mains was hopelessly inadequate, and I thought we could set up our own treatment plant, taking raw water from the reservoir at Eleiyele, treating it on campus and distributing it all over the campus. Fortunately, the scheme worked. Water from the plant was fed into a giant overhead tank on Amina Way, from where it found its way to various points on the campus, to everyone's relief, not least the students' in the halls of residence.

I did not have much to do to improve the supply of electricity. My predecessor, Professor Olayide, had installed huge generators more than capable of supplying the whole campus, and I only came into office during the finishing stages of the installation.

Turning my attention next to the structure of the university, I determined to complete the process which had started with the establishment of the College of Medicine.

In 1980, Council had received the O & M Report from its special committee which had been set up under the chairmanship of Justice Fakayode to review the administrative procedures of the university. The committee had recommended a collegiate system for the university and had proposed that the restructuring should start with the Faculty of Medicine, to test the waters. The experiment with the Faculty of Medicine had proved very successful, though somewhat expensive. As deputy vice-chancellor I had had the opportunity of closely studying the O&M report, and so, after settling into the position of vice-chancellor, thought it was time to complete the restructuring. After a prolonged debate, Council agreed.

I set up a committee under the chairmanship of the deputy vice-chancellor, Professor Peter Bodunrin, to liaise with the faculties and work out a proposal for the consideration of Council. This committee had a difficult time persuading the faculties to shed some of their powers, but in the end managed to get the faculties to agree to a five-college system; and provosts for the new colleges were appointed. Some of them encountered problems of acceptability, but I thought that would in the course of time be overcome.

This was the situation when I left office in 1991, but news soon reached me where I was spending my sabbatical at the University of Cambridge that the arrangement had unravelled and the faculty system had been restored. I considered it a major failure of my administration.

The four new Colleges approved by Council were:
1. College of Arts, Social Sciences and Law
2. College of Science and Technology
3. College of Agriculture, Forestry and Veterinary Medicine
4. College of Education.

***

My tenure experienced the effects of inadequate funding. The government withdrew support for the halls of residence, resulting in a dramatic fall of standards of maintenance of the halls. I thought the students bore the situation with understanding. Indeed, throughout my tenure the student union and ASUU showed considerable support for their vice-chancellor.

There was quite a hiccup when I approached the end of my first term in 1988. The Council, under the distinguished chairmanship of Alhaji Dr Liman Ciroma, unanimously decided to offer me an unprecedented second term, but for reasons best known to it, the ministry of education was totally unwilling. Council however stood its ground and the minster had to be prevailed upon to respect the wishes of Council. And that was how it came about that I became the first vice-chancellor to serve two terms at the university. I had a very fulfilling time and felt very grateful for the opportunity.

Following a series of send-off activities, I vacated office at the end of November, 1991, and on the morning of 1 December, I vacated the Vice-Chancellor's Lodge.

***

As I drove myself that day to my new abode at Villayo, 12 Oluga Street, New Bodija, Ibadan, it occurred to me that, at last, I was about to begin life as a 'town boy.' I had never earlier thought about it, but really, I had lived a protected life for most of my existence so far. Having lived the first ten years of my life on a college campus in Oyo which bore little relation to the ancient and traditional town of Oyo, I went on to Lagos to live in a vicarage which was protected from the hurly-burly of Aroloya, Lagos. Next I went to Igbobi, a boarding school. From there I went to the idyllic new campus of the Nigerian College of Arts, Science and Technology in Ibadan, which was a fully residential college. My next port of call was McBrayne Hall, University of Glasgow, where I spent the next four years. Back in the country, I continued to live on school premises at Ughelli and Ibadan.

That reverie brought me to my destination, where my family was waiting for me, and wondering, like me, how we were going to survive in the new environment. We now had, as a family, to provide for ourselves all those amenities that we had taken for granted since the children were born during my twenty-five years living on the campus of the University of Ibadan. Water, electricity, security and garbage disposal engaged our immediate attention.

We thought we could depend on water supply from the Water Corporation of Oyo State. But we soon found that there was no steady supply. In order to catch every supply that came, we had provided an underground water tank, a ground level water tank and an overhead water tank. But in spite of this, we once found, to our horror, that there was not a drop of water in the house. We therefore had to resort to the remedy which we found everybody in the city seemed to have adopted. We decided to drill a borehole. I consulted a senior academic in the geology department of the University of Ibadan, and he came over to the house to see how this could be done. In the end, he advised against drilling a borehole and suggested we should settle for a well instead. His reason was that the house was too close to a stream which might turn out to be a source of pollution of the water in a borehole. We took his advice, and in spite of the rocky nature of the terrain, dug a well. I sent a sample of the water to a professor in the chemistry department of the university, and he assured us that it was safe for consumption. In spite of that, however, we always took the trouble to boil and filter the water before using it.

With the onset of the dry season, we found the yield from the well drastically reduced , and so resorted to buying tankers of water from the water corporation; and when they could not supply, we approached private suppliers. It seemed incredible that for several months at a stretch, there was apparently no water supplied anywhere in the city by the water corporation. Excuses ranged from lack of water at the dam, to consistently broken pipes, which had to be repaired by the consumer.

While tackling the water problem, we also had to face the equally menacing problem of electricity. The most notorious supplier of electricity, possibly in the whole world, was the Nigerian Electricity Power Authority (NEPA), which everybody regarded as a joke because, whatever it found to engage itself in, it only very intermittently supplied electricity, and did not seem to know what to do about it. It had excuses galore – low level of water at the dam, broken-down transformers, inadequacy of gas supply, vandalism, broken lines at the slightest hint of a storm or drop of rain. It was clear that the lines were very poorly maintained, and consumers had to pay for repairs and replacements which ought to have been done by the suppliers themselves. The Authority, while complaining of inadequate funding, obviously knew that thousands – possibly millions – of Nigerians were consuming electricity without paying, at least officially, for it. It was generally believed that there was a big racket going on. Twenty-seven years on, and following privatisation, things have improved marginally, but we have not yet put the era of long outages completely behind us.

So again, we had to resort to self-help; and the obvious remedy was the acquisition of a generator, that hideous machine which produced annoying atmospheric and noise pollution.

However, buying a generator was one thing; maintaining it was quite another matter. At about this time, the prices of diesel and petrol were going up, at one time provoking a full-scale national crisis. The marketers of these products were kings. To sell above even the raised prices, they hoarded and then sold, often in the dead of night, at a scandalous price. At one stage, claiming a directive from the government, they declined to sell the products in jerry-cans. Since this did not result in any noticeable reduction in the noise pollution from generators, it was obvious that the products were, indeed, being secretly sold in jerry-cans. The only conceivable alternative would have been for people to make several trips to the stations to fill up the tanks of their cars and then empty the contents into jerry-cans at home.

Twenty-seven years on, the country is yet to solve the problem of supply of petrol at a reasonable price and in sufficient quantity. Yet the country is a major oil producer; but the Nigerian National Petroleum Corporation (NNPC) has been consistently mired in mind-boggling financial scandals.

The generator, alas, did not totally solve our energy problems. To prevent ourselves running the generator twenty-four hours a day, we had to acquire an inverter. By this means, and through an internal system of load-shedding, we were assured of power all day every day. We have also more recently been taking advantage of solar power.

Before having had time to settle down in our new house, we had been informed by one of the two original residents on our street in this new part of Ibadan, of the need to cooperate to ensure security in the area. It was a new area, a new extension to the well-known Bodija estate, and being as yet sparsely populated, was susceptible to brigandage at any time of day or night. The remedy was to form a neighbourhood assembly or association, and pool our resources together to employ security guards. I had previously thought that the first duty of any government was to ensure the security of its citizens; but obviously, I was wrong. The assembly increased numerically as more people came to settle in the area, and met every last Saturday of the month in the home of one of the first two residents on our street, Chief Omogbenigun, who hosted the meetings for many years until his passing. Even after that, his family urged us to go on meeting at the same venue.

The assembly did not just discuss security, even though that was always the most important item on the agenda. We also arranged to have our roads paved, arranged for street lighting and counselled one another on the need to minimize pollution from generators, which, of course, every household had.

It was a neighbourhood of enlightened and reasonably well-of families, but I found it incredible that members had to be cajoled to pay their subscriptions in order to maintain a tolerable neighbourhood. Hardly a quarter of members ever turned up for meetings, and on several occasions, the meeting ended by members making a round of the homes of the most notorious absentees. I stoutly refused to join in such demeaning campaigns; but on a few occasions the meeting received reports that some of the members targeted promptly shut their doors on sighting the delegation and, of course, did not answer any knocking. Yet they were not ashamed to enjoy the facilities paid for by the rest of us.

We had an energetic and dedicated secretary in Mr B.O. Oluga, a retired army officer who put his military training at our disposal. Twenty-seven years on, he is still stoutly running the show and fighting our battles, while ensuring that our guards are regularly paid – which is no mean feat. Our street bears his name, as he was the very first resident there. The whole area owes him an immense debt of gratitude.

So far, our own home has been broken into twice. On the first occasion, I was abroad with the family and we had securely locked up the house. The intruders must have been thoroughly familiar with the design of the house, for they got on to the ceiling from outside the house and walked along until they arrived on top of the main bedroom. They then removed the tiles and gave themselves a soft landing on the bed, and proceeded to pillage the room.

We were given an account of the escapade on our return. When the robbers had emerged on the street with their loot, the guards caught sight of them and raised an alarm. Mr Oluga immediately emerged from his house, rifle in hand. He personally gave the marauders a chase, fording the stream after them and firing warning shots in the air. In desperation, the thieves dropped some of the loot so that they could make good their escape. With the help of the guards, Mr Oluga salvaged what had been dropped and saved it until our return. He then ordered the guards to place a priority on the security of our house while we were away. Mr Oluga had displayed a rare and unspeakably admirable conduct, especially when it is recognized that he received no remunerations whatsoever for being our secretary.

The second occasion occurred when the whole family was at home and in bed. We must all have slept very soundly that night, but early next morning, as Tunde was on his way downstairs to the kitchen for his customary early morning cup of coffee, he noticed something odd about the family private sitting room. On a closer check, he found that the television was missing, and one or two items besides. He alerted the household, and it was confirmed that we had had unwelcome visitors during the night. We confirmed that the back door had been broken open and, this time, the guards had had no inkling of what had happened. So the robbers got away with the loot.

What immediately preoccupied our minds, however, was a sense of the danger which we had escaped. The intruders could have forced the bedrooms open to gather more loot and, more sinisterly, in the process, harm members of the family. We cut our losses and proceeded to make all our doors more impregnable. Actually, this must have worked, because there was indeed a third attempt to invade the house. Apparently failing on that occasion to gain access to the main house, the marauders turned on the house help's quarters, rudely woke up our steward and showed him the muzzle of a gun. Without much difficulty, they robbed him of his mobile telephone and all the money he had in his wallet. As we could see their footprints on the walls of the fence, we immediately arranged to put American barbed wire round the top of the entire fence.

On the whole, however, our guards, under the supervision of Mr Oluga, is doing an excellent job. There have been no reports of break-ins in the last few years.

While grappling with all these problems, we also had to find a way of disposing of our garbage. We found no signs of any agency being responsible for this, and therefore hired a private firm. The firm performed this function efficiently for many years; but recently the state (state, mind you) government intervened and took over the function. The fee previously paid to the firm is now collected by the government.

In all this, the reader would be justified to wonder whether there was a local government council in the area. Allegedly, there was and still is, but who they are and what they do is completely shrouded in mystery. In our twenty-seven years in the area, not a sound has been heard uttered by the chairman of our putative local government or any of his agents. If indeed there is a local government council, one would be interested to know exactly what it does, apart from paying staff salaries. Of course, it is possible that it does not receive funds for anything else.

One is reminded that a debate has arisen recently over the desirability of having a third tier of government at all. Apparently, state governors, or at least most of them, cannot wait to see the tier abolished. Yet in other parts of the world, this is the most relevant tier to the ordinary citizens, and even the country's constitution seems to recognise this. It is curious that in our country, the federal government revels in performing functions which properly belong to a state government, while the state government, in turn, is eager to perform the functions of a local government. Let us hope that a halt will be called one day to this confusion.

***

Having set up a new base in Ibadan, it was time to turn my thoughts to the plans that I had already concluded for my accumulated leave of one year, followed by my sabbatical.

The plan was to spend the first year as Visiting Fellow at Cambridge University's Research Centre for English and Applied Linguistics. By this time, three of the four children were already graduates. Bunmi had read English at the University of Lagos, and had returned to do her Masters under the supervision of Dan Izevbaye at Ibadan. She had already been in contact with Oxford Brookes University in England to do postgraduate work in Publishing. She would travel with us to Britain for this purpose. Tunde had read Law at Ibadan and had applied to the University of Dundee in Scotland to do a Masters in Oil and Gas. Dundee was reputed as the best university for the course in Britain. Yinka was in the process of completing her degree in English at Ibadan University in 1992, and was also planning, in the future, to study for an MSc in Occupational Safety and Health Management at the University of Middlesex in England.

The explanation for all this is that I had promised all the children that when they had taken their first degrees at home in Nigeria, I would be able and glad to support them for their Masters degrees in Britain. The basis of my promise was that I expected my FSSU – an insurance scheme that had covered all academics in the Commonwealth, and in Nigeria until the 1970's – to mature in 1994 when I turned 60.

Now, a tidy sum in pounds sterling had accrued to me from this pension scheme, and came in handy to pay Bunmi's fees at Oxford Brookes and, in the nick of time, Tunde's fees at Dundee. Indeed, the remittance for Tunde's board and tuition arrived by bank transfer at the University of Dundee on the very morning that he himself arrived there. A few years later, Yinka was to arrive in London after working in Nigeria for a while, and I was similarly able to support her at Middlesex University.

When Alice and I left for Cambridge, Dapo was in his first year in the Faculty of Law of the University of Ibadan. We had made adequate arrangements for his comfort, even bought him a small old car. In any case, during the long vacation, he was able to travel to Cambridge to join us. I had gone to London to meet him, and we had had a very pleasant train ride back to Cambridge, during which he had filled me in on all the latest developments at home in Nigeria. I was also surprised to discover that he had, from Nigeria, been following developments at Wimbledon.

After an enjoyable time in Cambridge, it was time for him to return to his studies at Ibadan. I went up with him to London and we reported at Heathrow for his night flight to Lagos. After he had checked in, we went to one of the lounges where he bought a hamburger. I kept an eye on my watch as I did not want to miss the last train to Cambridge. Eventually, I left him finishing off his hamburger and took the train back to Cambridge. Tunde and Yinka had been told to arrange to meet Dapo at Ikeja in the morning.

We were, however, startled to be told by Tunde and Yinka next morning that Dapo had not arrived on the arranged flight. I could not understand it, as I had seen with my own eyes his baggage being checked in. What could have been the reason for his missing the flight? Could he have failed to hear the boarding announcement? We expected to hear from him from London in the course of the day, but nothing happened. We then tried in vain to contact the airlines, and now wondered what we could do next. Then early next morning, we got a call from Lagos announcing Dapo's safe arrival twenty-four hours behind schedule! We were most relieved.

Dapo himself later recounted what had happened. Apparently, shortly after I left him at the airport, he began to think of a friend of his with whom he had been at the International Secondary School of the University of Ibadan, and decided he would go and visit him, as he had his address on him. So off he went, saw his friend and obviously had to spend the night with his friend's family in their home.

The next morning, he and his friend had gone to the travel agents and he had explained his predicament to them. They had then helped him to re-validate his ticket for that night. This time, he did not miss his flight, and his small adventure had come off.

***

One thing I looked forward to every morning in Cambridge was the long walk from our flat to the Centre. I had been asked on my arrival whether I needed to have a bicycle provided for me, but had declined. With a personal car and an official car in Ibadan, I had almost forgotten how to walk!

Life at Cambridge was, as expected, restful and fulfilling. Situated on the River Cam, the city of Cambridge was founded in the first century AD, and had been made famous by the university, founded in 1209. I had expected to see a city about as large as London, but it appeared the growth of the city had been constrained for the benefit of the university, whose many colleges dominated the city and its skyline. The population was only about 120,000, which made for serenity. It was, in addition, quality population, as I was told that forty percent of the workforce in the city had higher education qualifications – many times the national average. The favourite means of transportation within the city by students and staff was cycling, but I preferred walking and the bus. There was a modest railway station, and London was only about an hour away.

I was received at the Centre on my first day by Gillian Brown, professor and director of the Centre. Soft-spoken and friendly, she immediately made me feel welcome. I was shown to my room, and I noticed it was furnished with a computer and an electric typewriter. There was a communal printing room available to all staff.

I noticed that there was only one non-academic member of staff, the secretary, in the whole Centre. I assumed immediately that every member of staff had to fend for themselves in satisfying their secretarial needs. For me, this meant that I had to learn to be computer literate fast. The secretary advised that I should enrol in the beginners' course at the university's computer centre, and that was exactly what I did. Fortunately, my father had made me, as an adolescent, to acquire mastery of the keyboard of his typewriter. So, once I had learnt the ropes at the computing centre, I was able to make good progress immediately in the use of the computer and even enjoyed the self-sufficiency thus acquired.

Given my experience at Ibadan, I wondered how the Centre managed to cope with only one non-academic staff, but soon found the explanation. During the long vacation, a lady from town was hired to help with all the major typing needs of the staff. Each member submitted to her the handouts planned for the students for the next session. After working for several weeks, she put the handouts in staff individual pigeon holes and left, to return during the next long vacation. Thus the Centre was able to devote its resources exclusively to teaching and research.

The Centre did not engage in any undergraduate teaching, as all the students were enrolled for higher degrees. What I found particularly intriguing was the provenance of the students. Only a minority of them were British, and the rest had come from different parts of the world – the continent of Europe, the United States of America, Asia and Africa. Africa was represented by a student from Ghana who occasionally came in to discuss his Ph.D thesis with me. I however got an opportunity of lecturing to undergraduates in the Faculty of English. I was interested to find that English was in a faculty by itself.

For the most part, I was allowed to do my own private research. That left me with enough time to soak myself in the special atmosphere of Cambridge. I spent long hours in the Library and attended as many seminars as I could, particularly Commonwealth and International literature seminars, some of which were open to the public, but others, every Tuesday, which were held in Robert Fraser's rooms in Trinity College.

The African Studies Centre also organised seminars which I attended. That Centre was located on my way to and from work every day, and I made a habit of looking in on my way home in the afternoons. I made use of the library and occasionally had discussions with the Director, Keith Hart. The Centre subscribed to Nigerian newspapers which kept me abreast of developments at home.

On two occasions, I attended public lectures delivered by Nigerians. One afternoon, the secretary to the Centre asked me if I knew that Chief Ernest Shonekan was coming to give a public lecture. I thanked her for the information, and decided that Alice and I would attend, to show the flag. As we approached the venue of the lecture, we noticed an unusually large group of Africans, presumably Nigerians, heading in the same direction. We later learnt that they had come specially from London. If we thought they had come to cheer the lecturer, we were sadly mistaken, for it seemed the purpose of their presence was to object to the lecture – or more accurately, the lecturer. Chief Shonekan had been accompanied to the lecture by the late Ooni of Ife, Oba Sijuwade, and the Ooni's close friend, the late Emir of Kano, Alhaji Ado Bayero. However, the lecture went on as scheduled.

The second occasion was a lecture organised by the Commonwealth and International Literature group. I had noticed from the schedule of seminars that the Nigerian poet, Maja-Pearce, was coming to give a lecture. I went, only to discover that the speaker had come to paint his country in the most unflattering colours. I thought even the home audience was too embarrassed to ask questions.

***

Without any doubt, one of the high points of my sojourn in Cambridge came at Christmas. I had heard so much in the past about the famous service of carols and nine lessons from King's College, and Alice and I thought we should take advantage of being in Cambridge to personally attend the service. Having been warned that the service usually attracted a lot of people, we set out very early, as we thought. But more than an hour before the beginning of the service, there was already a long queue at the door, and we almost despaired. But we joined the queue as it moved slowly, and finally, we were at the entrance. The steward gave us a warm welcoming smile and led us to what I thought were the best vacant seats. It was almost an indescribable experience – the Gothic architecture of the chapel, the solemnity, the boom of the organ and the transporting sound of the choir.

Only one sad incident marred our experience in Cambridge. Weary of spending all day in the flat doing nothing while I went to work, Alice thought she could look for a casual nursing job. Many of her friends in Nigeria who had similarly trained in Britain in fact routinely retuned to Britain every summer to work. There was a small hospital up the road from where we lived; and so, one morning, Alice went up there to make enquiries. The Matron she spoke to could not have been more hostile. As soon as Alice left, the Matron called the police to report an 'illegal immigrant' in the neighbourhood. Next morning, two plain clothes policemen turned up at our flat and started questioning Alice. Two days later, we got a letter from the Home Office ordering Alice to leave the country within two weeks. This, in spite of the very clear explanations made to the two policemen.

I personally wrote a reply to the letter, pointing out that Alice was not an illegal immigrant – not even an immigrant of any description – as she had a valid passport and also a valid visa. I told them that she had accompanied me on my sabbatical at the university. I also immediately got in touch with the Nigerian High Commissioner in London. He wrote a stern letter to the Home Office, which promptly dropped the whole matter.

***

All too soon, my time was up. On my last day at the Centre, Gillian led all my other colleagues to fete me at lunch at Brown's Restaurant next door. They had been such wonderful people and had given me a memorable time.

We returned safely to Ibadan, but before really settling down, I had to prepare for the next phase of my travels which, this time, was to take me to Kristiansand, Norway.

***

Kristiansand was not going to be new to me, as I had been there some twenty years earlier to visit my old friend and former classmate, Peter Young, and his family. But that was in summer, and I wondered what living in Norway would be like in winter.

I indeed arrived at Kristiansand airport on a chilly February morning, and was happy to see Peter. As always, we relived old times as he drove me first to his residence, where I met his wife Lily, and their young son, Thomas. After a hearty meal, Peter drove me to the flat which had been hired for me. It was picturesquely situated in a high-rise building overlooking the fjords. I settled in, but Peter insisted that I should have breakfast with him and the family next morning, after which we would go together to Agder College, where I was to spend the next few months.

***

Kristiansand was even smaller than Cambridge, having a population of only about eighty thousand. It was a very carefully planned city, with streets parallel to or at right angles with one another. I told myself after a few days that I could never get lost in a city like this.

At the College, everyone was friendly, and I guessed that Peter had prepared the way for me. He took me round the English Department and introduced me to every member. Then he took me to the Rector's Office, where I met the Rector, Paul Flaa, who a few weeks later took me out to lunch. Not surprisingly, every one of them spoke impeccable English. I was assigned a cosy room furnished, now expectedly, with a computer. The college itself was located in one huge building and contained a bookshop and a restaurant on the ground floor. On the same floor as the English Department was an excellent library with a large holding of books written in English, which immediately made me comfortable, as I had been afraid that all the books would be in Norwegian.

Apart from giving a few lectures on the English language in Nigeria, I was not required to do regular teaching. Before my arrival, Peter had managed to secure a research grant from the Norwegian Research Council for both of us to press on with our work on the lexicography of Nigerian English.

***

Following the completion of my tenure as Vice-Chancellor at Ibadan, my friend Joop Berkhout, a publisher, had suggested that I should write a memoir recounting my experience, and I had tentatively titled the work *In the Saddle*, which also turned out to be the final title. In the very conducive atmosphere in which I found myself and, more important, given the fact that I was now quite proficient in the use of the computer, I decided to make a start with the memoir. I got absolutely absorbed with it and had written about three-quarters of the book by the time I returned home. At this point, I thought I must purchase my own personal computer, and with Peter's help I got a recommendation from the college's computing centre, which also got me a huge discount on the purchase.

As it turned out, I did quite a bit of travelling while in Kristiansand. I went up to Oslo a couple of times on lecture tours, where I was amazed at the lack of tight security around the king's palace. There was absolutely no fence. I was told that a visitor who had similarly been amazed, had asked the king where his security officials were. Whereupon the king took the visitor to the main entrance to the palace, which gave on to one of the major streets of the city and pointed to the citizens carrying on their business, saying: 'These are my bodyguards!' Coming from Ibadan, a city of well-barricaded private residences, I found this truly remarkable.

My next trip, to deliver a couple of lectures, was to Trondheim University in the north. I was told that this was the ancient capital of Norway where the kings were crowned. The university was much bigger than Agder, and the student life more boisterous. I was lodged in the university guest house from where I walked over to the university's refectory for all my meals. I attached myself to the English Department and saw how the business of the department was being conducted almost completely online. Among the staff was a Ghanaian, who seemed to be having the time of his life.

***

Meanwhile, Lily's parents had taken a liking to me and virtually regarded me as a member of the family. Her father was a highly-cultivated retired naval officer, and her mother gentle and kind. In the summer, Lily's father allowed Peter, who had turned out to be a very confident sailor, to take me in the family yacht to the family cottage at Hillesund, right on the edge of a river. Peter on some occasions simply sat on the bank of the river and caught fish! It was an utterly remote place.

After a few relaxing days we returned to Kristiansand, and I could not help admiring Peter's dexterity as he piloted the yacht towards home.

On another occasion, Peter hired a motorised canoe and we went out exploring the fjords. As we sailed along, we dipped our hands in the water and brought out shrimps, which we ate raw.

While in Kristiansand, I even had a quick trip back to Africa, to serve as external examiner at the University of Swaziland. It was quite a small university but well equipped with a library and other facilities. I was quite surprised to find that about half of the scripts that I moderated had the same surname, and was told that that was the name of the royal family. That gave me the impression that university education was highly privileged in the country.

This, in fact, was my second visit to Swaziland. Some six years earlier, I had attended a meeting of the Vice-Chancellors of Commonwealth Universities in the country, and had been struck by the stunning beauty of the country. On that occasion, we had paid a visit to the young king. He had just been recalled from a public school in England on the death of his father. He was still a teenager, but had already married three wives, the youngest of whom could not have been more than thirteen years old. The young king was very powerful and widely feared.

I had similarly served as external examiner to the University of Botswana. It was also a very small university which had managed to maintain high standards. I also found that the standard of living was quite high in the country.

***

While I was a boy at Igbobi, we had been told about the Kon-Tiki expedition led by a Norwegian named Thor Heyerdahl. The expedition had captured the imagination of the whole world. It was carried out in 1947 in a raft which went across the Pacific from South America to the Polynesian islands. The aim was to prove that people from South America could have crossed over to the Polynesian islands to settle there before the arrival of Columbus in America, despite the lack of the technology to build a modern boat. The experiment proved successful and I had been told that the raft could be viewed in Oslo.

When therefore Bunmi came over from Oxford to spend her Easter holiday with me, I decided that we should go and see Kon-Tiki in Oslo. Helge Ronning, an academic whom I had met through Peter Young, gladly invited us to stay with him in Oslo. The weather was agreeable and we went out to explore Oslo, the city of Nobel, ending up at the museum which housed the Kon-Tiki raft. The technology indeed looked rudimentary and one marvelled at the courage and doggedness of anyone who would commit such a fragile vessel to the fury of the Pacific. But then I recalled that the ancestors of Thor Heyerdahl had been the seafaring Vikings who had, in wave after wave, sailed across the North Sea and harried the English for many years before finally deciding to settle down with their victims by the close of the ninth century AD.

Back in Kristiansand, I re-immersed myself in the manuscript I was working on, but also made time to enjoy the colour, noise and good humour which marked the Norwegian national day.

My time was soon up, and after a series of farewell functions climaxed by a luncheon party hosted by the Rector Paul Flaa, I set out for home by way of London.

Joop Berkhout was glad to hear that my manuscript was all but ready, and in the course of the following year, I was able to hand it over to him. I had done all the typing myself and handed him the disc which, he told me, required no editing. Early in 1997, the book was published and was well received. I particularly enjoyed the reviews which were sent to me from Britain and the United States.

9

BACK IN IBADAN

On my return to the English Department in 1994, I wrote to the Vice-Chancellor, Kayode Oyediran, giving notice of my retirement from the university as I was sixty years old that year.

Kayode replied to my letter and graciously reminded me that the retirement age for professors had very recently been raised to sixty-five. I thanked him for the information but said I had already made plans to retire at that point.

Niyi Osundare, my former brilliant student and now my head of department, offered me the possibility of a contract appointment, but I thought, having declined Kayode's kind offer, it would be immoral to accept, as it would have meant being paid my pension and, at the same time, the remunerations of a contract professor, both payments from the resources of the same university. A week or so later, Niyi came over to tell me that since I would not accept a contract appointment, he was going to take immediate steps to recommend me for appointment as a Professor Emeritus. This carried no salary, but I was delighted to hear that it would entitle me to the continued use of Room 67! I finished off supervising one or two Ph.D students in the pipeline and, thereafter, made myself available every Wednesday to interact informally with staff and students.

***

Though now retired, I kept busy within and outside the campus. One of the commitments which kept me close to the faculty was my membership of the Nigerian Academy of Letters, and of the Ibadan Working Group of the Academy.

Following the Report of the Udoji Commission in 1974, the government had accepted the recommendation that an Academy be set up as an apex organization for scholarship and research in the country. For some time, this recommendation was not implemented, but the scholars in the sciences later began to set up a specific Academy of Science, as opposed to an Academy embracing all disciplines. Later, the scholars in education followed in the footsteps of science, and they managed to get President Babangida to come to the University of Ibadan in 1991 to launch the Nigerian Academy of Education. This was during my vice-chancellorship of the University of Ibadan.

Seeing these developments, three of us in the Humanities – Professor Emeritus Ayo Bamgbose, Professor Dan Izevbaye and myself – decided that it was about time to inaugurate the Nigerian Academy of Letters. Scholars in the other Nigerian universities were informed, and the Academy began to operate informally by holding public lectures. Three of such lectures were given at the University of Ibadan by Professor A. Afigbo, the historian, Professor J.P. Clark, the poet and dramatist and Professor Moses Makinde, the philosopher.

Meanwhile, arrangements were made for the incorporation of the Academy and for the formal launch of its activities on the national stage. The first President of the Academy was

Professor Emeritus Ayo Bamgbose, NNOM, and he was conferred with the title of Foundation President. All scholars in the Humanities who similarly held the NNOM were constituted into the first Fellows of the Academy. From 1998 the Academy has not failed to hold its annual convocation ceremony in the month of August at the University of Lagos. In addition, the Academy has held an annual lecture in February in different universities in the country.

Considering the amount of work necessary to launch the Academy and thereafter to plan the details of its activities, a group of scholars at the University of Ibadan agreed to meet every Wednesday at the University of Ibadan in a room which had graciously been made available by the university. This group later received the recognition of the Academy and has since been known as the Ibadan Working Group (IWG), which has continued to engage in detailed planning and reports to the Executive Committee of the Academy. I have been a member of the IWG from the very beginning, was elected Fellow of the Academy in 2000, President in the same year and gave the Convocation Lecture of 2007 on the subject: The Wages of Obsessive Materialism.

In matters of funding, the Academy of Letters has not been as fortunate as the two Academies that had been launched before it. It is believed that the Academy of Science receives regular subvention from the government, and grants from international agencies; the Academy of Education received a five million grant when it was launched personally by President Babangida. However, all attempts to get regular funding for the Academy of Letters from the government have so far failed. The only indirect support from the government so far has come from the Tertiary Education Trust Fund (TETFUND) in respect of the Academy's publications. Nevertheless, the Academy has been doing its utmost to focus on national problems at its annual lectures and Convocation Lectures, and has a consistent record of publications.

The view of the Academy is that all Academies in the country constitute a highly valuable human resource which, until recently, has been made scant use of by the public and private sectors. The Academy of Letters is, however, doing its best to remedy the situation.

***

At the same time, I have had the privilege of being involved with the Nigerian Literature Prize instituted by the Nigerian Liquefied Natural Gas (NLNG). In 2003, NLNG came up with a brilliant idea to aid research and creativity in the sciences and the humanities. The intention was to encourage scholars to find solutions to Nigeria's problems and to aid innovation generally as well as to spur creativity in Literature. To this end, the company set up a prize for Science and another one for Literature.

It was decided that the Literature Prize should run a cycle of four years spanning the genres of prose fiction, poetry, drama and children's literature. The first Literature Prize was to have been awarded in 2004 for prose fiction, but the Panel of Judges did not find a deserving entry. In subsequent years, however, entries for the prize have been impressive, and the cash prize has steadily risen to $100,000.

NLNG set up an Advisory Committee to oversee the award of the Literature Prize, and invited me to be Chairman. The other two members of the Board were – and still are – Professor Jerry Agada (Vice-Chairman) and Professor Emeritus Ben Elugbe. The Board then annually sets up a Panel of Judges appropriate for the genre in focus. The NLNG provides a secretariat for the meetings of the Board and of the Panel of Judges and, of course, also provides the prize money. But it has to be said to its credit that the NLNG exerts no influence whatsoever on the Board. The Board, in turn, exerts no undue influence on the Panel of Judges. In the fourteen years that the project has been executed, the Prize has been able to maintain its integrity. To further ensure comparability with global standards, the Board obtained the permission of NLNG in 2012 to appoint annually an appropriate external consultant. The final shortlist of three entries received from the Panel of Judges is sent to the consultant, who independently advises the Board on a winner, while the panel at the same time goes on to decide on the winner to recommend to the Board. The Board has been delighted to find that, since the institution of the participation of a consultant, the consultant's choice has agreed with the Panel of Judges'.

In all the fourteen years of the prize, there has been only one real hiccup, and that was in 2009 when, on the advice of the Panel of Judges, the Board was not able to announce a winner for the Poetry Prize. The media, claiming somehow to know better, launched an onslaught on the Board, and even personally on the Chairman, claiming that there ought to have been a winner. The Board however stood its ground, and soon the outcry died down.

That was the second occasion on which the Prize was not awarded. The third occasion was in 2015, when no Prize for Children's Literature was awarded, and this time, there was no upheaval. Both in 2009 and 2015, the money for the Prize was spent on organizing workshops for writers, which proved very successful.

The Nigeria Prize for Literature has indeed generated an encouraging degree of interest in writing and has introduced a fair number of new writers to the scene.

Post-Retirement Responsibilities

But I was not through yet with university administration. In 2000, I was appointed Pro-Chancellor of the University of Port Harcourt. The appointment took me completely unawares.

One evening, I was told that I had a visitor. When he came in, he introduced himself as Professor Nimi Briggs, a medical professor, and the incumbent acting Vice-Chancellor of the University of Port Harcourt. He told me that he knew my brother, Bayo, very well. He had come to see me, he said, because he had just seen the news item on television announcing the new pro-chancellors appointed to the federal universities. As the universities had been named in alphabetical order, he said he had been kept in suspense until it came to Port Harcourt and he saw my name. I was indeed surprised, but noticed what a very pleasant gentleman Nimi was. That first impression was confirmed during my dealings with him in the next five years; and we have, in fact, become firm friends ever since. I came to find that he was not only very pleasant but also thoroughly efficient.

When, shortly after I was appointed, the time came to appoint a substantive Vice-Chancellor, I had no doubt at all that Nimi was it. But the appointment exercise, to my surprise, did not go without a bit of drama. Some elements at the university, for reasons best known to them, had decided to scuttle the exercise. Following security reports, I was advised not to stay in the Pro-Chancellor's Lodge when I went down for the exercise, but to stay in a hotel in town, where the interviews actually took place the following morning. A Council meeting had been summoned for the following day when the report of the interview was tabled and Nimi's appointment was unanimously approved.

We thereafter settled down as a council and helped Nimi to pursue his vision for the university. We were fortunate to have committed members like Mrs Lateefat Okunnu who took their assignment very seriously.

Then one morning, as we gathered for a meeting of council, we got a big shock. The VC was nowhere to be found. I was very puzzled as he had, as usual, called at the pro-chancellor's lodge the previous evening to discuss the agenda of the following day's meeting with me. We sent across to the VC's lodge to find out what had happened and received the unbelievable news that some policemen had come early that morning and taken the VC away! I promptly adjourned the meeting of Council and sent a request to the State Governor, Dr Odili, asking him to receive the whole Council in audience. He graciously agreed, and we made our way from Choba to town. The governor was already waiting for us.

I narrated to the governor what we had learnt had happened to the VC, and wondered whether the governor would be kind enough to enlighten us about what was going on. I added that we had come to reassure the governor of our complete confidence in Nimi Briggs and to say that we could not imagine anything to have caused him seemingly to have been arrested. The governor reassured us that he would find out what was going on, as he never interfered with police investigations. We thanked him and left.

Back in Choba, Council continued its meeting. There we received further details of what had really happened to the VC, given by the VC himself. When he had left me the previous night, he had gone to his lodge to have a late lunch at about nine o'clock. He was still busy having his lunch when he was told that some policemen had asked to see him. He had asked the men what they wanted, and they had replied that they had been asked to bring him to the police station in town – several kilometres away – in connection with allegations which had been made against him. Obviously tired after a long day, he had told them to come back in the morning and they had gone away. The following morning, they had returned and taken him away. At the police station, he had been told the bizarre story that the police had received reports that he was gun-running in concert with some people planning to cause mayhem in the state. Dumbfounded, he had asked to see the report, and then asked to make a photocopy of it. They had allowed him to do so. He showed us the photocopy of a report written in scruffy handwriting and the most inelegant English. They had let him go after he had written his response, and that was why he was able to be with us at the adjourned meeting.

Various interpretations were placed on the incident, but the consensus was that someone, or some people, had planned to frame the VC and possibly eliminate him. Why, it was asked, should the invitation have been brought to him at about ten o' clock at night? Someone praised the VC's presence of mind in not allowing himself to go with them that night. Was it possible that they were planning to eliminate him on the way, claiming that he had tried to escape? Horror of horrors!

The whole matter blew over as mysteriously as it had come about. Presumably, the governor had been able to intervene effectively, and Nimi was left to carry on his good work.

***

The tenure of the Council of the University of Port Harcourt ended in 2005, and in the re-constitution of university councils which followed almost immediately, I was appointed Pro-Chancellor of the University of Ilorin, little realizing what I was in for. My appointment coincided with the height of a crisis at that university, shortly after a number of academic staff had been dismissed. This was after the staff had refused to sign back after a spell of industrial action. The staff concerned had gone to court to challenge their dismissal.

Almost the first mail I received as Pro-Chancellor was from Femi Falana, the aggrieved staff's lawyer, in which he suggested settlement out of court. I was delighted at the offer, hoping that we could speedily bring the bad blood poisoning the university to an end. I discussed the matter with the Vice-Chancellor, Shamsudeen Amali – incidentally a former student of mine at the University of Ibadan – who strongly advised me to ignore Falana's overtures. I was amazed, but thought that he had assumed that the university would win. So the malignancy at the university continued.

A few weeks later, judgment was delivered in the case, and it went in favour of the academic staff. Practically the day after the judgement was delivered, I read in the newspapers that the university had lodged an appeal, about which I knew nothing. Therefore when pressmen came to interview me on the matter at my residence in Ibadan, I told them quite clearly that the university had not lodged an appeal; indeed that the Council had not met to take such a decision. This of course was grist to the mill of the press: the vice-chancellor and the pro-chancellor seeming to be at loggerheads. Alarmed at the developing situation, the Minister of Education, Mrs Obaji, invited the vice-chancellor and myself to Abuja to see her.

In defence of the action he had taken, the vice-chancellor explained that time was of the essence and the appeal had had to be lodged immediately; whereupon the Minister asked him why he had not just picked up his telephone to seek the pro-chancellor's guidance. The vice-chancellor had no answer to that.

My position was that the Council was assigned the responsibility by law for the finances of the university, and lodging an appeal was committing, not the administration, but the Council of the University to unknown expenditures. Lodging an appeal which might possibly go from the Court of Appeal to the Supreme Court – which indeed turned out to be the case - was a matter to be carefully deliberated upon by the Council. The pro-chancellor, rather than the vice-chancellor, had the powers to take executive action on behalf of Council. The Minister appeared to have seen the point, and advised that a meeting of Council should be summoned without delay to deliberate on the matter.

But it turned out that the whole matter was more serious than I had realised. After the vice-chancellor and I had walked out of the Minister's office, she sent for me to come back to see her. She told me that she had never seen me before that day, but that she felt she should tell me that there was a conspiracy against me at the University of Ilorin, and that I should be very careful. I thanked her very sincerely and told her that when I get back to Ibadan, I would forward my resignation letter to her. She pleaded with me not to do any such thing as it might lead to an upheaval in the entire university system, and I would be held responsible for it.

As I was about to leave her office for the second time, one of her officials came in and handed a letter to her. She looked at it and, in turn, handed it to me. The letter was indeed addressed to me, care of the Minster. I opened it and found that it was from the President of the country, Chief Obasanjo, no less, asking me to come and see him about a week from then. The matter was getting 'curiouser' and 'curiouser'. I immediately called an emergency meeting of Council.

Before the emergency meeting of Council, reports began to reach me of the tension on the university campus, and I was told that the other members of Council had taken decisions on the eve of the meeting which might lead to a vote of no confidence being passed on me. Indeed, I was advised by well-wishers to make it a one-day trip to Ilorin and not stay at all in the Pro-Chancellor's Lodge. As if that was not bizarre enough, I was told that, should a vote of no confidence fail, a physical attack on me on my way back to Ibadan was being contemplated. At that point, I was absolutely convinced that there was more to this matter than met the eye.

As the meeting went on, things became clearer to me. As I had decided to return to Ibadan that evening, there was no time for beating about the bush; but a member asked for an item to be added to the agenda, namely, the pro-chancellor's statement to the press in Ibadan. I was sure that was the trigger for the no-confidence vote.

I put the matter very simply to my colleagues on Council: Who had the powers to decide to lodge an appeal in a case against the university: The vice-chancellor or Council? Considering the delicacy of the matter, I went round the table and asked each member individually to answer the question. I did not know what answers to expect, but there were two members whose views I had highly respected. One of them was a Senior Advocate of Nigeria (SAN), and the other was a high official of the Federal Ministry of Education. As I went round, everyone 'voted' for the vice-chancellor, but when I got to the SAN and he also voted as the others before him, I was deeply troubled. Finally, the government official voted with all the others. Without making any comments, I closed my files and pronounced the meeting closed.

A member then asked about the item earlier added to the circulated agenda, and the gentleman who had proposed the addition replied that it was no longer necessary!

I had plenty of time during my drive back to Ibadan to try and make sense of what had happened. Was this an aspect of the conspiracy that the Minister had talked about? Suppose I had insisted on my position and tried to argue my way through in the face of a SAN's opinion, the motion would have been moved that I was on my own and had lost the confidence of Council. The no-confidence vote would have followed, though I had no idea what implication that would have had. Anyway, I still had the appointment with the President to keep.

But before keeping that appointment, more information had filtered through to me from the university which seemed to explain it all. The information I was getting was in two broad parts. First, I was told of the strong resistance to my appointment in the first place. I was told that the Emir of Ilorin had even been approached to get the government to stop it. Apparently, the President had ignored the petition. And what were the grounds of the petition? The first was that I was not a Kwara indigene. The second was that I was not only a Christian but said to be the son of an Anglican priest. The third was that, according to them, I 'hated' Muslims because, as vice-chancellor at Ibadan, I had not agreed to remove the Christian cross to please them. No wonder the President had ignored the objections.

The second part of the information that got to me was to the effect that the President had made it crystal clear, long before my arrival in Ilorin, that under no circumstances should the dismissed staff be reinstated. It was said that this was because the President had been told that the staff concerned had on one occasion gone into an examination venue in the university and torn up the students' answer booklets. This would explain the university administration's attitude to Falana's overtures, but they had not disclosed their motives to me.

On the appointed date for the meeting with the President, I went over first to the Minister's office, as she had asked me to do, and my vehicle followed hers to Aso Rock, the seat of government. We climbed the stairs to the venue of the proposed meeting, but after we had sat for a few minutes, a number of high government officials walked in and sat opposite me on the other side of the table. They were the Attorney-General, the Head of Service and the Executive Secretary of the National Universities Commission (NUC). The Minster of Education, naturally, sat with them. As soon as they were seated, someone came in from downstairs and asked me to follow him. When we got downstairs, he told me that I had not been cleared to go upstairs, and so he gave me a form to fill in, and I returned upstairs. I had, of course, previously walked up with the Minster.

By the time I got back upstairs, the Minister had left her seat. Then to compound the mystery, a camera crew of the Nigerian Television Authority (NTA) came in, panned round the room and left.

I wondered what this was all about. Even if I was about to be relieved of my duties at Ilorin, was it necessary to make such high drama of it? We waited, while the Minister's seat remained vacant. Then after a long while, she returned and resumed her seat. A few minutes after that, the President himself walked in and sat at the head of the table, with all his officials to his left, and lonely me to his right. As he walked in, he surprised everyone in the room by greeting me and addressing me in Yoruba, saying he had not seen me for a long time. Was I being sweetened up before the hatchet? But that turned out not to be the case. After engaging in small talk with me for a few minutes, he rose and made his way out, this time passing behind me. I could not help myself but asked him if I could come to see him at a later date. He replied that that could be arranged.

I gathered later that the real purpose of the meeting had indeed been to relieve me of my duties at Ilorin, and it would have been a news item on the NTA that night – with appropriate footage; but the Minister – bless her – had prevented that from happening.

Apparently, during her prolonged absence from the room, she had gone to see the President to try to persuade him from carrying out the plan, insisting that I was a completely innocent man; and it took her a long time to achieve this, what with the President's chief of staff – an Ilorin man – mounting a fierce opposition to her. I myself had not the faintest idea what I was being accused of. The President had, at any rate, quietly made up his mind and surprised all the officials present when he turned the meeting into a purely social one.

I wondered how I could possibly have a one-on-one interaction with the President, to find out from him exactly what was going on. Then it occurred to me that a very close friend, Professor Ladipo Akinkugbe, might be able to help, as he was often in Abuja helping out with government health policy matters.

On returning to Ibadan I called up Ladipo and told him about the strange meeting that I had just had at Aso Rock, and asked if he could possibly help me to fix an appointment to see the President. He was most willing to help and said he would see what he could do about it.

True to his word, Ladipo called me a few days later to say that he had managed to secure an appointment for me to see the President. More than that, he had arranged for me to be met at the airport in Abuja and taken to a hotel which he had very kindly booked for me. He even gave me a phone number to call on my arrival at Abuja. He truly could not have been more helpful.

I called that number even before embarking at Ikeja airport, just to confirm the appointment, but there was no response. I then had to take a quick decision, ticket in hand, as to whether to abort the journey or to continue in the hope that the arrangements were in place. I decided to press on with the journey. Ladipo – bless him – had indeed sent a driver to meet me at the airport. I asked the driver to take me straightaway to Aso Rock where, at the first barrier, I was asked to wait, to confirm that I did have an appointment. I was later told that my name was not on the register of expected visitors.

By now I was feeling famished. It was already late afternoon, and I had not had any meal since breakfast. I told the driver to head to the hotel where a reservation had been made for me. Fortunately, they had my booking, and once I had settled into the room, I ordered an early supper and then called Ladipo to tell him about my experience at Aso Rock. He said he would find out what had gone wrong and get back to me. I had my meal and waited. After about half an hour, Ladipo rang back to say that my name was now on the register and I should go back there. I told him it was already past nine o'clock in the evening, but he said that did not matter. And so, in a very heavy downpour, I made my way back to Aso Rock. This time, the guards at the gate were most apologetic and let me in.

As I entered, the sight that met my eyes was truly surreal. There was an enormous sitting room filled with people sitting around coffee-tables and presumably waiting to see the President. I was ushered to a seat and asked whether I wanted tea or coffee. I ordered a tea and looked round. Quite a number of people in the room were white, and it was like a night market. Seeing the number of people that had arrived before me, I truly wondered whether I was going to be able to see the President that night, and whether the President was going to have any sleep at all.

***

Adjoining the large sitting/waiting room was what I discovered later to be a very small room where the President received each visitor in audience. He was alone in the little room and came to the doorway personally each time to select who was to be his next visitor. I wondered if he would know the order in which the visitors had arrived because he conducted the whole exercise entirely on his own. After about an hour, he came to the doorway as usual, and I was relieved when he recognised me and said he would see me after the visitor he had just called in. Obviously, it was not 'first come, first served,' as I had been the latest arrival at the table where I sat.

Finally, I was invited into the little room. There were two easy chairs in the room and hardly any space for more furniture. The President led me in and sat in one, beckoning me to sit in the other one. The atmosphere was very relaxed, and almost conspiratorial. Considering the crowd waiting next-door, we went straight to business. I spoke first, telling the President that I could not understand what had been happening to me since I was posted to the University of Ilorin, climaxing with the meeting I had had with him and his officials at Aso Rock.

The President then proceeded to the heart of the matter which, at the end, made everything plain to me. He told me that when pro-chancellors had originally been assigned to universities, I had been assigned to the University of Jos. When the list had come to him for final approval, however, he had personally made an alteration and assigned me to Ilorin because, according to him, he wanted a 'good academic' there. But he had been dismayed to find that as soon as the list was published, people had started coming to him (obviously from Ilorin) to say that the man he had appointed as Pro-Chancellor of Ilorin was, in fact, the Grand Patron of the Academic Staff Union of Universities (ASUU). He had then told them that, clearly, I could not be the Grand Patron of ASUU and at the same time Pro-Chancellor of Ilorin. I even learnt later that the national ASUU was believed to be undermining the government with a view to overthrowing it!

It was now all clear. The local branch of ASUU at Ilorin had broken away from the national body, apparently sure of the firm support of the President. So when the argument between me and Amali arose, the President had apparently been told that it represented an argument between the local union at Ilorin (which allegedly had the sympathy of the President) and the national body, of which I had been falsely labelled as Grand Patron. I was thus portrayed as fighting the corner of the national body. I now realized that that was why, at that emergency meeting of Council, all my colleagues had voted solidly for the Vice-Chancellor. Not to have done so would have seemed to them treasonable, and they were sure that I was on my way out of the job, if not worse.

At this point, I reminded the President of his unsolicited but extremely kind gesture towards me when, as Vice-Chancellor at Ibadan, I had had a dispute with the then Minster of Education who had been set to hound me out of office over the Christian cross. Chief Obasanjo's spontaneous intervention had greatly impressed me and I had felt very grateful. I then asked him if he thought I could now turn round and be part of any possible attempt to overthrow his government. I was sure he did not, and by now I thought he had begun to see through the stratagems of my false accusers. The meeting ended on a cordial note.

I was told some people in Ilorin were nonplussed when they saw me arrive to preside over the next meeting of Council. For my part, I was determined not to let matters degenerate to a breakdown of personal relationships between me and my former student, Amali, and his very competent deputy, Is'haq Oloyede. We worked cordially together until all councils of universities were dissolved in 2007, but not before I had supervised the emergence of Oloyede as the next Vice-Chancellor. He hit the ground running and proceeded to push the university to higher and higher levels.

***

Just about the time that I was being appointed Pro-Chancellor of the University of Ilorin, I received an invitation from the Right Revd G.I Olajide, retired Bishop of Ibadan, to be a member of a planning committee that he was putting together for the establishment of the first Anglican university in Nigeria. The proposed university was to be sited on the grounds of the old St. Andrew's College, Oyo. I was excited at this prospect of returning to Oyo, the town where I had spent the first ten years of my life, to participate in planning the upgrading of the college where my father had, for almost twenty years, been tutor and senior tutor.

We set to work in earnest, meeting in the conference room of the Bishopscourt at Arigidi Street, New Bodija, Ibadan. After many brainstorming sessions, we broke up into groups which were to make proposals to the main body on the philosophy, logistics and funding of the proposed university. We were guided by the requirements provided for us by the National Universities Commission (NUC).

We were fortunate in the composition of the committee. Not only did we have highly respected academics like Professor Emeritus Ayo Bamgbose, a product of St Andrew's College, Oyo and current President of the Old Boys Association (SACOBA), Professor Bolanle Awe, Professor Bisi Sowumi and Professor Tunde Ogunmola, we also had retired Justice Ogunade (another Old Boy of the College) and retired Chief Judge Sidney Afonja who, together, furnished the committee with an excellent draft of a proposed law of the university. We also had Sir Gbolahan Folayan and Toyin Okeowo to advise on the financing of the university.

Under the inspiring leadership of Bishop Olajide, we strove hard to fulfil all the conditions imposed by the NUC. The intervention of Ven. Archdeacon Alayande (affectionately called Papa Alayande), for a long time President of SACOBA, helped us at some critical stages of our planning.

The presence of prominent members of SACOBA on the committee was by no means fortuitous. The idea of a St Andrew's University was first planted in the minds of the members of SACOBA as they gathered to celebrate the centenary of the foundation of their alma mater in 1996 in St Michael's Church, Oyo. On that occasion, the Primate of the Anglican Communion in Nigeria, the Most Reverend Abiodun Adetiloye, in his sermon had challenged SACOBA to think of the upgrading of their alma mater to a university. SACOBA had enthusiastically accepted the challenge and immediately started to mobilize its members.

The question of proprietorship of the proposed university naturally came up, and it was assumed that that role would be best played by the Anglican Communion in Nigeria. In order to confirm our assumption, we arranged to have a meeting with the newly enthroned Primate, the Most Reverend Peter Akinola. He agreed to meet a delegation from us at his private residence in Abeokuta. There, our enthusiasm was somewhat dampened by what he had to tell us. He told us that on a recent first review of the current assets of the Church, he had discovered that the Church was in a very bad way financially and could not possibly play the role that we were inviting it to play.

The fallback position was to invite the western part of the Communion (the Supra-Diocesan West) to take up the responsibility. The leaders of SACOBA had already paved the way for this, and the leaders of the five ecclesiastical Provinces of Lagos, Ibadan, Ondo, Kwara and Bendel had apparently agreed to pick up the gauntlet. Indeed, it was they who had asked Bishop Olajide to constitute and chair the Planning Committee.

As we found out shortly afterwards, this was the point at which the seeds of the early and enduring problems facing the project were planted. While SACOBA understood the Supra-Diocesan West to be accepting the role of proprietor, the Church leaders, it would appear, were merely offering to give SACOBA their moral support while SACOBA, or any other body, would effectively take up the role of proprietor. Of course it was clear that SACOBA could not possibly be expected to play that role. The alternative explanation was that the Church leaders had indeed agreed to be the proprietors but did not realise the responsibilities going with that position.

Undeterred by this conundrum, the Planning Committee pressed on with its work, with Bishop Olajide exhibiting uncommon faith and courage. We assumed that Supra-West was our proprietor and expected it to give seed money to the Planning Committee and, in addition, commit itself to an annual subvention once the university was established. I personally addressed the Bishops on more than one occasion asking them to give maximum support to the institution during the first ten years of its life and thereafter leave it to exist on its own, having built up enough internally generated revenue. It was however frustrating to find that neither of these expectations was fulfilled, and the enormity of the problem stared us in the face. Our proprietors left it to the individual dioceses to provide whatever help they could to the university, and it emerged that dioceses were only prepared to invest in hostel accommodation for the students. This, though very limited, was useful, as we had planned for the university to be fully residential. The investing dioceses were, however, insistent on the returns on their investments, which meant that a substantial portion of the accommodation fees received from students had to be remitted to the investors.

Fortunately, the bishops had their annual conference in January on the campus of the university, and the university took the opportunity to appeal to them to save the university from strangulation. They decided at one point to involve the congregation of every Church in Supra-West by taking special collections in aid of the university. Much later, it was even decided that on a particular Sunday every year, the total collections from every Church should be forwarded to the university. But all this made very little impact on the university's finances.

***

Meanwhile, having got all our documents ready, we had applied to the NUC for a licence to run the university. Everything went smoothly until the NUC informed us that no university bearing a name suggestive of a religious affiliation would be granted a licence. Led by Papa Alayande and Bishop Olajide, we managed to secure an appointment to explain our situation directly to the President, Chief Olusegun Obasanjo.

We were well received by the President and explained to him the background to the projected St Andrew's University. He was happy about the initiative but immediately dropped the bombshell. With the name we were proposing for the university, there was no way we could obtain a licence, he told us. There was a brief silence in the room. Then Papa Alayande, himself a proud alumnus of St Andrew's College, stood up to present a strong argument for letting us retain the name. But the President was unyielding, and then casually asked us: Why not name the institution after Ajayi Crowther, the first African bishop? He might well have added that Ajayi Crowther had been born not too far from Oyo town. Another brief silence. The delegation thought, in unison, that if we had to give up St Andrew's, we could do a lot worse than adopt the name of this icon of our Church. We agreed, and the President even arranged some refreshments for us before we left.

One immediate step we had to take was to retrieve the documents we had already submitted to the NUC and change 'St Andrew's' to 'Ajayi Crowther' wherever it occurred. With that, we were very reasonably assured of a licence.

The expected letter from the NUC eventually arrived, inviting us to come to Abuja to receive the licence on 7 January, 2005. I joined a delegation, this time led by the Archbishop of Lagos, the Most Reverend Ademowo, who received the licence on behalf of Supra-Diocesan West, the Proprietor. We heaved a sigh of relief, even if we had been made to make a concession regarding the name of the university.

The visit to Abuja on this occasion was made memorable by the fact that, owing to severe fog, we were unable to travel back to Ibadan that afternoon after the presentation as had been planned. Having waited at the airport till near midnight, by which time the only option open to us would have been to fly to Lagos and find our way to Ibadan next morning, we were turned away and asked to report early next morning. At this point, Professor Ayo Bamgbose and I found ourselves in the eminent company of Archbishop Ademowo, who was in the same situation with us. He graciously led us to a hotel run by the Anglican Church in Abuja where we had a comfortable night. At the crack of dawn next morning, we were on our way back to the airport. The fog had obviously persisted overnight, and there was utter confusion at the airport. We therefore decided to hire a cab to take us to Ibadan, where Bamgbose and I would alight and the cab would then take the Archbishop to Lagos.

In spite of the length of the journey, we had a pleasant ride to Ibadan, most of the time listening to the Archbishop's anecdotes. He had a service to conduct at the Cathedral in Lagos that afternoon, he told us, and we wondered whether he would make it. We arrived in Ibadan in the early afternoon, and Bamgbose and I made our way to our homes in a jalopy of a cab.

***

Having secured a licence for the university, the Implementation Committee proceeded to set up a Governing Council for the university and invited me to be the pioneer Pro-Chancellor and Chairman. It was a star-studded Council, and we were determined, and had the capacity, to make a difference in university education in the country, if only the funds were available. At the same time, the Anglican Primate of All Nigeria, the Most Rev. Peter Akinola, was appointed pioneer Chancellor of the university.

The new Council advertised for a pioneer Vice-Chancellor and had no difficulty in offering the job to Professor Jire Olaniran. Professor Olaniran had been the last Provost of St Andrew's College as a college of education after the government of Oyo State had taken over the old St Andrew's College. Though himself not an Andrian (i.e. old student of the original St. Andrew's College), he had had a keen sense of history, and had cultivated and retained the support of SACOBA all through his tenure as Provost. When the implementation committee for the proposed university was set up, he had gladly accepted to serve as the secretary, using his time and resources generously to ensure the success of the project.

Later, a pioneer Registrar was appointed in the person of Dr Josephine Oyebanji. Having just left her post as Deputy Registrar at Obafemi Awolowo University, she had come to us with a rich experience in university administration, which helped the administration of the new university to settle down speedily.

Starting modestly with the Faculties of Arts, Science and Social Sciences, plans were made for the systematic growth of the university. Plans were also made for a Faculty of Law, and when these were realised, thanks to the generosity of the Alakijas of Lagos, it turned out to be, as we were told, the best Faculty of Law complex in Africa. Before this, General Danjuma had donated to us a most befitting library. Both benefactions came through the good offices of the chairman of the Board of Trustees, Professor Ladipo Akinkugbe. For our campus further down Ogbomoso Road, we had planned the Faculties of Engineering and Medicine, which are yet to take off.

Meanwhile, the Council had to struggle for the very survival of the university. In spite of the robust support of the Lagos West Diocese, and of a number of individuals, we were nearing the end of our tether. We felt let down by our Proprietor and were forced in desperation to consider taking a loan of one billion naira from any bank that would offer us favourable terms; and that bank turned out to be First Bank of Nigeria. It is worth emphasizing that this loan was obtained, not by the Proprietor but by Council, though two of the Bishops, on their own, kindly provided us with collaterals. The downside, of course, was that we had to devote a considerable proportion of our meagre resources to the servicing of the loan.

With the bank loan, we were able to stabilize our infrastructure somewhat. Water supply improved and solar energy was provided to supply power in the buildings and for street lighting.

But it was not long before problems arose with the management of the hostels, which were developing into a republic within a republic. Against the better judgment of some members of Council, including myself, the management of the hostels was handed to each owner diocese, as that seemed the only way to have the hostels at all. The result was that the staff in each hostel were not part of the university staff, a situation which the students were not slow in exploiting.

The current thinking is that the university should arrange to buy off the dioceses and make the hostels proper halls of residence. Moreover, serious attempts are now being made to provide a secure financial future for the university, and when this has been done, the university will be able to make the envisaged impact on university education in Nigeria.

Within its limited means, the institution has been pulling its weight. After the excellent work of Jire Olaniran as pioneer vice-chancellor, it has had the benefit of the leadership of Canon Professor Kola Jaiyeoba who, on completing his tenure, handed over to the Right Rev. Professor Dapo Ashaju, who is putting all his energy into transforming the university. By this time, I had succeeded Ladipo Akinkugbe as the Chairman of the Board of Trustees.

***

Meanwhile, I have given NLNG notice of disengagement effective from the end of the year 2018 and also, while remaining a member, I have given up office in Educare, a very innovative organization originated by the doctor-artist Tony Marinho. Tony had devoted a great deal of his time and resources to this organization which is designed to add value to the education of school children in the city of Ibadan. My remaining main involvement with voluntary work in Ibadan is my continuing membership of the Initiative for Information, Arts and Culture Development in Nigeria, previously known as the Nigerian Society for Information, Arts and Culture (NSIAC).

NSIAC had come about when the British Council was closing its public library in Ibadan and a group of public-spirited citizens of Ibadan decided, at their own expense, to take over the library and keep it going. It was undoubtedly an ambitious project, but it did help that the Leventis Company, the erstwhile landlords of the British Council, agreed that we should have the free use of the building.

We appealed to other citizens of Ibadan who might be interested in the venture, but with little success. Still we continued, broadening the activities of the Centre as reflected in its new name. Money continued to trickle in, thanks to the efforts of the President of the Board of Trustees, Professor Ladipo Akinkugbe and, very recently, the energy of the current Director, Mrs Femi Bucknor-Arigbede, effectively guided by the deputy chairman of the executive committee, Kolade Mosuro, the famous bookseller. I have served as the chairman of the executive committee for a number of years now. The Centre is surely an asset to the city of Ibadan, and we had hoped that the government of Oyo State would take an interest in it and offer a modest annual subvention. But perhaps that can still happen.

***

Meanwhile, as must have been noticed, I had been seriously considering slowing down on my activities. However, shortly after notifying NLNG of my intention to step down as Chairman of the Advisory Board for the Literature Prize, I received a totally unexpected invitation to serve as the Chairman of the Board of the National Universities Commission. The current Executive Secretary, Professor Abubakar Rasheed, is a scholar that I know very well and for whom I have a great deal of respect. So I accepted the offer, in spite of a serious health challenge which I suffered in July 2017, and from which, through the grace of God and the expertise of the consultants at University College Hospital, Ibadan, particularly Dr Salami, I was swiftly restored to good health. I feel truly blessed.

It is early days yet, but I am impressed by the zeal for reform which pulsates in the National Universities Commission. At the new Board's first formal meeting on 19 April, 2018, I presented an address which is provided as an Annex to this work.

The whole family was thrown into a great turmoil with the passing of Alice on 30 November, 2014, six months after my 80th birthday. For such a closely-knit family, her sudden departure caused a great deal of pain and anguish, but the children have since risen to the occasion most wonderfully, as have the larger Banjo family.

***

Two recent acts of recognition have, on the other hand, to be recorded with great appreciation. In the year 2009, I was put up by colleagues – particularly Munzali Jibril, my former student and erstwhile Executive Secretary of the National Universities Commission – for the ultimate prize in scholarship – the Nigerian National Order of Merit (NNOM). After a slight hiccup, the ceremony took place on 2 December, 2010, and I went up to Aso Rock with Alice to receive the honour. Earlier, in 2001, the country had graciously conferred on me the honour of Commander of the Order of the Niger (CON), which I had gone up with Alice to accept.

Sadly, Alice was not there when the University of Ibadan decided to bestow on me the highest honour in its gifts in 2015. Forty-nine years after I joined the staff of the English Department as a lecturer; forty years after I became a professor in the department; fifteen years after my two-term tenure as Vice-Chancellor, the university graciously put the icing on the cake by awarding me the degree of D.Litt *honoris causa*. The University of Port Harcourt had, ten years earlier, similarly conferred the honorary degree of D.Litt on me. These, together with the Order of Merit and the Fellowship of the Nigerian Academy of Letters, are honours, late in life, which I treasure beyond any others and which give me a profound sense of fulfilment.

At eighty-four, I am still in reasonable shape and hope to continue to play my humble part in elevating the standards of university education in the country.

Ph.D., Ibadan 1969

Ph.D, Ibadan 1969

Ibadan, 1969

With wife and first child, Bunmi

With nephews: David and Layi

At Georgetown University, Washington, USA

Tobago, May 1981

At lunch with students in the Students Cafeteria, U.I., 1986

With the Deans, U.I., 1987

With the UI Pro-Chancellor (L) Alhaji Ciroma, and Chancellor (R) the Oba of Benin

Congress of the National Parent Teacher Association of Nigeria, Lagos, 22nd April, 1999

With family members after a UI Convocation

At the Award of Hon. D. Litt, University of Port Harcourt

In the Department of English, UI

Fellow of the Nigerian Academy of Letters

Induction as Fellow of NAL, 2000

At a NAL Convocation

At the conferment of Hon. D. Litt., University of Port Harcourt

Receiving the CON award from Chief Obasanjo

Some Fellows of the Nigerian Academy of Letters

At a NAL Convocation

With Ayo Bamgbose and Olu Osoba

At a UI Convocation

Congress of the National Parent Teacher Association of Nigeria, Lagos 22nd April, 1999

With son, Tunde, on his graduation day.

With Brother at Bunmi's Graduation

Brother Bayo with Bunmi (and Alice in the background)

Bunmi's Graduation Day

With Val in London

CON Award Day

With Wife, Alice

With Ladipo Akinkugbe

Children and Grandchildren

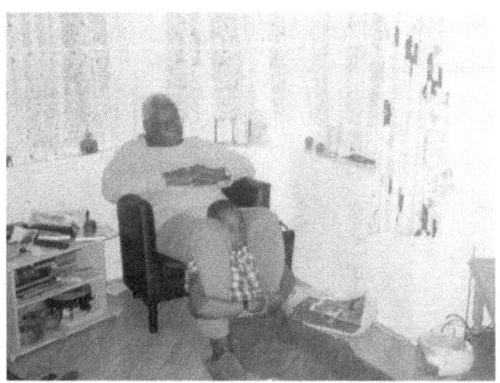
With Gbenga in London

Bunmi and the children in London

With Children in Ibadan

With Grandchildren in London

In London

With Daughter and Children at St. Paul's Cathedral, London

Yinka with Bunmi, Gbenga and Tobi

With Gboyega, Brother Bayo and Tobi, Gbenga and Dupe

Yinka and her uncle

Papa with his great grandchildren

With Dupe, Tobi and Gbenga in London

In Barbados

At the beach in Barbados

At a Niece's Home, London

A family get-together

On the steps of St. Paul's Cathedral, London

70th Birthday, 2004

Alice

David, Nephew at his wedding

Tunde, at Call to Bar

With Takena Tamuno and Joop Berkhout

With Joop Berkhout

With Subomi Balogun

The girls with their uncle

With brother (and Gbenga)

Bunmi and Yinka

St. John's, West Hendon, London

At brother's wake

Bunmi on her wedding day

Bunmi and Yinka

Yinka

Lagos, 15th August 2000

Abuja, June 2002

On my 70th birthday

With Jide Desalu

With Kayode Oyediran

With Jide Desalu and Gay Odia at Igbobi College

Old Igbobi Classmates

Alice at a family wedding

At Home

With Subomi Balogun

At St. Paul's Cathedral, London

2008, With Ayo Bamgbose and Kayode Oyediran

Dapo

Alice with Chief Akomolafe

With Brother, Bayo

With Biola Irele

Abuja, June 2002

With brother (Dr. Bayo Banjo) &
sister (Mrs. Tokunbo Ogunbawo)

Lakeside House, Surrey

Pro-chancellor, Ajayi Crowther University, Oyo

EPILOGUE

As I look back over the years, I cannot help calling to mind the changes that have taken place in me as related in the foregoing pages, but also in the country, Nigeria.

When I was born, Nigeria was a colony of Great Britain. As I write this, the country has arrived at the position of a deeply troubled independent republic. How has this transformation taken place? In one sense, there has, undoubtedly, been an enormous progress. There has been a population explosion, which one would have expected to aid economic development. But unfortunately, the middle class has not grown proportionately with the total population.

The elite of Lagos, made up largely of the earliest professionals in the country, were so few that boys like me knew their names, their residential addresses, and even the registration numbers of their cars. This obviously provided a lot of inspiration. Among the elite were such names as Herbert Macaulay, Dr Nnamdi Azikiwe, Mr Ernest lkoli, Sir Kofo Abayomi, Sir Adeyemo Alakija, Mr Olorunnimbe and a number of other prominent figures. In the Provinces, such names as Obafemi

Awolowo, Sir Francis Ibiam, Ahmadu Bello and Tafawa Balewa began to be heard consistently.

With the presence of such men in the country, it was a matter of time before agitation for independence emerged and political parties began to be formed. Hopes were kindled for a free and prosperous country which would be the redemption of the black race.

As the colonial government found the demand for independence irresistible, arrangements were made in London for the leaders of the Regions – Ahmadu Bello, Awolowo and Azikiwe – to have a series of meetings in that British city to decide what form an independent Nigeria should take. This was a very significant step, because it followed the procedure by which federal governments had emerged in different parts of the world, namely, by federating units establishing federal governments and determining their relationship with them. It indicated that the federating units owned the federal government rather than the federal government owning the States to the extent of creating as many States as it pleased and thereby generating rancour in the land.

A true federation was thus set up after independence, leaving the States, which were the federating units, with a large measure of independence. These units each had their own constitutions distinct from the constitution of the federation. Each had its own Chief Justice and its own police force. Not surprisingly, healthy rivalry was engendered and the pace of development gathered momentum. In the Western Region, for example, where free primary education had been established even five years before independence, the rate of development was phenomenal, with impact felt particularly in the areas, apart from education, of health services and agriculture.

One remarkable feature of this period of the nation's development was that the various leaders in the States managed to gather around themselves the most competent people – the brightest and the best-available. Nigerians trained abroad and at the nation's only university at Ibadan – soon to be joined by the Universities of Nsukka, Ahmadu Bello, Lagos and Obafemi Awolwo were enthusiastically pressed into service to ensure success for the venture. The measure of the patriotism of these political players could be seen in the fact that many, if not all, of the members of the State Assemblies held on to their primary jobs and only received allowances for attendance at the Assemblies.

How was the dream shattered? The conventional wisdom is that the steep decline was set in motion by the military intervention of 1966, followed by the internecine three-year war of 1967 to 1970. This is largely true, but does not represent the whole truth. The ominous signs were discernible before the army struck. It was evident in the unhealthy rivalry building up among the regional leaders. Azikiwe was unhappy at not being allowed to lead the government of Western Region. The pace at which Western Region under Awolowo was developing was said to make the other leaders uncomfortable.

Agitations for more States in the north and the south erupted, and the manner in which the leaders responded showed that Awolowo was a marked man. While the North and the East decided that Midwest Region should be created, presumably to clip Awolowo's wings, nothing was done about the equally vocal demands for a State in the country's middle belt or in the minority areas of the East. It was clear that rather than cooperating to ensure the country's rapid development, the leaders were beginning to fight their own seemingly ethnic battles. Awolowo ended up being humiliated with a prison term until he was released by the military government of Yakubu Gowon, and he then joined in prosecuting the Biafran war, to the great displeasure of the separatists.

Things began to slide so rapidly that idealistic young army officers decided to do something about it. Unfortunately, their plans misfired and ironically ended up by intensifying ethnic animosities.

The situation was worsened by the ensuing military regime, which brought instability to the country because of the incessant coups. Moreover, the army, never having had training in statecraft, were inclined to impose the command structure of the army on the country. The basis of creating more States, until today there are thirty-six of them, was not always clear; and in any case, the effect has been to impose a unitary system of government on the country.

Deterioration became evident in every department of governance, particularly in the management of the economy and in the administration of education.

It is well known that, before the end of the military regime, the country had received an enormous boost to its economy as a result of oil sales. It would appear that the military rulers did not know what to do with this bonanza. That being the case, the rulers settled down to enriching themselves. Greed inevitably set in, hotly pursued by corruption. The country accepted with equanimity the anomaly of a military regime and hoped that with the return of civilian rule, the country would be returned to the path of economic development with the appropriate use of the oil revenue.

If anything, the situation worsened with the return of a civilian regime. The new rulers did their best to copy the arbitrariness that had characterized the military experience. Worse still, they seemed not to know what to do to harness and grow the economy. A mind-boggling national assembly was set up to gobble up the nation's resources. Greed continued unabated, and corruption became more or less institutionalized.

The country had missed the opportunity, hopefully not for good, to deploy its oil wealth to building a strong infrastructure and establishing an enduring education system which would have lifted the masses out of abject poverty and released their energies to intensify national development.

Interestingly, it was not as if the leaders were unaware of the right thing to do; what was amiss was either the ability or the willingness to do it. Scholars in and out of the universities were very active in analysing the nation's problems and proffering solutions, but little heed was paid to them. In education, for example, which was central to any efforts to effectively develop the country, a sad confusion arose, particularly in the supposedly pace-setting Western Region, between access to education and the genuine building of human capital.

An attack seemed to have been aimed, on ideological grounds, at the elite schools – King's College, lgbobi College, CMS Grammar School, Methodist Boys High School, in Lagos; Government College and the lbadan Grammar School in lbadan – and similar institutions up and down the country. The governments took over the schools and reduced them almost to shambles. The number of schools was multiplied producing barely literate boys and girls at the end of their secondary school careers who swiftly returned in many cases to a state of complete illiteracy.

At the federal level, the government similarly took over the universities that had been established by the regional governments in lbadan (later moved to lfe), Nsukka and Zaria. Everywhere, the government was biting more than it could chew.

Meanwhile, huge sums of money were spent on universal primary education and, later, universal basic education, with results that were not at all commensurate with the expenditures. Instead of listening to scholars at home, the government listened to foreign experts who advised them to divert expenditures from the universities to the primary schools. And that was the beginning of the decline of the universities, some of which had been leaders in the Commonwealth.

When the government held negotiations with the staff of the universities in 2000, one of the recommendations was that the country should, in accordance with the cited recommendation of

UNESCO, devote 26% of its annual budget to education. There was an immediate outcry from some quarters. The government itself was not comfortable with the recommendation, and its advisers asked for proof that such a recommendation had ever been made by UNESCO. Other ministers in government asked for the same percentage on health, on agriculture and other budget heads, thereby ridiculing the recommendation. It was in vain that the negotiating parties, incidentally under my chairmanship, pointed to Awolowo, who had reputedly devoted about 40% of the Region's budget to education to execute the free primary education scheme in Western Region. It was reported that when that amount proved not to be enough, he had imposed an education tax which many citizens enthusiastically paid because they could see the transformation being brought about to their lives. Attention was also drawn to contemporary Ghana which was devoting a similar percentage to education. Twenty years later, Nigerians were flocking to Ghana to take advantage of the education system there. Difficult as it may seem, a bold decision has to be made on this matter, realizing that the dividends are unquantifiable and pervasive in their effect over the rest of the economy.

The other question is whether more money should be spent on basic education than on tertiary education. This discussion is often rightly reduced to the chicken-and-egg syndrome. Obviously, we cannot have a sound and productive primary and secondary system without a sound tertiary system. People who argue otherwise seem to forget that, ideally, all teachers at the secondary level should be graduates, while the teachers at the primary level are produced by university graduates. At the same time, of course, good products from the primary and secondary tiers obviously strengthen the universities. The tragedy of the recent past is that neither the universities nor the other tiers have managed to impact one another fully and meaningfully. There are enough experts in the universities and in the Nigerian Academy of Education who can be challenged to produce a bespoke model of education for the country and save it from shopping around the world for models.

At the moment, the only passable primary and secondary schools in the country are privately owned. The public system, and the majority of the privately-owned schools too, are highly unsatisfactory, though some States are beginning to remedy the situation. For a start, models for construction and maintenance of the schools should be prescribed and enforced by the governments. Mandatory features should include well-designed structures with functional toilets and running water. Spacious playground should also be required and, in the case of secondary schools, access to sporting facilities, whether on site or nearby, should be made compulsory. Most of these were standard features of schools in the pre-independence era.

In contrast, the government goes to great lengths to prescribe the lay-out of universities regarding physical features, adequate facilities and staffing etc. Yet no such prescriptions seem to be made with regard to primary and secondary schools. It needs to be emphasized in particular that children go to primary school not just to learn to read and write but, more importantly, to be acculturated to a civilized mode of living; and an enabling environment has to be provided.

The Nigerian Academy of Letters has as its mantra: 'Development is about people', and it is about time the governments took this to heart. Once the people are developed, and keep developing themselves, development in other spheres will follow, and myriads of societal problems will be resolved, not just by the governments, but by the populace itself.

The future of the country fills all thinking Nigerians with forebodings, but as the country prepares for new elections in 2019, the line seems to be firmly drawn between those who desire a root-and-branch reform, and those who are content to leave things as they are and prayerfully await a *deus ex machina*.

Appendices

Appendix 1

∞∞∞∞

Time to Pause and Reflect
Professor Emeritus Ayo Banjo,
NNOM Chairman, Board of the NUC

First of all, I should like to congratulate all of you for the honour and privilege of being appointed to this new Board of the National Universities Commission.

It is my hope that we shall work assiduously and harmoniously to bring about a much-needed improvement in our country's university system.

Next, I am grateful to have this opportunity of addressing this highly distinguished group on a subject that is dear to all our hearts for, in a non-trivial sense, the future of this country lies in our collective hands.

The Nigerian University System

The Establishment of Universities

I do not have to persuade an audience of this calibre of the importance of education to the total development of a nation, nor to demonstrate the crucial importance of a sound system of higher education, not only to the lower tiers of education, but indeed to everything that happens in a country. Nigeria has come a long way since the first university institution, University College Ibadan (UCI), was established in 1948. Not only do we have now over a hundred universities in the country – and the number is growing – but the variety has also grown, from UCI established by the colonial government of the day, to a mixture of federal and state universities, and finally to these two categories of public universities strengthened with the establishment of private universities. Understandably, access to university education had begun to loom large in the minds of the authorities.

Perhaps we should first of all pause and consider the justification for this impressive growth in numbers and variety. We recall the meticulous planning that preceded the founding of UCI, and the elaboration of the rationale for taking this bold step. We may also recall that some of the country's political leaders at that time did complain that, even at that stage, Nigeria needed more than one university. Left to them, they would have sought for balance and political correctness by having one in each of the constituent regions of the country. But the costs of establishing a university institution which would bear the name of the University of London naturally weighed heavily on the minds of the colonial government of the day. Gradually, however, the first generation of universities emerged, taking its cue from UCI, except for Nsukka, which took its inspiration from the United States of America, thereby enriching the Nigerian university culture.

However, the preoccupation with access led the government of the day in the 1970's to create seven new universities without any visible planning. But then, that was the era of military government. Once this floodgate had been opened, however, another seven new universities were added in the 1980's, again without any visible careful planning. The consequence of this rapid development was, not unpredictably, that the funding of the existing universities began to decline dramatically, until it intermittently reached a crisis point. Undoubtedly, we are here up against the old tension between access and quality, a tension which remains with us even today, and which we must have a rational way of resolving.

There is no way of running an acceptable – not to talk of a first class – university with grossly inadequate funds. Vice-chancellors have repeated this all the time, but the authorities seemed to believe that there was a way of squaring the circle without adequate funding. One remedy that they decided upon was to open the system to private participation. But this has not quite solved the problem because, even as private universities were opening, the federal government continued to open more universities of its own. The result would appear to be, not private/public collaboration, but duplication, which has resulted in an alarming number of unemployed graduates. What remains apparent is an absence of clear planning. Instead of collaborating with the private sector to ensure that universities are evenly spread across the country, the federal government appears to be pursuing a policy of spreading universities across the country on its own. The financial crisis in the federal universities has thus remained hardly abated.

In addition, the inequity of a system in which some students enjoy tuition-free university education, not necessarily because they are the best material, while others have to pay heavily for it, also needs to be resolved. The private universities, meanwhile, have been seeking support from the federal government, arguing, for example, that they should be eligible for financial support from TETFUND. Only one or two of the private universities appear at present to be financially buoyant; so the funding problem cuts across the whole spectrum.

The Funding of the University System

I have, in a 1997 convocation address at the University of Uyo (In Olayinka, ed. 2014), made a revolutionary suggestion of solving the problem, or at least mitigating it holistically, by involving every tier of government, and the beneficiaries themselves, in the funding of every university. Each of them would contribute according to an agreed ratio. Perhaps this suggestion can still be examined to see if it can help towards a solution to the problem.

Governance of the Universities

The federal universities are situated, naturally, under the purview of the federal ministry of education, which represents the proprietor. Following the first wave of new universities, the federal government deemed it expedient, in 1974, to set up the National Universities Commission as a body corporate, through an Act. Thus, at last, a mechanism for the planning and upkeep of the university system was set up. It should be observed, however, that the government seemed to have only the federal universities in mind at this time, though that was not explicitly stated. When state universities came on board, no such mechanism was set up for them by their proprietors, and such universities were, in effect, part and parcel of the state ministries of education, and seemed to be run directly by the state commissioners for education.

University Autonomy

It had been found in the older universities in other parts of the world that, in order to be maximally innovative, a university must enjoy a certain degree of autonomy. Such autonomy extends to the setting up and maintenance of academic standards, the appointment of staff and admission of students, the internal administration of the institutions and the operation of their finances; all this, of course, under the laws of the country.

Such autonomy was enjoyed by UCI for the first twenty years of its life. During that period, the two successive vice-chancellors were appointed by the Governing Council of the university. Then came the successive military governments with their military mindset. The law of UCI was brusquely amended by the then head of state and, among other things, vice-chancellors now had to be appointed by the government. This military attitude to the universities was countered by the growth of militant unionism by academic and non-teaching staff; and thus began an era of intermittent breakdown of communication between the government and the universities. Happily, the situation is now improving, and councils have again been empowered to appoint vice-chancellors for their universities, The issue of funding, the other enduring flashpoint, however, remains a sore point.

The argument over autonomy can be explained in terms of a simple misunderstanding of the meaning of the term in a university setting. For example, one government official was reported to have said that 'who pays the piper dictates the tune', which elicited the quip from within the universities to the effect that the tune sounds a lot better when dictated by the piper himself! However, recent trends are reassuring, though there is still a considerable way to go.

Academic Autonomy

As to academic autonomy, this has always been guaranteed. There may, however, have been some grey areas, such as the minimum standards document provided by the NUC, and which, apparently, some universities take to be the curriculum to be strictly followed. The emphasis is, of course, on 'minimum', and the document is obviously intended to guide universities, particularly the new ones, in designing their own curricula.

Student Admissions

More problematic, perhaps, is student admissions. While universities are absolutely free to handle postgraduate admissions, the admission of undergraduates is done through a 'third party'. Some conflict has been observed between the law which empowers JAMB to do this and the laws of the universities which vest the senate of universities with the power to admit all students. However, the situation has so far been imaginatively handled, and no students are imposed on universities.

Financial Autonomy

Unfortunately, the universities would appear to have suffered a setback with respect to financial autonomy. At the beginning, UI's subvention for a whole session was paid up front. This enabled the institution to plan its finances with certainty and even invest some of the funds. As time went on, however, grants were paid on a 'term' basis, and even sometimes in arrears. The difficulties posed for the universities can be imagined.

Moreover, Ibadan and the other federal universities had been able, through the relevant committees of council, to award contracts for the development of the universities. By the beginning of the current century, however, universities were ordered in this respect to follow the practice in the civil service, which is rather cumbersome and cuts off the councils of the universities from having a say in this important aspect of university governance.

Public Perception of Nigerian Universities

It is worth asking: What does the Nigerian public think of its universities? While all Nigerian parents ardently desire to have their children attend university, they observe some unsatisfactory features of the institutions at present. In many cases, they are disappointed with the prevailing atmosphere in the universities, which lacks the kind of serenity and seriousness of purpose found in the best universities in the world. One cause of this, surely, is the prevailing 6:3:3:4 model of education delivery adopted in the country, which makes it possible for fifteen and sixteen year olds to enter university, bringing with them their secondary school habits. If the overwhelming majority of entrants were to come in with 'A' levels, the situation is bound to improve. This was the practice at Ibadan in its halcyon days. In this connection, it may well be worth considering encouraging as many secondary schools as possible to go up to sixth form and provide a firmer basis for university entrants. As it is at the moment, there is serious disquiet, particularly among employers of graduates, about the competence of fresh graduates.

Added to this is the unsatisfactory arrangement regarding accommodation, which leaves a lot to be desired in quantity and quality. Most universities appear overwhelmed by this problem; yet a satisfactory solution has to be found.

University Calendar

To compound the problem, parents increasingly find that they cannot predict how long a four-year course will take their wards to complete. This is due to union activities at staff and student levels, and this situation demands very serious attention if Nigerian universities are to conform with global norms. Apart from the problem that this creates for students and their parents, it has a serious effect on the academic staff, who cannot attend the many academic conferences on offer in the northern hemisphere during the summer months, with telling effects on the quality of research and teaching in the universities.

Underlying all this instability, of course, is the chronic shortage of funds.

Financial Autonomy

There was a misconception at one stage that financial autonomy for the universities meant that the institutions should be made to source all their funding from outside the government, which is the proprietor in the case of federal universities. This led to a meeting of pro-chancellors with the President of the day and his officials, in the early 2000's, at which I was asked to chair a committee to look into this important matter of funding.

The committee conducted extensive research and determined the real cost of producing graduates in the different disciplines, and then arrived at a total cost of running each university. The recommendation of the committee was that, to begin with, the government should provide each of its universities with 70 per cent of those total costs, while each university should internally generate the remaining 30 per cent. The committee added that, as time went on, internally generated revenue (IGR) would increase in the universities and the subvention from the government would go down correspondingly until, perhaps, it stabilized at about 20 percent. Unfortunately, nothing came of these recommendations, and the financial conundrum persisted.

The University Committee System

One area which appears sacrosanct, however, is the running of the universities through their own tested committee system, though there was a period when government circulars for civil servants were routinely sent to the universities. This practice was stoutly resisted, as much by the staff of the universities as by their governing councils.

University Councils

The logical end of the current trend regarding autonomy, surely, is to put the university councils firmly and unambiguously in charge of the running of the universities. For this to take place, however, a number of steps must necessarily be taken. The first step, obviously, is to ensure that councils have an optimum degree of capability and capacity to do the job. It is derisively – and, I am sure uncharitably, in many cases – claimed that many members of council are awake only when there are contracts to be awarded.

Federal university councils are set up by the federal ministry of education, and it would be helpful if the ministry were to draw on the large pool of competent people in the country to constitute the councils, leaving the NUC to perform the necessary oversight functions. The NUC, in turn, should be a repository of all information relating to university education and should stand ready to offer advice, particularly to the younger universities. With this kind of arrangement, there need never be the necessity for direct interface encounters between the government and university unions. Each council should resolve its internal problems and, when necessary, take up unresolved problems with the NUC which, in turn, if necessary, would relate to the ministry. On its part, the NUC has a ready reservoir in the nation's academies to help it in ensuring the highest standards in all its undertakings.

The question may be asked as to the limits of the powers of council under such a dispensation. Can we go to the extent of, for example, asking each council to decide the salary structure of the staff? Those who think that they should, argue that salaries should ideally be tied to local cost of living; but the problem is that this is generally not the practice in this country, though there would be nothing wrong with the universities leading the way.

Global Perception of Nigerian Universities

The fact that all universities in the world operate within a global context has been brought home more forcefully to us in recent times by the phenomenon of global rankings of universities. The idea is that, though universities may differ in character between one country and another, and even within the same country, they all have the common purpose of seeking knowledge, of creating new knowledge and of disseminating knowledge in the most effective manner. The point has been made that there is a cultural bias in the criteria currently being used, and in the weighting of those criteria, by the ranking entities; but we are reassured that active work is still going on to refine those criteria and, hopefully, make them even more culturally inclusive. In the end, though, each country, in addition to being ranked globally, will have to do its own internal rankings, as many countries, like Britain, already do.

Recently, the latest world rankings were released by QS (Quacquarelli Symonds), an entity in UK which started its rankings in 2004. It is remarkable that only two African countries feature, in low positions, in the rankings, namely South Africa and Kenya. It is even more remarkable that a university in Singapore which is only twenty-six years old features more prominently, and is expected to move into the top one hundred before long.

Fortunately, the NUC has bought into the idea of university rankings, to promote excellence here at home. It remains to be seen how different the criteria to be employed – and particularly the weighting of those criteria – will be, to suit the local environment. It is, however, unlikely to be so radically different that our universities will be portrayed as pursuing completely different objectives from the universities in the rest of the world. We will profit, therefore, from examining the criteria employed by QS.

The criteria used by QS, together with the weighting attached to each of them, are six in number, as follows (*www.thechronicleofeducation.com*):

1. Academic reputation   40%
2. Employer reputation   10%
3. Staff:student ratio   20%
4. Citations per faculty member 20%
5. International faculty ratio 5%
6. International student ratio 5%

A cursory look at the above data explains why no Nigerian university is even in the top 500 of the rankings.

When we talk of academic reputation, the older universities clearly have an advantage. The oldest university in Nigeria is still less than seventy years old whereas the universities which feature regularly in the top twenty positions tend to be old universities like Cambridge (founded 1209), Oxford (founded about 1096) and Harvard (founded 1636). But it is worth noting that a relatively younger university like MIT, founded in 1861, currently occupies the top position; so age need not determine everything. Nevertheless, one may legitimately question why as high a percentage as 40 should be attached to this criterion. The lesson we can learn is that, globally, academic reputation is considered very important indeed.

Employer reputation is not clearly defined and is, in any case, a criterion that must be considered culturally skewed in favour of industrialized societies. If it refers to the reputation that a university has as an employer, by way of attractive conditions of service, this is justifiable, but in a country like Nigeria, the opinions held by employers of the products of a university would also be a desirable criterion. We unfortunately have to accept the fact that Nigerian universities at the moment do not measure very well even in this latter respect.

Staff:student ratio carries 20%, the second highest percentage, and rightly so, as it indicates the degree of effective teaching and learning. A high staff:student ratio makes it possible to operate with small tutorial groups or even, as in some universities, with assigning a tutor to each student.

Another 20% is assigned to citations per faculty member. This encourages universities to place a high premium on the excellence of their academic members of staff. It encourages the staff to publish seminal works. This emphasis is unexceptionable, and a university ignores it at its own peril.

No true university can thrive in isolation. To prevent insularity, both staff and students need to be exposed as widely as possible to different world cultures, and to as many divergent viewpoints as possible. This criterion carries 5% but is clearly related to the sixth and last criterion, which also carries 5%.

The final criterion is international student ratio, which emphasizes the importance of students living and studying in an international setting to develop a broad world outlook. This criterion, together with the previous one listed above, emphasizes the essential international essence of the university enterprise and together, they attract 10%.

This is not the occasion to embark on a detailed critique of the practice by QS and other rankings entities, all of which, even considering their objectives, are basically similar. Rather, we should consider the implications of these rankings for the management and development of our own universities.

It is all too clear that the basic determinant of excellence is adequate funding, without which none of the criteria discussed above can be met to any appreciable degree. It takes money to build up a reputation, to which, really, the other criteria contribute – an international mix of staff and students; attractive conditions of service to attract scholars from all parts of the world, and an optimal system of course delivery.

We may recall that Ibadan, in its first twenty years, showed promise of scoring high on each of these criteria, and the other universities of the first generation took a cue from Ibadan. The universities were, indeed, international centres of learning and research, and the salaries were adequate for both local and expatriate academic staff. For some time, when salaries began to be inadequate, Britain helped by offering its nationals on the staff at Ibadan supplementary emoluments payable into their accounts in Britain. The oil boom came, and the supplementation was withdrawn. Expatriate staff petered out in the universities, and it is possible that there are now scores of Nigerian universities which are completely without expatriate staff, or expatriate students, for that matter. These are matters on which we must spend considerable thoughts as we reform and shape our university system in coming years.

Ayo Banjo
April, 2018

Appendix 2

∞∞∞∞∞

Summit on Elements of Statutory Governance, Procurement and Financial Accounting in Nigerian Universities

An Overview of the Nigerian University System
Ayo Banjo NNOM, FNAL,
Chairman of the Board of NUC

In order for the Nigerian university system to deliver fully on its mandate, it is important to keep it under constant review, especially on those important occasions when the universities receive new Councils under new pro-chancellors. This collaborative effort by the NUC, the Committee of Pro-Chancellors and the Committee of Vice-Chancellors of Nigerian Universities is a welcome step in this direction.

The remit of the summit is expectedly wide, but with emphasis on financial matters. I have been asked to provide an overview of the system as a background to the specific issues that will be discussed by other speakers.

On November 17 this year, the university system in Nigeria will be seventy years old. As university systems go, therefore, ours can be regarded as still being in its infancy; and while it is expected to exhibit appropriate innovations here to appropriate the global system to local existing circumstances, it is necessary to bear in mind the important fact that universities all over the world bear the same basic responsibilities, which are to preserve knowledge, to create new knowledge and to find the most efficient ways of disseminating that knowledge among its students.

Excellence is an attribute that all universities aim at, in teaching, research and organization of the university community. Excellence in research means that the academic staff are engaging in the business of creating new knowledge which, apart from being desirable in itself, also holds out the possibility of the new knowledge being applied to the problems of the society. Excellence in teaching holds out the prospect not only of the present researchers replacing themselves, but also provides for the society a constant stream of individuals whose intellect has been consciously developed and who can turn that fine intellect to any of the professions of their choice. And finally, excellence of the university environment entails the provision of a suitable atmosphere, for staff and students alike, which is conducive to prolonged meditation.

University College Ibadan, when established in 1948, was fortunate, through the University of London, in having founders who strongly believed in excellence. Indeed, some politicians at the time had thought that the country already needed more than one university institution and that, in any case, it would have been more politically correct to have three, to satisfy each of the three political Regions of the country. But the University of London would not lend its name to what would have resulted in watering down the excellence. The colonial government of the time then proceeded from the beginning, to make the college a world class university institution. Scholars were assembled from all corners of the world, and the doors of the college were thrown open to students from all over West Africa, and somewhat later, all parts of the world. A beautiful parkland campus was in place.

It is also worth noting that the colonial government, having established a university institution in Ibadan, to which the most promising students from all over the country were admitted, followed up with the establishment of a three-campus College of Arts, Science and Technology, this time managing to be politically correct. We should also note the ratio of one university institution to three colleges of technology, and note further that the three colleges of technology were made complimentary, so that engineering was available only at the Enugu campus, architecture at the Zaria campus, and business studies at the Ibadan campus. All campuses, at the same time, offered 'A' level courses which provided entrants to Ibadan and other universities inside and outside Africa, thus facilitating the political integration of the country.

We may ask at this point: What is the duty of a university? The current popular formulation is: teaching, research and public service. In a sense this is true, but it is important to examine what comes under the rubric of teaching. From mediaeval times, students have been very important products of universities. Particularly in developing countries, governments are now insistent on universities which are 'relevant', defining relevance in terms of what the university contributes to aid the country's economic development. In Europe, the idea that universities should be agents of national development only goes back to the eighteenth century, following the industrial revolution. Before then the motto was, basically, 'education for the development of the intellect.'

Even though today every university attempts to be relevant, the duty of a university is not just to produce professionals who can walk straight from the university into a profession for which they are immediately well suited. Except for academic professionals, it is possible to produce other professionals from outside the university. One can be a lawyer, a doctor, an engineer without attending a university. Presumably, a lawyer, doctor, engineer produced by a university is expected, in addition to whatever training he has received, to have had his intellect developed, simply by having been to a university.

In an early response to the growing strident demand for relevance, Cardinal John Henry Newman, in his seminal book *The Idea of a University* published in 1852 affirms that "the ideal university is a community of thinkers engaged in intellectual pursuits not for any external purpose but as an end in itself." Many a leader in developing countries would be horrified by this affirmation, but indeed a graduate who cannot think properly is unworthy of his degree. After the university makes a good thinker of him with a bias towards the medical sciences, a tertiary hospital makes a good doctor out of him. Certainly, if a graduate doctor turns out to be an incompetent surgeon, you blame the tertiary hospital, not his university, for it.

In answer to the question, what is the soul of a university? Sophia Deboick, writing recently in the *British Guardian* newspaper, says, "A university's soul lies in the mark it leaves on students," adding for good measure, "Narrow specializations produce narrow minds."

The first generation Nigerian universities were able to come close to Newman's ideal, but by the close of the twentieth century, a sea change had come over the system, brought about by a blurred focus and desperate underfunding.

The general feeling among the Nigerian population is that the university system is performing below expectation. There is no meaningful calendar anymore, except in a few private universities. The quality of products is called to question because of the fall in the quality of research and teaching. The system was once able to cream off the best graduates and train them for a career in the universities, but not anymore, given the vibrancy of the private sector. A summit of the leaders of the universities such as one gathered here surely has its job cut out for it bringing about appropriate remediation of the situation; and I am glad that finance features on the programme.

No university can successfully operate outside the global system, and so there are currently strenuous efforts by universities to occupy as high a position as possible on the global rankings. We may argue about the criteria – and the weighting of those criteria – by current ranking entities, but we ignore what they do at our peril. While the entities are attempting to refine their systems, it is gladdening to know that the NUC intends to firmly establish the local rankings of Nigerian universities, devising appropriate criteria and appropriate weighting. Other countries, such as Britain and the United States, do the same.

In order to understand the prism through which the rest of the world views our universities, it would be helpful to examine the criteria employed by one of the ranking entities, namely, Quacquarelli Symonds (QS} entity. QS employs six criteria weighted as follows:

1. Academic reputation   40%
2. Employee reputation   10%
3, Staff: student ratio   20%
4. Citations per faculty member 20%
5. International faculty ratio 5%
6. International student ratio 5%

In the opinion of QS, these are the criteria necessary for determining the excellence of a university. Some critics in Nigeria have argued that there ought to be a criterion for determining the contribution to national development. There may be a way of working this into the local set of criteria.

When it comes to weighting, it has been wondered why academic reputation, important as it is, should be assigned 40% – almost half of the total points. It may be argued that this criterion is skewed in favour of the very old universities, which have had time to acquire a reputation. Indeed, among the top twenty positions in last year's rankings were Cambridge University, founded in 1209, Oxford, founded about 1096, and Harvard, founded 1636. In contrast, the oldest university in Nigeria is only 70 years old this year. All the same, age does not tell the whole story, as the Massachusetts Institute of Technology (MIT}, found in 1861, topped the list last year. Moreover, a much younger University of Singapore has been moving up rapidly and is expected to be in the top hundred before long.

Employee reputation is an ambiguous criterion as it is not clear whether it refers to the university as the employer in relation to its staff, or to the opinions of the employers of the university's products. If it refers to the latter, it has to be admitted that the employers of the products of Nigerian Universities do not have much to say that is flattering on the whole.

Once there is funding at an appropriate level, the Vice-Chancellor takes over from the Pro-Chancellor in enabling the university to score highly on all the criteria and, most importantly, help to produce graduates whose intellects have been stretched in different directions to make them efficient thinkers and go on to raise the general level of intelligence in the country.

Staff: student ratio determines the quality of teaching. Obviously, teaching an inordinately large class is not the same as teaching groups of five or six. There are even universities where much of the teaching is done in 1:1 interaction between staff and students.

A university is judged largely by the quality of its academic staff, and one pointer to quality is the number of times members of faculty are cited in other people's works. This assumes, of course, that research is being seriously engaged in.

The last two criteria, which together carry 10 percent, emphasize the international nature of universities. There can be no insularity in the make-up of staff and students, if the students are to be exposed to different cultures and different points of view. Nigerian universities would at present score quite low on these two criteria. There may well at present be scores of universities without a single expatriate staff or students. Nigerian universities can, for a start, open their doors to West African students, as Ghanaian universities seem to be doing. It would also improve their revenue.

It is evident from all of this that, for a university to achieve a high ranking – and indeed to be able to fulfil its mission – it must be well funded in order to obtain high scores on all the six criteria. Government subventions need to be substantially increased, but so also does the inflow from internally generated revenue. This places a heavy responsibility on Councils. Many universities at present manufacture bottled water and bread, but it is doubtful if substantial revenue can possibly be generated from this. Pro-Chancellors will have to think of huge investments in agriculture, which has the advantage of providing practical experience for their students, real estate and investments in big companies. They may also try to persuade the government to make the beneficiaries make a contribution.

Once there is funding at an appropriate level, the Vice-Chancellor takes over from the Pro-Chancellor in enabling the university to score highly on all the criteria and, most importantly, help to produce graduates whose intellects have been stretched in different directions to make them efficient thinkers and go on to raise the general level of intelligence in the country.

Ayo Banjo
May, 2018

Appendix 3

Address by the Vice-Chancellor, Professor Ayo Banjo On the Occasion of the 43rd Foundation Day Anniversary of the University of Ibadan on Monday, 18 November, 1991

The Visitor, Commander-in-Chief of the Armed Forces, Federal Republic of Nigeria, General Ibrahim Badamasi Babangida;

General Officer Commanding, 2 Mechanised Division, Nigerian Army, Ibadan;

Millitary Governor of Oyo State, Colonel Abdulkarim Adisa;

Hon. Minister of Education, Professor Aliu Babatunde Fafunwa;

Your Royal Highness, Omo N'Oba N'Edo Uku Akpolokpolo Erediauwa, Oba of Benin and Chancellor, University of Ibadan;

Visiting Chancellors of other universities;

Dr A. Liman Ciroma, Pro-Chancellor and Chairman of Council;

Pro-Chancellors of other Universities;

My Lords and Kabiyesis;

The Executive Secretary, National Universities Commission, Professor Idris Abdulkadir;

Your Excellencies;

Members of Council;

Visiting Vice-Chancellors;

Deputy Vice-Chancellor;

Registrar;

The University Bursar;

The University Librarian;

Provosts of Colleges;
Honorary Graduates;
Deans of Faculties and of the Postgraduate School;
Directors of Institutes;
Members of Senate;
Heads of Departments;
Members of the University Community;
Distinguished Guests;
Ladies and Gentlemen.

I should like to add my voice to the warm welcome to everyone already expressed by the chancellor and pro-chancellor. We are particularly delighted to have in our midst this morning the Hon. Minister of Education who, I am pleased to say, has paid several visits to us since his appointment and who has graciously closely identified himself with our efforts to consolidate academic excellence and to improve student and staff welfare. We are deeply indebted to him and wish him continued success in his onerous responsibilities.

I am happy that His Excellency, the military governor of Oyo State, is able to be with us today as this provides me with my last opportunity to use this forum to thank him personally for being such a wonderful pillar of support to the university. As I have had cause to remark on a previous occasion, to judge by Governor Adisa's concern for this university, one would have thought it was a state, rather than a federal, university. In addition to his numerous gestures of solidarity and support, he has, this year, given our College of Medicine a thirty-seater bus to facilitate the operation of the outside postings and has further, personally endowed prizes in the Postgraduate School and the Department of Communication and Language Arts in the College of Arts, Social Sciences and Law. The university is profoundly in his debt, and so am I personally for keeping the door of his office and his lodge open to me at all times. There are rumours that he, too, like the other governors, may soon be moving on. If so, all of us here wish him every success in his future endeavours.

I should also like to express our pleasure at seeing so many friends of the university here this morning. I bid them all welcome, as I do our graduands of today and their families and friends. I congratulate the graduands on reaching this important milestone in their academic careers. I hope you will forgive me if I single out for special welcome one of my illustrious predecessors in office, Professor T. Adeoye Lambo, and his wife. It is a great pleasure to welcome him back to the university on this occasion, and we would like to take this opportunity of letting him know how proud this university has been of his achievements at the W.H.O., and wishing him every happiness in his retirement.

We have just witnessed the admission to higher degrees and awards of postgraduate degrees and diplomas in respect of 2,911 candidates. Of this number, 129 received doctorate degrees, 18 M.Phil. or M.P.H., 1,697 Masters and 67 diplomas. I should wish each one of them a successful career. It is my hope that, in spite of present conditions, such a career in some cases will be here and elsewhere within the university system in the country.

There is, naturally, the urge to convert this particular address into a valedictory one. It is, however, an urge that I intend to resist, for valedictory addresses are in order only when one is taking a final leave, which I do not intend to do for another few years. What I think is rather called for here is a vote of thanks, and I will begin by doing this, officially and for the last time, as vice-chancellor before expressing my own personal thanks.

This university has been sustained in these anxious times through the generosity and support of its friends too numerous to list fully in the time available here. I hope they will all accept our most grateful thanks. But there are a few names which it would be grossly ungrateful not to mention, and I hope you will pardon me for mentioning them now.

One of the most notable changes in the landscape of the university in the last three years has been the appearance of U.I. Ventures Ltd. The measure of the success of this company, which is wholly owned by this university, is indicated by the presentation, during the company's last Annual General Meeting, of the sum of half a million naira to the university in addition to the reduction in the university's expenditure which the company has helped to bring about. This company has done what was thought impossible and, as is expected, has blazed the trail for the other universities. This university owes a great debt of gratitude to the board of directors of the company, and particularly to its chairman, Otunba Dr Michael Olasubomi Balogun, an honorary alumnus and great benefactor of this university. He has given to the company the same touch of excellence which has made his own companies the toast of the Nigerian private sector. We are also indebted to Mr Ewa Henshaw, member of Council, who has made it his personal responsibility to ensure the success of the company, and to Alhaji Dr Adebayo Adetunji, who has also given the company the benefit of his fabled business acumen. It is my hope that the company will continue to grow and that its contributions to the revenue of the university will increase by leaps and bounds.

A welcome relief in the encircling financial difficulties was the special grant, towards the end of the 1989/90 session, of the sum of twenty million naira to this university which has helped us to improve the university skyline by completing long abandoned student hostels at Idia Hall and Obafemi Awolowo Hall. Parts of the grant were also used to effect improvement in staff welfare. I should like to renew the profound thanks of this university to the Visitor for this timely help. But even more profound are our thanks to him for the special grant of ₦297 million to this university to build a waterworks in a bid to solve once and for all the acute water shortage on the campus. We were delighted that the president found it possible on 2nd August this year to perform personally the commissioning of the project. Thanks to the completion of the project, we are now able to maintain a very high standard of sanitation in the halls of residence.

One of the indefatigable benefactors of this university is the Ogbeni Oja of Ijebuland, Chief T.A. Odutola. His latest benefaction is a library building to the Faculty of Law. I am very pleased to say that that building is now just being completed and should be available for use in the course of this session. The university is immensely grateful to the Ogbeni Oja, who is also an honorary alumnus of this university, for his abiding interest in the progress of the university.

Sadly for us, in the course of last session, we lost another legendary benefactor of the university in the person of Sir Mobolaji Bank-Anthony. It is difficult for me to express, let alone quantify, the extent of the late Sir Mobolaji's love for this university. He never missed joining the academic procession if he was in the country on Foundation Day. Indeed, he was always the very first person to send someone all the way from Lagos to collect his cards for the ceremonies. One of his last acts was to persuade his wife to endow a building to the university, and those present at last year's Foundation Day ceremony will recall Lady Lande Bank-Anthony making a presentation of a cheque for half a million naira personally towards the cost of the building. I am pleased to say that Lady Bank-Anthony also personally performed the turning of the first sod at the site of the building on her 82nd birthday on 27 September this year. We are deeply grateful to her and do pray that Sir. Mobolaji's soul may continue to rest in peace.

It is a well-known fact that the Zard family of Ibadan have for many years identified themselves with the progress of our Faculty of Agriculture by regularly offering scholarships to many students there. Dr Raymond Zard has personified that interest and extended his philanthropy to other areas of the life of the university. Recently, he has been giving very strong support to the music life of the university. We are truly grateful to him for his generosity.

Bashorun Abiola has been well-known for his public-spiritedness, and the universities in recent years have been beneficiaries of his philanthrophy. Our university benefited from the grants that he made to the universities during the last three years, and we have just received further generous grants from him to our Postgraduate School to the tune of ₦1.8million. I do express our grateful thanks to him and renew our congratulations on his recent appointment as the chancellor of Oyo State University at Ogbomoso.

It now remains for me to add my personal thanks, and I shall begin with my great indebtedness to the chancellor, Omo N'Oba Erediauwa for his strong and fatherly interest in the university which he has graciously extended to me as an individual. I have, in the last eight years, spent many happy hours discussing the affairs of the university with him and have never been left in doubt as to his commitment to the university and his profound interest in its well-being. I have constantly received encouragement from him and do believe we have been singularly lucky in having him as our chancellor. To him, I offer my deep personal thanks.

As if it was not enough to have His Highness as chancellor, our cup runs over with the presence of Dr Liman Ciroma as our pro-chancellor and chairman of Council. His deft handling of Council; his commitment to truth, justice and fair play; his humaneness, have helped in the last six years to produce an era of stability and progress in the university. He has been, to me, a tower of strength, an inspiration, an exemplar of what is possible in human refinement. I owe him more than I can express, and to people who have been wondering how I have managed to survive this long on the job, I confess that Dr Ciroma is one of the secrets. I am most grateful to him.

I have been supported in office by colleagues too numerous to mention here. In big ways and small, they have provided the seat-belt to last me through many a turbulent episode. I would like in particular to express my gratitude to the principal officers who have often with me been exposed to the heat of the kitchen. I make no apologies for having worked closely with them in what I believe to be the civilised and democratic way that a university should be run. I am happy that one of my former deputies, Professor Peter Bodunrin, has since earned the richly deserved preferment of the vice-chancellorship of Ondo State University where, by all accounts, he is proving his mettle. I thank him for his loyalty and support while he was here. In Professor Olusola Akinyele I was blessed with another deputy with sterling qualities. I am deeply thankful to him. I am grateful to the registrar, Chief Ekanem-Ita, for keeping the administration of the university on an even keel, and to the bursar, Mr Philip Omoregie, for imposing order on the chaos of the bursary that he inherited. I am, of course, also grateful to the members of the Ceremonials Committee under the able leadership of Professor Laolu Akinyele, and to the Alumni Association under the admirable leadership of Chief Osita Okeke.

Surrounded by all these wonderful people and sustained by God, I have been inspired to give of my very best to this university during the last eight years, and now the time has come to say goodbye, and I do so with infinite thanks for an opportunity given and, I hope not misused. I do so with a clear awareness of what more could have been done if more resources had been available. And above all, I do so with a solemn prayer that Ibadan may continue to flourish.

Goodbye, and God bless the University of Ibadan.

Ayo Banjo
Vice-Chancellor, 1984-1991
University of Ibadan
18th November, 1991

Appendix 4

∞∞∞∞∞

Dearest Ayo,

Do spend this five guineas to buy any thing you fancy as the token of my joy at your acquisition of a doctorate degree. It is my prayer that you should use the knowledge for the good of the community.

Your joyful
Daddy

Index

'A' level qualifications, 146
Abayomi, Kofo 199
Abimbolu, Bimpe (later Bimpe Ike), 51
Abisogun, Gbolahan 79 - 80
Academic
- Autonomy, 213
- community, 133
- Staff Union of Universities (ASUU), 151, 155, 188
Academy of Science, 174-176
Achebe, Chinua 51
Action Group, 85
Adadevoh, Kwoku 29
Adamolekun, Nathaniel 111
Ade Ajayi, Prof. 112, 114
Ade Ojo, S. 125
Adebayo, Augustus 112
Adebo, S.O. 125
Adefarasin, 29
Adejumo, Nike 22
Ademowo, Most Reverend 193
Adesina, Lere 33, 40
Adetiloye, Abiodun 190
Adetugbo, Biodun 119
Adokpaye, Godwin 90
Afigbo, A. 174
Afolayan, Bisi 119
Afonja, Sidney 33,190
Agada, Jerry 176
Aggrey, 35
Aghadiuno, Patrick 33, 65, 70
Agyeman, Ossai 51
Aig-Imoukhuede, Ikpehare 32
Aina, Olu 33
Ajayi Crowther University, 8
Ajayi, Gbenro 73, 81
Ajibade, 40
Ajose, Oladele 125
Akande, Jade 2
Akinkugbe, Ladipo 185-186, 195, 197
Akinloye, Adisa 137
Akinola, Peter 190, 194
Akinyele, I.B. 10, 18

Akomolafe, Ade 8, 22, 40
Alaafin, 6
Alafe Aluko, Dr 34
Alakija, Adeyemo 199
Alakijas, 195
Alayande, Rev. Canon 95, 190, 192
Alexander, Peter 62
Alhaji Ado Baiyero (Emir of Kano), 166
Ali, 44
All Saints Church Jericho, Ibadan 41
Allen, Major 41
Allsopp, Richard 125,129
Alo, Jide 79
Amali, Shamsudeen 180, 188-189
Anene, J.C. 48
Annan, Brian 99
Apartheid regime, 59
Appointments and Promotions Committee, 118
Arobieke family of Oke-Ijaga, Ijebu-Igbo 1
Ashaju, Dapo 196
Awe, Bolanle 2, 189
Awe, Muyiwa 93
Awolowo, Obafemi 85, 199-201, 204
Azikiwe, Nnamdi 85,199-201

Babangida, President 174-175
Balewa, Tafawa 200
Ballroom dancing, 50
Balogun, Subomi 49 -51, 73, 81, 94
Bamgbose, Ayo 22, 118-120, 174, 189, 193-194
Banjo, Abimbola Olugboyega 11, 27, 43, 95, 125
Banjo, Aduke Tokunbo (later Mrs. Ogunbanwo) 10, 27, 125
Banjo, Alice (nee Mbamali) 71, 81, 94, 96, 101 -102, 110, 114, 115, 124-125, 132, 162, 166-167, 198
Banjo, Ayodapo 121, 163
Banjo, Ayotunde 121, 160, 162-163

Banjo, Ayoyinka 121, 162-163
Banjo, Comfort Jokotola (nee Osinuga) 1 - 2
Banjo, Dorcas 1
Banjo, Femi 27
Banjo, John 1
Banjo, Kunle 27, 125
Banjo, Ladipo Ayodeji
- admitted to CMS Grammar School, 23
- appointed
  - as Deputy Vice-Chancellor, 133
  - as Professor Emeritus, 173
  - at University of Ibadan, 109
- as
  - acting Vice-Chacellor, University of Ibadan
  - Captain, Oluwole House, 40-41
  - Chairman, NLNG Advisory Committee, 176
  - Chapel Monitor, 40
  - Commander of the Order of the Niger (OON), 198
  - Dean, 122
  - Education Officer, Abraka, Government Teacher Training College, 85-92
  - Education Officer, Queen's School, Ede
- External Examiner,
  - University of Botswana, 171
  - University of Swaziland, 171
- Head of Department of Engilsh, 121, 130
- Library Monitor, 40
- Pro-Chancellor,
  - University of Ilorin, 180
  - University of Port Harcourt, 177
- School goalkeeper, 41
- School Prefect, 40-41
- Sub-Dean, 120
- Associate Editor, English Worldwide, 120
- at
  - Christ Church Cathedral School, Lagos 8
  - Igbobi College, 8, 28-43
  - Kindergarten School, St. Andrew's Primary, Oyo 3
  - Kristiansand, 168-172
  - Nigerian College of Arts, Science & Technology, Ibadan 47-51
  - St. John's Aroloya, Lagos 17
  - University of Besancon, 79-81
- Award of D.Litt honoriscausa by University of Ibadan & University of Port Harcourt, 198
- Awardee of Major Allen Prize, 41
- back at Government College, Ibadan 92
- back in University of Leeds, 98-107
- becoming a Professor, 122
- Chairman,
  - Board of NUC, 197, 209
  - Board of Trustees, 196
  - Committee of Deans, 122
- *contributing Editor to the Annual Bibliography of English Language and Literature,* 120
- end of tenure as Vice-Chancellor, 155
- engagement party with Alice 81
- Fellow, Nigerian Academy of Letters, 198
- Fellow of Academy, 175

- founding Editor, *Ibadan Journal of Humanistic Studies*, 120
- home coming (from Britain), 82
- in
  - Boy's Brigade, 18
  - Glasgow, 57
  - Great Britain, 55
  - Leeds, 74-78
  - UCLA, USA 101-119
- inducted to Boys Scout, 4
- involved in production of Oxford Primary Dictionary, 120
- love for Music/Church Music, 7-8
- member,
  - Ibadan Dining Club, 125
  - Nigerian Academy of Letters, 174
  - Planning Committee for establishment of Anglican University, 189
  - School Cricket Team, 42
- on Sabbatical leave
  - at University of Cambridge, 155, 163-168
  - at University of West Indies, Cave Hill, Barbados 123, 125-129
- Order of Merit, 198
  - participation in production of Longman Primary Dictionary, 120
  - pioneer, Pro-Chancellor, Ajayi Crowther University, 194
  - Vice-Chancellor, University of Ibadan 120,125
  - Vice President, International Federation of Modern Languages, 120

Banjo, Olubunmi   109, 114, 162, 172
Banjo, Olumide Adebayo (Bayo, Banjo) 2, 13, 18, 20, 25 – 27, 95, 109, 111, 125, 131, 178
Banjo, Samuel Ayodele 1, 11, 122, 238
Banjo, Valerie 111
Barber, Kehinde 22
Bello, Ahmadu 85, 200
Berkhout, Joop 169, 172
Biafran war, 201
Bishop, Mr 44
Black, Joseph 60
Blaize, Rotimi Alade   14
Blakely, Dr 63, 72
Bodede, Bayo 33
Bodunrin, Peter 123, 154
Bowden, Prof. 102
Bowman, Ian 48, 51, 62
Boy's Brigade, 18
Briggs, Nimi 177-180
British
- Council, 52, 55-56, 70, 76, 94, 97 – 99, 109, 119, 196
- District Officer, 5
- Expatriate Supplementation Scheme (BESS), 144

Brown, Gillian 164, 168
Bucknor-Akerele, Femi   197
Bullock, Derek 94
Burns, Robert 63
Burtler, Lord 64
Burton, George 10
Burton, Mrs. 10
Busari, Alarape 76

Cain, Ellen   48
Cambridge
- School Certificate, 40
- examination, 42
- University, 79

Carter, Nick   90 - 91
Chomskyan linguisgtics, 108, 115

Christ Church Cathedral School, Broad Street 17, 19 – 21, 28
Christ Church Cathedral, Lagos 11 - 12
Churchill, Winston 102
Ciroma, Liman 155
Civilian regime, 202
Clark, J.P. 91, 174
Clinton, Christine (later Christine Obumselu), 49, 51
CMS Girls' School, 21
CMS Grammar School, Lagos 20, 29, 57, 203
Coker, F.C.A. 29
Coker, G.B.A. 29
Coker, Segun 33, 50
Collegiate system, 154
Commonwealth and International Literature group, 166
Concessional entrance examination, 146-147, 149
Convocation Ceremony, 175
Cowley, A.P. 100
Crowther, Ajayi 192

Dalton, Mrs. 76, 101
Daniel, Ladipo 65
Danjuma, General 195
Davies, Dr 63
Davis, Norman 63
Dekalu, Ade 105 -107
Dekalu, Akin 105
Desalu, Jide 33
Dike, Kenneth 51, 111
Doherty, Adebayo 16
Doherty, Akanni 24 – 25
Doherty, R.A. 125
Dudley, Billy 114

Echeruo, Michael 121-123
Edgal, S.F. 87, 89, 91
Education tax, 204
Effiong, Charles 75, 87
Elder, Senator 127

Elias, Teslim 29
Elugbe, Ben 176
Empire Day, 5 - 6
Establishment of Universities, 141-143, 209-211
Esubiyi, Talabi 34 – 35, 39
Ethnic animosities, 201
European powers, 96
Extra-curricular activities, 4

Fagbenro, Mrs. 135
Fagunwa, D.O. 3
Fakayode, Justice 51, 154
Falana, Femi 180, 184
Falase, Ayodele 41
Federal
- Civil Service Commission, 40
- universities, 150-151
Ferguson, Alan 90 – 91
Financial Autonomy, 213, 215-216
Financing the Universities, 149-152
Flaa, Paul 169, 172
Folayan, Gbolahan 90
Fordyce, Christian J, 61
Free primary education, 200
- scheme, 204
Freeman, Thomas Birch 35
Funding of the University System, 211

Giwa-Amu, Idowu 88
Global Perception of Nigerian Universities, 217-220
Governance of the Universities, 212
Governing Council of the university, 133, 136, 138-140
Government College, Ibadan 90, 92 – 93, 97, 100, 203
Government College, Ughelli 89-92
Gowon, Yakubu 201
Gregory, Michael 100
Grieve, D.W. 111
Groves, Chris 94

Hallidayan model, 108, 115
Hall-Partee, Barbara 104
Harrison, 124
Hart, Keith 45, 166
Hetherington, Hector 60
Heyerdahl, Thor 171-172
Higher School Certificate (HSC), 146
Hinds, 125
Holy Trinity, Ebute Ero 17
Hough, S.S.G. 34
Howells, Adelakun Williamson 12
Hume, David 59
Hunponu-Wusu, Ladipo 33

Ibadan Grammar School, 203
Ibadan working Group (IWG), 175
Ibiam, Francis 200
Ibru, Michael 29, 40
Igbo Irunmole, 3
Igbo Olodumare, 5
Igbobi College, Yaba, Lagos 2, 27 – 43, 49, 203
Ighodaro, Mr 27
Ijagbemi, 122
Ike, Vincent 51
Ikime, Obaro 91, 123
Ikoli, Ernest 199
Institute of African Studies, University of Ibadan, 127
Izevbaye, Dan 116-117, 123, 134, 162, 174

Jadesinmi, I.G.A. 94 - 95
Jaiyeoba, Kola 196
JAMB, 145, 149
Jeffares, Norman 100, 116-117, 121
Jeyifo, Biodun 117
Jibowu, Olumuyiwa 125
Jibril, Munzali 198
Joint Admissions and Matriculation examinations, 144-145, 147
Jolaoso, Olujimi 29, 34
Jones, Eldred 117

Kale, S.I. 12, 23- 24
Kalejaiye, Mr 27 - 28
King's College, Lagos 41, 203
Kolawole, Taiwo 130-132
Kon-Tiki expedition, 171-172
Kudeti Girls' School, Ibadan 2
Kujore, Obafemi 123

Ladefoged, Peter 104
Language-learning methodology, 4
Language tutorials, 15
Lasebikan, G. 4
Lewis, Arthur 126
Lewis, Mrs. 22
Linguistic Society of America, 108
London 'A' Level certificates, 146
London 'O' Levels, 147
Lugard, Lord 91

Macaulay, Herbert 16, 199
Maja, Akinola 17
Maja-Pearce, 166
Majekodunmi, Mr 19, 26
Major Allen Prize, 41
Makeba, Miriam 109
Makinde, Moses 174
Manuwa, Samuel 84
Marinho, Tony 196
Massachusett's Institute of Technology (MIT), 104
Maxwell, Desmond 109 -110
Mbamali, Ernest 94
Mbamali, Felicia 95
Mbamali, Mr 44
Mbamali, Theresa 95
Mckenzie, Miss 65
Mensah, E.T. 50
Methodist Boys High School, Lagos 21, 29, 42, 203
Methodist Girls' High School, Yaba, Lagos 42
Military intervention, 201
Military regime, 202

Mitchell, Terry 100
Modern Humanities Research Association, 120
Momoh, Tony 88
Moody, L. 94, 97 -98
Moorehouse, Mr 34
Morgan, Edwin 62
Morgan, Timi 58
Morris, Norman P. 28, 30 – 32, 34
Mosuro, Kola 197
Mother tongue, 108
Musical Society of Nigeria (MUSON), Lagos 43

National Assembly, 40
National Universities Commission (NUC), 143-144, 184, 189-190, 192-193, 197, 212
Ngugi, James 100
Nigerian
- Academy of Education, 174-175, 204
- Academy of Letters, 174, 176, 205
- Broadcasting Corporation, 50
- College of Arts, Science and Technology, Ibadan 45, 155
- Electricity Power Authority (NEPA), 157
- English Studies Association, 119
- Liquefied Natural Gas (NLNG), 176-177, 196-197
- Literature Prize, 176-177
- National Petroleum Corporation (NNPC), 158
- Society for Information, Arts, and Culture (NSIAC), 196
- University System, 209-220
  *overview of, 221-227
Noam Chomsky's transformational-generative theory of grammar, 104

Nwagwu, Mark 124
Nwoga, Donatus 79 - 80

Oba
- Olagbegi, (Olowo of Owo), 124
- Sijuwade (Ooni of Ife), 166
Obaji, Mrs. 181
Obasanjo, Chief 182, 188
Obi, Chike 94 - 95
Obumselu, Ben 51
Odia, Gabriel 33
Odili, Dr 179
Oduaran, 111 -112
Odugbesan, Mr 44 - 45
Odulate, Segun 33
Oduntan, Sam 57
Odunuga, Segun 122,132
Odunze, Fred 50
Odutola, Bishop 94, 95
Oduwaiye, Admiral 33
Ogedegbe, 43 - 45
Ogunade, Justice 190
Ogundipe Molara 116-117
Ogunlesi, Remi 33
Ogunmola, Tunde 190
Ogutuga, Bandele 33, 73 – 74, 81
Ojo, Joko 2
Ojo, Sina 67, 69
Okeowo, Toyin 190
Okoisor, Frank 76
Okojie, Christopher 137-139
Okoli, Christie (later Christie Achebe) 51
Okpara, Dr 85
Okpewho, Isidore 124
Okunnu, Lateefat 178
Olafimihan, Kola 40
Olaitan, Yinka 29
Olajide, G.I. 189-192
Olaniran, Jire 194
Olayide, S.O. 130-139,153
Olisemeka, Ignatius 29

Olivier, Lawrence 65
Oloko, Atinuke (later Atinuke Ige), 14
Olorunnimbe, Mr 199
Oloyede, Is'haq 189
Oluga, B.O. 159-161
Olunloyo, Mololu 93
Oluwole, Bishop 35
Omogbenigun, Chief 159
Omololu, Dr 15 – 16
Onosode, Gamaliel 91
Onwukeme, 44
Oredugba, Mrs. 83
Oruwaiye, Dr 48
Oruwaiye, Mrs. 48
Osayimwese, Iz 129
Osinuga, Jonathan 2
Osofisan, Femi 93
Osundare, Niyi 142, 173
Oundle School, Britain 31
Oviawe, 41
Oxford Brookes University, England 162
Oyebanji, Josephine 194, 196
Oyediran, Kayode 173
Oyelese, Dejo 50
Oyesanmi, Bola 33
Oyewole, 116
Oyo Empire, 96

Parker, Reginald B. 31- 32, 34, 39, 42, 69-71
Phillps, T.K.E. 16,19
Phonetics laboratory, 104
Political
 - controversy, 77
 - independence, 85
Post-Retirement Responsibilities, 177-180
Powell, V.B.V. 90, 92
Prator, Clifford 103
Private universities, 143, 150-151

Public
 - Perception of Nigerian Universities, 214
 - Service Commission, 112

Queen's College, Lagos 79

Rasheed, Abubakar 197
Recruitment of Academic Staff, 143-144
Riba, Shayiwe 58
Ritchie, Dr 58
Ronning, Helge 172
Rowlands, A.C. 118
Russell Group, 75

SACOBA, 189-191, 194
Sagay, John 33, 40, 49 -50
Sagoe, M.N.Q. 29
Sagoe, Moyo 70 - 71
Salami, Dr 197
Sandey, Mr 18 – 19, 26
Schachter, Paul 104
School Certificate examination, 147
School's Cup, 41
Secondary school system, 148
Senate (of the University), 133-134, 136, 140
Sessford, Father 65
Shonekan, Ernest 166
Sigma Club, 50
Sikuade, Seni 58
6-3-3-4 system of education delivery, 144, 147
Sixth Form classes, 146-147
Smith, Adam 59
Sofenwa, Lamidi 91 – 92
Solarin, Seun 76
Sowunmi, Bisi 189
Soyinka, Wole 93
Spencer, John 100

Index

St.
- Andrew's College, Oyo 1 – 2, 7 – 8, 18, 26, 40, 189, 192-194
- Anne's Girls School, Ibadan 94
- David's Church (now Cathedral), Kudeti, Ibadan 2
- David's Primary School, Kudeti 1
- Gregory's College, Lagos 41, 76, 94,
- John's Church, Aroloya Lagos 12, 17, 24, 26
- Luke's College, Molete Ibadan 26, 47, 82, 95, 112
- Michael's Church (now Cathedral), Agunpopo, Esiele, Oyo 7, 14 – 15, 190
- Paul's Breadfruit, 17
- Peter's Church Aremo, Ibadan 112
- Peter's Faji 17

Staff development programme, 114
State Universities, 143, 150-151
Stocwell, Robert 104
Student
- Admissions, 213
- Enrolment, 144-149

Supreme Military Council, 33
Swallowbeck music scholarship, 40
Sylvester, Victor 50

Tamuno, Tekena 134, 137
TETFUND for tertiary institutions, 151, 175, 211
Theory of stylistics, 116
Thomas, Horatio Oritsejolomi 29
Thompson, Lloyd 122-123
Thompson, Trevor 124, 129
Tomori, Oyewale 91
Tomori, S.H.O. 119
Townsend, Bishop 35

Toye, Afolabi 131-132
Tuition- free education, 150,152

Udoji Commission report, 174
Ukoli, 124
UNESCO, 204
UNESCO, 149
United Missionary College (U.M.C.), 29
United Missionary College (UMC), Ibadan 2
Universal primary education, 203
University
- Autonomy, 212-213
- Calendar, 215
- College Ibadan (UCI), 34, 47-51, 79, 84, 87, 100, 104, 142, 146, 209-210
- Committee System, 216
- Councils, 216-217
- education, 194, 198
- of
  - Besancon, France 76 – 80
  - California, Los Angeles (UCLA), 98
  - Dundee, 162
  - Glasgow, 51
  - Ibadan, 22, 41, 43, 75, 91, 98, 109 -111, 113, 125, 127, 134, 136, 142, 146-148, 156,163, 174-175,180-182
  - Jos, 187
  - Lagos, 95, 162, 175
  - Leeds, England 72, 75, 98, 100, 116, 121
  - London, 1, 51, 97, 113, 118, 121, 142
  - Middlesex, England 162
  - Nigeria, Nsukka 80, 121
Unoh, Solomon 123

Vanderpuye, Mr 44
Vaughan, Funso 14 - 16, 19 - 20

Vining, Leslie Gordon 20
Voluntary agencies, 152

Walsh, William 75
Watt, James 60
West African
- Linguistics Society, 119
- Modern Language Association, 120

Western Nigeria Public Service Commission, 112
Whitaker's Almanack of Public schools, 42

Whitehall, Harold Fritz 113, 115, 117, 122
Williams, Adeniyi 112
Wright, Dr 48
Wusu, Ladipo (Ladi), 23, 65, 70

Yoloye, Tunde 124
Yoruba
- poems, 4
- Studies Association, 120

Young, Peter 117, 121, 168-172

Zarpas, J.N. 38

www.ingramcontent.com/pod-product-compliance
Lightning Source LLC
Chambersburg PA
CBHW070810300426
44111CB00014B/2465